W9-DGM-864

DATE DUE

PROSTITUTION IN THE DIGITAL AGE

PROSTITUTION IN THE DIGITAL AGE

Selling Sex from the Suite to the Street

R. Barri Flowers

PRAEGER

AN IMPRINT OF ABC-CLIO, LLC
Santa Barbara, California • Denver, Colorado • Oxford, England

Library of Congress Cataloging-in-Publication Data

Flowers, R. Barri (Ronald Barri)
   Prostitution in the digital age : selling sex from the suite to the street / R. Barri Flowers.
      p. cm.
   Includes bibliographical references and index.
   ISBN 978-0-313-38460-8 (hardback: acid-free paper) — ISBN 978-0-313-38461-5 (ebook) 1. Prostitution—United States. 2. Prostitutes—United States. 3. Digital media. 4. Sex-oriented businesses. I. Title.
   HQ144.F59   2011
   363.4'40973—dc22   2010050952

ISBN: 978-0-313-38460-8
EISBN: 978-0-313-38461-5

15   14   13   12   11   1   2   3   4   5

This book is also available on the World Wide Web as an eBook.
Visit www.abc-clio.com for details.

Praeger
An Imprint of ABC-CLIO, LLC

ABC-CLIO, LLC
130 Cremona Drive, P.O. Box 1911
Santa Barbara, California 93116-1911

This book is printed on acid-free paper ∞

Manufactured in the United States of America

In memory of my father, Johnnie Henry Flowers, Sr.,
who instilled in me the confidence to follow
my dreams and passions in life till I exceeded them, and beyond.
And my mother, Marjah Aljean Flowers, to whom he was
married for nearly 57 years and who continues
to be a loving and influential person in my life.

Lastly, to my wife and best friend of 30 years who has been
my greatest source of motivation as an author, H. Loraine.
Thanks for seeing me through yet another book project.
Your support has been invaluable.

Contents

Introduction

Prostitution has long been referred to as the "world's oldest profession." Clearly, it has flourished for centuries, as documented through historical and religious books, literature, fiction, criminological and true crime writings, exposés, memoirs, and Hollywood. The trading of sexual favors for currency has proven to be resilient as part of our society and social consciousness with little indication of becoming a thing of the past.

In the 21st century, prostitution continues to thrive as a major part of the commercial sexual exploitation of females and males throughout the world, along with pornography, pedophilia, and related avenues of sexual commerce. In the digital age, prostitutes and customers have found new ways to connect with each other through the Internet, smartphones, picture and video messaging, text messaging, cable television, and various other wireless devices. Popular social networking sites such as Facebook, MySpace, and Craigslist have proven to be fertile virtual ground for prostitution-involved individuals to advertise themselves or others and for those who seek prostitutes to fulfill their sexual needs.

The commercial sex trade today is a multibillion-dollar industry on a global scale, with prostitutes and customers operating within countries and crossing borders, almost with impunity. Every year, millions of mostly women and teenage girls and boys are being bought, sold, forced, or coerced into the sex trade as streetwalkers; brothel, massage parlor, or escort service prostitutes; and other means of sexual exploitation. With this comes a high rate of sexually transmitted diseases, substance abuse, violence, and victimization.

The sexual exploiters of prostitutes for pleasure and profit are customers, pimps, sex traffickers, pornographers, gangs, organized criminals, and sometimes even family members. Runaways and thrownaways are especially preyed on by pimps and other sexual exploiters, who take advantage of their dire predicament as homeless or drug-dependent street youth to lure them into the sex-for-sale business. International sex traffickers set their sights on susceptible poor women and children with promises of employment, high earnings, and a good life that typically turns into sexual slavery and forced prostitution.

Apart from the involuntary or survival prostitution that played a big role in the commercial sex trade of the early decades of this century, there are perhaps as many, if not more, prostitution-engaged women and men who voluntarily sell a variety of sexual services for high earnings, targeting wealthy clients who have no problem paying for what they want. Upper-class sex workers may be the most suited to capitalize on the potential for money-making that exists in the online marketplace, often using a combination of Internet savvy, proven marketing techniques, and the lure of sexuality to find success in the sex trade.

Legal prostitution and brothels have increased in recent decades in countries throughout the world, including in the United States, which allows some form of government control and regulation over a certain segment of the adult sex-for-sale business. However, in most such instances, legally permitted prostitution is in direct competition with illegal prostitution that generally brings in greater revenue and includes many more active participants.

In the United States, only a few counties in Nevada allow prostitutes to operate through legal brothels. That means prostitution is illegal everywhere else, and there are many laws to that effect and occasional prostitution arrests by local and federal law enforcement seeking to contain soliciting sex and procuring sex workers. Unfortunately, that caveat does little to prevent the proliferation of the commercial sex trade industry in this country as sex workers on all levels offer their bodies for currency, profit, survival, shelter, drugs, and, for some, the comfort of love and companionship.

Prostitution in the Digital Age explores the commercial sex-for-sale business in the United States and the components that make it work as a successful enterprise, as well as the dynamics of sexual exploitation, vulnerability, desire, commerce, and implications.

PART I

Commercial Sexual Exploitation in the 21st Century

Chapter 1

Business of Sexual Exploitation

In the United States, the sexual exploitation of women and children has become a multibillion-dollar business with no end in sight. Prostitution, sex trafficking, pedophilia, and pornography are at the core of commercial sexual exploitation. Those profiting from this business include pimps, pornographers, purveyors, organized crime, gang members, drug dealers, and parents of sexually exploited minors. Others who make money from sexual exploitation include prostitutes themselves, particularly high-end call girls, porn actors, the adult entertainment industry, modeling industry, hotels, bookstores, and those who cater to the needs of sexual exploiters. Use of the Internet has precipitously increased revenues for many involved in this business through social networks, advertising, and other means; as well as use of other digital mechanisms such as cell phones and text messaging. The fact that so much money is exchanging hands through both legal and illegal sexual exploitation enterprises, with willing and unwilling participants who are legally of age and minors, makes it nearly impossible to control, much less eliminate the business of sexual exploitation.

Prostitution

Prostitution is perhaps the most visible means of illegal commercial sexual exploitation, with countless young women and men peddling flesh on the streets, in cars, massage parlors, hotels, and elsewhere. Worldwide revenue from the sex trade industry is estimated to exceed $100 billion annually.[1] In the United States alone, an estimated $14 billion, or $40 million each day, is generated in the sex-for-sale business each year in the United States.[2]

According to Norma Almodovar, a former Los Angeles traffic cop turned prostitute and author of *Cop to Call Girl*, "You have thousands and thousands and thousands of people in prostitution that are working in the business, and so you multiply that by the number of encounters with the number of clients they have and you're talking about serious money."[3]

Much of the profit from prostitution goes to those providing prostitution services, including pimps, madams, gangs, drug dealers, escort services, brothels, sex rings, strip clubs, sex traffickers, and pornographers involved in the sex trade. But others also profit from the sex trade, such as hotels and motels where much of the sexual activity takes place, related adult entertainment establishments, local businesses, Internet providers, phone companies, etc. Basically, for prostitution to survive and, indeed, thrive, it requires many elements of society to operate in conjunction in successfully selling sexual favors.

High-class prostitutes can earn considerably more than middle-class hookers or lower-level streetwalkers who often have to split their earnings with madams, pimps, and others supplying prostitutes for an endless supply of johns. Infamous madams such as Heidi Fleiss, dubbed the "Hollywood Madam;" Sydney Biddle Barrows, known as the "Mayflower Madam;" and Deborah Jeane Palfrey, called the D.C. Madam, reportedly raked in millions by supplying attractive young women to clients. According to the CNBC documentary *Dirty Money: The Business of High-End Prostitution*, some elite high-class call girls can earn as much as $100,000 a day plying their trade. Most were said to pull in around $12,000 per day.[4] The Emperor's Club, a prostitution operation believed to have supplied the prostitute that led to the downfall of former New York Governor Eliot Spitzer, charged up to $5,500 an hour for services by a prostitute in its stable.[5]

Though streetwalkers' earnings pale by comparison, typically charging anywhere from $10 to $50 to perform sex acts, many charge more to prostitute themselves, depending on the request, experience, pimp, city, need for drugs, and other factors. Streetwalkers are also more likely to have multiple johns on a given day or night than their high-class counterparts, increasing their earnings that much more. All told, the money lower- and middle-class prostitutes make can still add up to hundreds of thousands of dollars and more over a lifetime.

Online prostitution has lead to increased revenue on all levels of prostitution from streetwalkers to high-class call girls. Prostitutes, pimps, and clients typically use the Internet these days and such sites as Craigslist and popular social networks like MySpace, Facebook, and YouTube to solicit, promote, arrange meetings, and otherwise ply their trade or satisfy a desire to sexuality exploit persons in the sex trade. A street prostitute or her pimp can earn as much as 30 times more by setting up a job online rather than on a street corner.[6]

Child Prostitution

The prostitution of children or minors is a subset of the lucrative sex trade industry and arguably as profitable for sexual exploiters as adult prostitution. Hundreds of thousands of teenagers and possibly more than 1 million are active participants in the U.S. sex trade.[7] Many of these youths are also involved in sex trafficking, pedophilia, and pornography, giving those who sexually exploit them multiple ways to profit from their victims. Though it is unknown precisely how much money teenage prostitutes bring in nationwide, indications are that underage prostitutes earn hundreds, if not thousands, of dollars a night turning tricks.

According to Rachel Lloyd, the Executive Director of Girls Educational & Mentoring Services (GEMS), five prostituted girls can earn $1,500 a night for pimps, charging $40 to $50 for oral copulation, $75 for sexual intercourse, and $150 for out calls or when the prostitute services the client at his hotel or house.[8] Researcher Mia Spangenberg suggests that an attractive young prostitute servicing 10 clients can feasibly and singlehandedly bring in $1,500 on one good weekend.[9]

Most prostitution-involved female teenagers often have quotas they are required to meet by their pimps, who force them to work the streets 7 to 10 hours nightly for as many as six days a week—bringing in potentially hundreds of thousands of untaxed dollars annually from a pimp's stable. More money can be made when teen prostitutes also double as drug dealers or thieves, often under the guidance of their pimps to whom most of their earnings go.[10]

Online child prostitution has been increasing in recent years as a means to attract clientele, increase revenue, and reduce risk. Law enforcement has countered by cracking down more on Internet prostitution involving minors, in particular.[11] However, all too often determined and computer-savvy pimps are managing to circumvent the authorities while utilizing current digital technology to boost their earnings.

Pornography

Pornography is another means of sexual exploitation that is big business and has moved into the mainstream in society. It is estimated that $10 to

$13 billion is generated in the U.S. porn industry annually.[12] Of this, $4 to $6 billion is made from legal adult entertainment, including videos, magazines, pay-per-view, the Internet, and sex toys. A 2001 *Forbes* report broke down yearly revenue derived from the business of pornography as follows:[13]

- *Videos:* $500 million to $1.8 billion
- *Magazines:* $1 billion
- *Internet:* $1 billion
- *Pay-per-view:* $128 million
- *Cell phones:* $30 million

Consumer demand for adult entertainment in the 21st century rivals that of paying to see professional sports, motion pictures, and buying music, as reported by *60 Minutes*. As a result, big companies such as Comcast, DirecTV, Time Warner, and General Motors are raking in millions selling pornography and erotica. Comcast alone was said to have earned $50 million from adult entertainment in 2002.[14] One industry observer estimated that DirecTV could earn up to $500 million from pornography each year.[15]

Huge profits from pornography are also made by some of the nation's largest hotel chains. According to a CBS News study, hotels such as the Hyatt, Sheraton, Marriott, Hilton, and Holiday Inns offer adult entertainment on pay-per-view. An estimated 50 percent of their guests purchase access to this material, comprising almost 70 percent of in-room revenue.[16]

The wealth of the porn industry is generated through and shared by its various entities including those who manufacture, produce, distribute, and supply pornography; as well as wholesalers; retailers; and cable, satellite, and foreign TV buyers. Additional prominent players in the pornography business are operators of adult nightclubs, sex shops, and other types of legal and illegal sexual exploiters. All target the consumer of adult entertainment and profit from it.

In 2003, more than 800 million adult DVD and videotapes were rented and sold in stores across the nation, with some 11,000 adult titles released the prior year, according to Paul Fishbein, the founder of *Adult Video News*, a trade publication for the porn industry.[17] Though females are typically the ones sexually exploited in adult entertainment films, more women are now producing and directing adult material, thereby gaining a bigger slice of the pie.

Pornography on the Internet, webcams, cell phones, and other digital devices has given pornographers and related profiteers of sexual exploitation new means to find customers and generate revenue. For example, a *USA Today* report alleged that in 2003 adult entertainment Web sites such as Cybererotica.com had revenue of around $2 billion, constituting about 10 percent of the domestic pornography market.[18] With ever-increasing inroads in online pornography, erotica, and other sexual exploitation, this percentage has very likely grown in the subsequent years.

With the proliferation of Internet porn, many sites have sprung up in recent years such as desperateamateurs.com, amateurallure.com, and barelylegalpersonals.com where attractive young women are being sexually exploited for pay as "amateurs" in the world of pornography, designed to titillate customers and capitalize on the lucrative worldwide pornography market.[19]

Child Pornography

Child pornography is a branch of pornography and child sexual abuse in which children are being portrayed in sexually explicit terms or actions in photographs, films, computer images, or writings. As with pornography in general, child pornography is a multibillion-dollar international sexual exploitation industry in and of itself. Unlike pornography, it is a crime to "knowingly possess, manufacture, distribute, or access with intent to view child pornography."[20]

An estimated 20 percent of U.S. pornography is child pornography.[21] Anywhere from hundreds of thousands to well over a million children are believed to be sexually exploited by child pornographers and pedophiles, many of whom are considered "dual offenders" in possessing child porn and sexually victimizing children.[22] Pedophiles view and collect child pornographic materials for personal use, trading among pedophiles, in relation to "child grooming," or preparing a victim for child sexual abuse, or other means of sexual exploitation such as child prostitution or producing more child pornography.[23]

According to the U.S. Department of Justice's Child Exploitation and Obscenity Section, producing child pornography has now become a simple and low-priced process with the Internet enabling pornographers to create digital movies and images for reproduction and dissemination to countless individuals through Web sites, instant messaging, e-mail, chat rooms, bulletin boards, and other means.[24]

As a result, the Internet has become a boon for child pornographers and others capitalizing on the commercial child porn business, such as pimps, organized criminals, and gangs, with the amount of child pornography available to pedophiles and other users larger than ever before. It has been reported by the National Center for Missing and Exploited Children that since 1997, online child pornography has risen by 1,500 percent.[25] There are more than 1 million child porn images on the Internet at any given time with 200 new images placed on the Web every day.[26] This growing global problem of commercial child sexual exploitation has led to efforts to criminalize the production and use of child pornography on an international scope.

Sex Trafficking

Sex trafficking is another type of commercial sexual exploitation that is menacing to society. It is defined as a "modern-day form of slavery in which a commercial sex act is induced by force, fraud, or coercion, or in which the person induced to perform such an act is under the age of 18 years."[27] Although federal laws, such as the Trafficking Victims Protection Act of 2000, ban sex trafficking[28] especially concerning minors, the trafficking business is flourishing in this country and elsewhere. Revenue generated from trafficking of persons is estimated to be $10 billion annually. At least $4 billion of this is earned in the global brothel industry.[29]

Most victims of sex trafficking are women and children, who "are forced into various forms of commercial sexual exploitation including prostitution, pornography, stripping, live-sex shows, mail-order brides, military prostitution, and sex tourism," according to the U.S. Department of Health and Human Services.[30] Trafficked persons are often compelled to sell sex as streetwalkers, but can also be found in brothels, massage parlors, private residences, and other locations.

It is unknown just how widespread sex trafficking is. However, estimates on the number of sex trafficking victims globally illustrate the severity of the problem. An estimated 800,000 to 4 million persons are trafficked across borders worldwide every year, as reported by United States Agency for International Development.[31] A large percentage of these are women and children who are prostituted for profit. UNICEF estimates that 1.2 million children alone are trafficked every year.[32] Anywhere from 50,000 to as many as 100,000 women and girls are estimated to be trafficked into the United States annually and are sexually exploited commercially by international criminal syndicates, pimps, pornographers, and other exploiters.[33]

However, domestic sex trafficking is a greater problem. It is estimated that between 100,000 and 300,000 children are sex trafficking victims within this country every year, turned into moneymaking sex slaves by pimps, gangs, and even parents.[34]

Like other sexual exploiters, sex traffickers have turned to the Internet and digital devices such as cell phones to recruit and abduct victims, advertise, and increase revenue from sexual slavery, as well as try to evade law enforcement.

Mass Media and Commercial Sexual Exploitation

Aside from prostitution, sexual slavery, and pornography through various venues, mass media plays a big role in the business of sexual exploitation. Millions upon millions of dollars are being made through films, television series, books, magazines, music, fragrances, and advertising through sexual exploitation of adults and teenagers. In taking full advantage of society's apparent obsession with youthfulness, beauty, sexuality, fitness, and imagination, many brand names and successful businesses have profited handsomely from commercial sexual exploitation of women and children, in particular.

Popular magazines such as *Cosmopolitan* and *Maxim* routinely offer provocative covers, scantily clad young men and women in photographs and online videos, as well as sexually explicit articles.[35] Similarly, trendy perfumes and colognes often rely on sexy commercials with attractive young actors to help sell the product.

Commercial sexual exploitation is also abundant in American cinema and television series. Many of the most successful movies in recent times have brought in millions, largely through sexually exploiting mostly youthful cast members. The same has been true for popular TV series such as *Sex and the City, Friends, Silk Stalkings, Baywatch, One Tree Hill, The O.C., Beverly Hills 90210*, and *Cougar Town*.

Moreover, some producers have tackled prostitution or pornography directly with art imitating life in sexually exploiting young actors and actresses commercially. Examples of this include the movies, such as *Pretty Woman*, which grossed more than $463 million,[36] and *The World of Suzie Wong*, along with television series and miniseries such as *Satisfaction, Secret Diary of a Call Girl*, and *Human Trafficking*. Recently reality television shows such as *The Hills, Big Brother, Survivor*, and *Jersey Shore* have also jumped on the bandwagon in sexually exploiting young people for big profits.

The literary world has also capitalized on the public's fascination with the life and times of actual prostitutes, ex prostitutes, madams, and pimps—leading to numerous memoirs and exposes of the business with such titles as *The Happy Hooker, Mayflower Madam: The Secret Life of Sydney Biddle Barrows, Secrets of a Hollywood Super Madam, Cop to Call Girl*, and *Callgirl: Confessions of an Ivy League Lady of Pleasure*.[37]

This commercialization of sexual exploitation through mass media aptly reflects popular culture and the profitability that comes from fueling the public's growing appetite for such material and items. It also allows a context for exploring the commercial sex trade industry in the digital age.

PART II

Commercial Sex Trade Industry

Chapter 2

Dynamics of Sex-for-Sale Industry

Prostitution has become a thriving enterprise in the United States today and involves women, men, and children in the trading of sexual favors, sexually transmitted diseases, pornography, pedophilia, skirting the law for prostitution services and servicing, and various related dynamics such as substance abuse, violence, and even death. Though prostitution is often depicted as taking place on street corners, in alleys or vehicles, most prostituting occurs behind closed doors in elegant hotels, private residences, massage parlors, and other places well out of public view where much of the money exchanges hands and both prostitutes and their clientele are not as easily detected. The result is that much of the activity in the commercial sex trade industry goes on regularly with little fear of interruption or arrest by law enforcement. With access to the Internet and cell phones, prostitutes, pimps, and clients have 21st-century digital devices at their disposal, making it very easy to communicate with each other and promote sex for sale with those who have the means to deliver and pay for it.

Defining Prostitution

Prostitution has been regarded by many as the world's oldest profession, with prostitutes, pimps, and customers operating to one degree or another since the beginning of time. Although some definitions of what constitutes prostitution have evolved over the centuries—particularly with regard to gender—and may vary from country to country, what defines the fundamental act of prostitution has generally remained steady from past to present. The *Merriam-Webster Dictionary* definition of prostitution is typical in the modern era as "the act or practice of engaging in promiscuous sexual relations, especially for money," or "the state of being prostituted."[1]

Charles Winick and Paul Kinsie's *The Lively Commerce* defined prostitution as the "granting of nonmaterial sexual access, established by mutual agreement" of the prostitute, customer, and/or pimp, which accounts for most of or all of a prostituted person's income.[2] In *The Comfort of Sin*, Richard Goodall defined prostitution as the selling of sexual favors by one who "earns a living wholly or in part by the more or less indiscriminate, willing, and emotionally indifferent provision of sexual services of any description to another, against payment, usually in advance but not necessarily in cash."[3]

According to Abraham Flexner, three elements are necessary for actions to be considered as prostitution: barter, promiscuous sexual behavior, and emotional indifference. He explained this:

> The barter need not involve the passage of money. . . . Nor need promiscuity be utterly choiceless: a [person] is not the less a prostitute because she [/he] is more or less selective in her [/his] associations. Emotional indifference may be inferred from barter and promiscuity. In this sense any person is a prostitute who habitually or intermittently has sexual relations more or less promiscuously for money or other mercenary consideration. Neither notoriety, arrest, nor lack of other occupation is an essential criterion.[4]

A legal definition of prostitution can be seen in the New Mexico Statute as follows:

> Prostitution consists of knowingly engaging in or offering to engage in a sexual act for hire. As used in this section "sexual act" means sexual intercourse, cunnilingus, fellatio, masturbation of another, anal intercourse or the causing of penetration to any extent and with any object of the genital or anal opening of another, whether or not there is any emission. Whoever commits prostitution is guilty of a petty misdemeanor, unless such crime is a second or subsequent conviction, in which case such person is guilty of a misdemeanor.[5]

By its very nature, for prostitution to achieve its objective, it requires the active participation of the prostituted person, either voluntarily or involuntarily, and those to whom prostitution services are aimed at and solicited.

Defining the Prostitute

The prostitute represents the most important person in the world of prostitution in order for it to function successfully. A prostitute is defined as one who engages in sexual intercourse indiscriminately with other people for monetary or other forms of payment such as drugs, food, or shelter. The dictionary defines the prostitute as "one hired as a sexual partner." To proffer yourself as a prostitute is therefore to "offer oneself to another as a paid sexual partner."[6]

Prostitutes are often referred to by other terms, including whore, harlot, sex worker, streetwalker, call girl, escort, and white slave. The term *prostitute* derives from the Latin words *pro* and *statuere*, meaning "to expose" and to "place up front."[7] Historically, prostitution and thereby prostitutes have been viewed as gender-specific, or as involving entirely females. According to Howard Woolston in *Prostitution in the United States*, prior to 1918, the only statutory definition of prostitution was found in the Indiana Law, as such:

> Any female who frequents or lives in a house of ill-fame or associates with women of bad character for chastity, either in public or at a house which men of bad character frequent or visit, or who commits adultery or fornication for hire shall be deemed a prostitute.[8]

Though many still tend to associate prostitutes in narrow or sexist terms, most general and legal definitions of prostitutes today identify those in the sex trade as female, male, and juvenile, as well as heterosexual, homosexual, and bisexual. Further classifications categorize prostitutes in terms of services performed, earnings, and place of business, such as a street corner or posh hotel.

Defining Customers of Prostitutes

Aside from prostitutes, other key participants in the sex trade industry are the customers. Also referred to as clients, johns, tricks, and kerb crawlers, among other slang names, customers are the persons who solicit prostitutes for sex. It has been suggested that the word *john* could have emerged from prostitutes' clients routinely identifying themselves with the common name "John" to remain anonymous.[9]

Though the vast majority of prostitute customers are adult males who solicit prostituted females and males, clients can also be females or juveniles. Many johns are also involved in other illegal activities such as pornography, pedophilia, drug dealing, gangs, and even murder. History is replete with serial killer johns such as Jack the Ripper, Robert Yates, and Gary Ridgway.[10]

Defining Pimps and Madams

Pimps and madams also play a major role in prostitution, acting as facilitators and operators of prostitution stables while using different means to maintain the cooperation of prostitutes and keep the operation running smoothly. They are seen as panderers or procurers of johns for prostitutes. A *panderer* is also legally defined as a manager for prostitutes and a person who entices or coerces a person into the sex trade industry.[11] The procurement of prostitutes includes running a prostitution business, bringing persons across borders for the purpose of prostitution, and the transporting of a prostitute to a location for sexual favors.

Pimps are primarily male and largely do their business at the street level of prostitution, controlling as much as 95 percent of female teenage prostitution.[12] They are also often involved in sex trafficking, pornography, drug dealing, and other illegal activity. Pimps typically take most of a prostitute's earnings and rely on a combination of psychological persuasion and physical abuse or threats thereof to keep their stable in line. A 1999 documentary, *American Pimp*, explored the gritty world of pimps in the United States.[13]

Madams are women who run brothels and escort services or defined as "the female head of a house of prostitution."[14] Their prostitutes are predominantly female and their clients male. Well-known madams include Sydney Biddle Barrows, known as the Mayflower Madam; Heidi Fleiss, dubbed the Hollywood Madam; Deborah Jeane Palfrey; and Xaviera Hollander.[15] Unlike pimps, madams do not need to rely on violence or intimidation to recruit prostitutes, as their stable is often self-sustaining due to the higher earnings that can be made for brothel and escort prostitutes, as well as safer conditions.

The Scope of Prostitution

How many people are involved in the United States as prostitutes, procurers, or customers? There are no estimates that account for total numbers of participants in the sex trade industry. What figures are available likely underestimate the actual scope of prostitution-involved individuals, given the surreptitious nature and range of prostitution-related activities. The yearly prevalence of prostitutes in the business full-time in the United States was estimated in a 1990 study at 23 per 100,000 persons.[16] With opportunities and perhaps a need for turning to prostitution increasing in the digital age of the 21st century and the downturn in our economy, many more people may have entered the sex trade industry as a result.

Most data on prostitution focus on female prostitutes. According to *The Prostitution of Women and Girls*, there are millions of females actively plying their trade as full-time prostitutes.[17] When adding part-time prostitutes and those labeled as mistresses for one client, the numbers could easily double or triple. One recent report estimated that active female prostitutes in this country averaged 868 male partners per year.[18] In a 2008 self-report survey of persons voluntarily entering a substance abuse treatment program, 41.4 percent of the females admitted prostituting themselves in the previous year compared to 11.2 percent of the males.[19]

Although data on male prostitutes are even more limited than data for female prostitutes, some findings suggest that there may be as many males selling their bodies as females. Since lower-level male prostitutes are not as conspicuous as their female counterparts are, assessing their incidence becomes all the more challenging.

Child prostitution appears to be every bit as big a problem as adult prostitution, especially where it concerns teenagers selling sex. Conservative estimates of underage prostitution places the number of prostituted youth at anywhere from 162,000 to 300,000 on U.S. streets.[20] In *Runaway Kids and Teenage Prostitution*, it was reported that upward of 500,000 persons under the age of 16 are actively involved in the sex trade in this country; with the number doubling or tripling when including 16- and 17-year-olds.[21]

Aside from domestic prostitution, there is a growing incidence of trafficking of individuals into the United States for purposes of sexual slavery. The U.S. State Department estimates that as many as 100,000 women and girls are trafficked into this country from abroad annually.[22] There is also an indication that sex trafficking within U.S. borders exists as well. Some 240,000 to 325,000 minors are believed to be victims of domestic trafficking annually, with runaway and thrownaway youth especially at risk.[23]

Not too surprisingly, little information exists on the scope of customers of prostituted individuals in the United States. The use of the Internet to solicit prostitutes has become a way of life for many johns and those they pay for sex, making it that much more difficult to track and for authorities to apprehend. Based on a 2004 poll, it was estimated that 15 percent of men in this country have paid for sexual relations at one time or another, with the number doubling for single men over the age of 30.[24] According to detailed interviews conducted in Chicago of acknowledged johns, 83 percent described paying for sex as an addiction, while 40 percent reported being under the influence of alcohol when purchasing the services of a prostitute.[25]

Types of Prostitution

Illegal Prostitution

Prostitution is illegal in the United States in every state except Nevada, where it is legal in a number of rural counties. Sex for sale or purchase was banned in Rhode Island in 2009, after being legal for three decades in the absence of a law that strictly forbade the act of prostitution, per se.[26] However, as with all other states, related actions were against the law, such as soliciting on the street, acting as a pimp, and operating a brothel. In 38 states, payment for prostitution services is prohibited, and solicitation laws are on the books in 44 states and the District of Columbia. Other states ban prostitution through laws against vagrancy and loitering.[27]

Prostitution is generally considered a misdemeanor, typically resulting in a fine or up to 6 months in jail. However, related charges such as pandering, sex trafficking, child pornography, assault, drug possession or dealing, money laundering, and income tax evasion can carry much stiffer sentences.[28]

According to the CBS News report "Sex Work Emerges from Shadows," vice squads across the United States average more than 82,000 prostitution-related arrests annually.[29] The U.S. Department of Justice estimated that in 2008 more than 75,000 arrests were made for prostitution and commercialized vice nationwide.[30] Female prostitutes are more likely to be arrested and incarcerated than male prostitutes, customers, or pimps, although more efforts have been made in recent years to reduce the disparity.[31]

Legal Prostitution

Legal prostitution in the United States exists only in the state of Nevada, where in eight counties licensed brothels are permitted for prostitution services between consenting adults. However, in Clark County, which includes Las Vegas, and Washoe County, including Reno, any kind of prostitution is banned. There has been much debate on the issue of legal prostitution versus illegal in this country as well as abroad, where in countries such as the Netherlands, Germany, New Zealand, Australia, and Turkey, prostitution is legal to one degree or another for adults or licensed brothels. In spite of the fact that regulated prostitution in Nevada seems to be working insofar as protecting prostitutes from sexually transmitted diseases and violence, there appears to be little chance that prostitution will become a legal enterprise across the country anytime soon, as opponents point toward everything from sexual immorality to a rise in the crime rate where prostitution is present to the recruitment of juveniles or the disadvantaged for commercial sexual exploitation.

Categorizing Prostitutes

Researchers have categorized prostitutes based on motivation for entry into the sex trade and situational or occupational variables. In *Prostitution and Morality*, Harry Benjamin and R. E. L. Masters described prostitutes as voluntary or compulsive, although neither was mutually exclusive.[32] Voluntary prostitutes come into the business rationally and of their own accord; whereas compulsive prostitutes are driven by psychoneurotic needs or narcotics addition.

Paul Goldstein's book, *Prostitution and Drugs*, broke down prostitutes as related to *occupational commitment* and *occupational milieu*.[33] Occupational commitment, or the frequency of prostitution, is further divided into three types of prostitutes:

1. *Temporary prostitute:* an episode of prostitution lasting no more than 6 months in a specific occupational milieu.
2. *Occasional prostitute:* two or more instances of prostitution in a specific occupational milieu, with each lasting no more than 6 months.
3. *Continual prostitute:* prostitution that lasts more than 6 months on a regular basis in a specific occupational milieu.

Occupational milieu refers to the types of prostitutes in the sex trade industry, such a streetwalking prostitutes, call girls, mistresses, and barterers.

Anthropologist Jennifer James classified prostitutes as *true prostitutes* and *part-timers*, for which they played roles.[34] Examples of true prostitutes, include rip-off artists, outlaws, old-timers, ladies, hypes, and thoroughbreds. *Part-time prostitutes* are those who have no style or are amateurs. James found that the roles were not mutually exclusive of each other, as they described different behavioral aspects as opposed to complete behavior sets for prostitutes.

Prostituted individuals can also be identified in terms of income, class, race, ethnicity, education, and opportunity to varying degrees and in conjunction with one another. In general, white call girls tend to make the most while working the least, often independent of other variables, whereas minority street-level prostitutes are more likely to earn the least for their services while putting in the most time plying their trade.

Types of Prostitutes

Prostitutes fall into several general groups based on earnings, work status, location, gender, age, and services rendered. Depending on the prostitute and circumstances of their prostitution, prostitutes can move between types or occupy more than one at a time.

Call Girls

Call girls represent the top echelon of female prostitution. Often referred to as upper-class prostitutes or high-class hookers, they range from super-elite prostitutes servicing a very wealthy clientele to middle-class prostitutes. They work as self-employed entrepreneurs or through escort services operated by a madam. Most are young, attractive, fit, well-dressed women who pride themselves on appearance and professionalism. Many are college educated and use this to their advantage in setting up a successful career as a call girl prostitute. They often ply their trade at five-star hotels, private residences, or another agreed-on meeting place. Some boast of their earnings, which can be hundreds of thousands of dollars per year. Experts estimate that call girls represent at least one-fourth of all prostitutes in the United States.[35]

Streetwalkers

Streetwalkers are at the low end of the prostitution hierarchy. As the most visible type of female prostitute—often seen on and around street corners in scant or sexual attire as they offer their services to men in cars passing by—street prostitutes are also the most vulnerable to violence, arrest, and other hazards of street life. It is estimated that streetwalkers constitute anywhere from 10 to 15 percent to as many as three-fourths of all working women in the U.S. sex trade industry.[36] Within this group, one in five are under the age of 20.[37] The vast majority of teenage prostitutes are streetwalkers and most have pimps, are forced into survival sex, abuse alcohol and drugs, and rarely advance into a higher class of prostitute.

In-House Prostitutes

Many prostitutes ply their trade in brothels, massage parlors, spas, saunas, modeling agencies, strip clubs, and other enterprises, some of which may operate as legitimate businesses but are actually places of prostitution and/or pornography. These gullible young women are often lured into the business through advertisements promising high earnings and successful careers, only to end up selling their bodies and engaging in other crimes such as drug abuse. In-house prostitutes generally fall between high-class call girls and streetwalkers in terms of prestige and earnings potential. Although law enforcement is aware of such fronts for illegal prostitution (as noted earlier, brothels are legal in certain counties in Nevada), they are often tolerated if not condoned due to the enormity and diversity of these establishments and other criminal activity that is given higher priority.

Male Prostitutes

Male prostitutes may rival female prostitutes in numbers and levels of prostitution with some high end and others low end in the sex trade. However, whereas the vast majority of prostituted females service heterosexual male clients, prostituted males' clientele include heterosexual men and some women, as well as homosexual men. The male (and female) prostitute's services rendered are more about what clients are willing to pay for than the prostitute's sexual orientation. Male prostitutes have been given various labels, often related to their customer's sexuality or gender. These include heterosexual prostitutes known as *gigolos*, homosexual prostitutes called *hustlers* or *rent boys*, and *chickens*, who are young boys and teenage males as the objects of desire by older men known as *chicken hawks*.[38] Prostitution-involved males ply their trade and solicit customers on the streets, in bars, spas, through escort services, and from advertising on the Internet and print materials that cater to their clientele.

Lesbian, Gay, Bisexual, and Transgender Prostitutes

Many prostituted persons are lesbian, gay, bisexual, and transgender (LGBT) or sexual minorities. Research indicates that anywhere from 20 percent to

50 percent of the homeless are LGBT.[39] Within this group, a high percentage are involved in street prostitution and survival sex. Although it is unknown how many upper-class prostitutes are LGBT, the indication is that the numbers are relative to the percentage in society at large.

LGBT prostitutes' clients are heterosexual, homosexual, and bisexual; and not necessarily indicative of the prostituted individual's sexual orientation or gender identity, per se, but rather a willingness to provide sexual services for survival or profit based on their clients' needs. Most prostitution-involved LGBTs are more susceptible to discrimination, violence, and victimization than heterosexual prostitutes are. They also have a high rate of mental disorders, substance abuse, HIV infection, and other negative experiences.[40]

Child Prostitutes

Child prostitutes include any prostituted youth under the age of 18. Most prostitution-involved juveniles are teenagers. Female and male teens are equally represented among child prostitutes. They number into the hundreds of thousands and perhaps well over a million such child prostitutes are active in the U.S. sex trade.[41] A high percentage of prostituted children are runaways and thrownaways who have been recruited for sexual exploitation by pimps, pornographers, organized criminals, and sex traffickers, or have been forced into survival sex to pay for food, or shelter, or to support drug habits. Although many teenage prostitutes come from abusive, impoverished, broken, or otherwise dysfunctional homes, some entered the business in spite of stable backgrounds or upper-middle to upper-class lives, often to escape boredom, make extra money, acquire drugs, peer pressure, or as a reflection of popular culture and the glorification of prostitution and promiscuity.[42] Many child prostitutes become drug-addicted adult prostitutes in a cycle of sexual abuse and exploitation.

Sex Trafficked Prostitutes

Sex trafficked prostitutes are among the most sexually exploited prostituted individuals commercially.[43] The trafficking of persons, usually woman and children, is sexual slavery that involves the forced or fraudulently induced participation in commercial sexual exploitation. This includes prostitution, pornography, live sex shows, and sex tourism. Hundreds of thousands of victims are trafficked across international borders and into the United States for purposes of prostitution and other sexual exploitation each year, with a growing number trafficked from within our borders by human traffickers, pimps, and crime syndicates.[44] Sex traffickers often engage in illegal debt-bondage practices to coerce victims into paying off debts through prostitution and other sexual services. Prostitution-involved victims of sex trafficking are often found selling sex on street corners, massage parlors, brothels, strip clubs, spas, and private residences.

Entering and Exiting Prostitution

For many prostitutes, leaving the commercial sex trade business has proven to be as difficult as entering it, if not more so. Most prostitution-involved individuals at all levels are primarily driven by the money that the sex trade offers, which is often more (and for many upper-class sex workers, much more) than can be earned through traditional work. Giving up the earnings and potential thereof, which is relative on the prostitution hierarchy, has been a powerful enough incentive to keep many in the business for years or till their services were no longer needed.

The average age of entry into prostitution for females is 12 to 14, although many become prostitution-involved at earlier ages.[45] Male sex workers tend to enter the business most often between the ages of 11 and 13, but are often younger when they have their first homosexual experience in which some form of payment is involved.[46] Most prostitution-involved individuals entered the sex trade as runaways or thrownaways and often came from sexually or physically abusive homes or foster care. Many become homeless or street youth due to substance abuse or sexual orientation/gender identity issues. Virtually all homeless persons at some early stage find themselves engaging in survival sex before progressing into full-blown prostitution.

Most young prostitutes may enter the sex-for-sale business seeing the sex work as only temporary. Often it becomes full-time prostituting as a necessary means to satisfy basic needs, to pay for drug habits, and as a requirement for prostituted females with pimps. The supply and demand of the flourishing commercial sex trade industry dictates that many sex workers ply the trade on a regular basis.

Most prostitution-engaged males tend to exit the business by their mid-twenties, primarily because their clientele often favors young prostitutes. However, female prostitutes can work well into their thirties and forties, as a market still exists for them, particularly for low-end prostitution, though most johns also tend to prefer prostitutes who are teenagers and in their twenties.

Beyond the money that the commercial sex trade industry offers prostitutes, exiting the prostitution business is hampered by such issues as having few workable skills to compete in the legitimate job market, drug dependency (drugs are readily available in the prostitution subculture and may often act in lieu of cash payment for drug-addicted prostitutes), the lifestyle itself that can be addictive to those involved in prostitution, and losing status and a sense of belonging that sex work can bring. Furthermore, for many low-end female prostitutes who work for pimps, leaving the business is not an option, as threats of bodily harm or even death are enough to keep them in a pimp's stable often for years till he replaces them with someone younger and healthier.[47]

Sexually Transmitted Diseases and Prostitutes

With the nature of commercial sex work that often involves multiple anonymous sexual partners for unprotected sex, intravenous (IV) drug use, and other risky behaviors, a high rate of sexually transmitted diseases (STDs) exist among female and male prostitutes, and often their customers. These include HIV/AIDS, genital warts, gonorrhea, syphilis, herpes, and hepatitis B. Studies show a strong correlation between prostitutes and exposure to STDs, with prostituted women, teenagers, and males at relatively equal risk. According to one researcher, more than 85 percent of prostituted teens have contracted an STD while working the sex trade.[48] The National Center for Missing and Exploited Children's report, *Female Juvenile Prostitution*, pointed toward STDs as a common issue of susceptibility for girl prostitutes.[49]

HIV infection is of particular concern as an STD or drug-related disease for prostitution-involved individuals. In the publication *AIDS, Drugs, and Prostitution*, the author found that high-risk sexual activities were commonly associated with heavy use of drugs and alcohol, along with a depression of the immune system.[50] Streetwalking prostitutes, many of whom continue to have unprotected sex (or inconsistent use of condoms) with numerous partners, may face the greatest threat of becoming HIV-positive. In a study by the University of Miami, 41 percent of the streetwalkers sampled were HIV infected.[51] Another study of streetwalkers found that around 4 in 10 of those who were IV drug users tested positive for HIV.[52]

Homeless prostitutes are also at high risk for contracting the AIDS precursor HIV. One study found that the "HIV prevalence rate for homeless youth was up to 10 times higher than other youth in the United States; with homeless teenagers seven times as likely to die of AIDS and 16 times more likely of being diagnosed with HIV than youth in the population at large."[53] According to the largest New York City shelter, Covenant House, girl runaways who offered their bodies daily to johns could have a rate of HIV infection that exceeded 50 percent.[54]

Other research reveals that the high-risk activities of prostitution-involved males put them in the greatest danger of HIV exposure. In one study of male prostitutes in New York City, over half who engaged in homosexual prostitution tested HIV-seropositive.[55] A Chicago survey of self-reported risk factors among homeless male youth in contracting the AIDS virus found that 87 percent of the respondents had engaged in one or more risk factors such as prostitution, having high-risk or multiple sex partners, anal sex, and IV drug use.[56]

Violence and Prostitution

Lower-class, homeless, and teenage female prostitutes are frequently the victims of violence by pimps, customers, pornographers, gang members, homeless persons, the mentally ill, and others, leading to serious injuries and even death. The Department of Justice reported that the rate of mortality among prostitutes is 40 times greater than the national average.[57] According to one source, around 80 percent of prostitutes have been rape victims, with an average of 8 to 10 rapes a year.[58] Another study found that 70 percent of prostitution-involved females are raped regularly by customers, with 65 percent victims of physical assaults by johns.[59]

Experts believe the percentage of pimp-generated physical and sexual assaults of prostitutes is even higher.[60] Pimps often resort to violence as part of the control mechanism for controlling their stable and keeping them from leaving. Violence is also used by pimps to make an example of one prostitute to ensure his hold over others.

Although violence is less of an issue for high-end prostitutes, some have been the victims of rape, assaults, and fatalities by violent johns or others in the course of their profession. Given the greater anonymity of upper-class sex workers, victimization is less likely to come to the attention of authorities and researchers.

Prostitution-engaged males are frequently the victims of physical and sexual assaults by customers, as well as bias crimes and threats of bodily harm as a result of their sex work and/or perceived sexual orientation. One expert on violence in the male prostitution subculture referred to it as rampant and "endemic to this lifestyle."[61]

Gay, bisexual, transgender, or questioning boy prostitutes have one of the highest risks of being physically attacked, sexually assaulted, or robbed. The National Runaway Switchboard found prostitution-involved homeless youth identifying as sexual minorities seven times more likely to be victims of violence than their heterosexual counterparts.[62]

Chapter 3

Causes of Prostitution

As the so-called world's oldest profession, theorists and criminologists have long debated and theorized on the causes of prostitution and what forces draw women, men, and children into a world of paid sex that is generally seen as taboo. For moral, legal, health, personal, or safety reasons, certainly most people would never consider selling their bodies, often to multiple customers, for money or material items, regardless of their circumstances. Yet, by most accounts, the business of prostitution is flourishing in the 21st-century digital age as supply and demand are both in abundance, with little indication of slowing down and law enforcement unable to keep pace. Persons enter the sex trade for a variety of reasons relating to economics, earnings, family dynamics and dysfunction, child sexual and physical abuse, sexual orientation/gender identity issues, sex trafficking, pimps, survival, sex addiction, drug dependency, mental issues, low self-esteem, promiscuity, adventure, peer pressure, and often a combination of factors. The fact that there is a constant source of buyers for sexual services and multiple means to bring prostitutes and customers together to do business with the relatively low risk for detection, makes the sex for sale industry a powerful draw and, as such, perhaps the primary cause and effect of prostitution.

Theories on Prostitution

Early theories on prostitution tended to focus largely on prostitution-involved females and biological, psychological, and sociological hypotheses in explaining entry into prostitution and continual participation. Many such theories have since been dismissed for their gender biases and weak methodologies, while some have been modified or modernized to account for gender-neutral and the wider ranging prostitution in today's world.

Biological Theories

One of the first people to study female criminality was Cesare Lombroso, an Italian psychiatrist. Thought by many to have founded the biological-positivistic school of criminology, in 1894 Lombroso and his son-in-law, William Ferrero, wrote *The Female Offender*. In using quantitative and qualitative research, they theorized that female criminals, and particularly those engaging in prostitution acts, were biologically predisposed to criminality or in effect "born deviants."[1] These women were seen as atavistic or having primitive genetic characteristics not present in normal females. As an example, it was thought that prostitutes were "likely to have very heavy jaws, large nasal spines, simple cranial sutures, deep frontal sinuses, and wormian bones. A fallen woman usually possessed occipital irregularities, a narrow forehead, prominent cheekbones, and a 'virile' type of face."[2]

Though the Lombroso-Ferrero atavism theory had support from some such as Harvard anthropologist Earnest Hooton, it has been largely rejected by such critics as Charles Goring, a British physician, as methodologically flawed and gender based.[3] Other criminologists such as Enrico Ferri favored a broader approach to explaining prostitution and other criminal behavior by including socioeconomic and political variables.[4] Modern biological research on female deviance has tied hereditary factors to promiscuity and such hormonal issues as menstruation and premenstrual syndrome to criminality.[5] These theories also have been controversial and limited in their acceptance as a result of methodology and biases.

Psychological Theories

Much of the early psychological approaches to prostitution were influenced by Sigmund Freud's psychoanalytic writings.[6] Similar to Lombroso, Freud believed prostitutes to be biologically deficient and consequently unable to resolve the Oedipus complex. He regarded them as "morally inferior and less able to control their impulses than men, implying an inherent pathology existed in females who prostituted themselves."[7]

A number of Freudian supporters saw prostitutes as frigid with "immature psychosexual development and severely deficient object relationships."[8] Case studies of prostitutes have not shown any general degree of abnormality. The notion of frigidity among prostitutes has also been called into question. In Jennifer James's study of prostitutes, she found that the rate of achieving orgasm among them was actually higher than the general public.[9]

Freud's propositions regarding prostitution have been largely rebuffed by contemporary psychiatrists and psychologists for their biases, psychological shortcomings, and lack of social and economic principles.

Recent studies of prostitution-involved individuals, however, have found a psychological component to prostitution, linking it to clinical depression, emotional deprivation, psychosis, suicidal ideation, and schizophrenia.[10] Researchers have found that between 10 and 20 percent of prostituted girls have spent time in psychiatric institutions, with half having been hospitalized more than once.[11] Studies indicate that up to half of all female prostitutes have attempted suicide on at least one occasion.[12]

Sociological Theories

Sociologists have also offered theories in attempting to explain prostitution. One of the earliest was William Thomas, who rejected the biological inferiority approach to female prostitution, believing gender differences in criminal behavior could be attributed to social factors and acquired characteristics.[13] He offered a dyadic goals-means theory instead, indicating that everyone has four basic desires: security, recognition, new experience, and response. Thomas believed that criminal behavior was influenced mostly by the desire for new experience and response. He theorized that female prostitution reflected a need for excitement and response, arguing that for women, "prostitution in one form or another was the most likely avenue to satisfy those needs."[14]

Critics have dismissed Thomas's theory as sexist, paternalistic, and unproven. Similar criticism was leveled at Sheldon and Eleanor Glueck's 1930s research on female delinquents, many of whom were prostitutes, that concluded a high percentage were mentally defective with their criminality intergenerational.[15]

In 1950, Otto Pollak published *The Criminality of Women*, considered at the time to be the authoritative work on female criminal behavior.[16] Although Pollak was influenced by Lombroso and Freud, he developed new theories of female criminality, especially prostitutes, arguing that their crimes were largely sexually motivated (compared to the economic motivations of male criminals). He contended that the hidden nature of prostitution made it more difficult to be properly assessed in the statistics and that females were addicted to offenses that were easily concealed. Pollak's hypotheses have been mostly rejected as biased and lacking substantiation. Arguably female streetwalkers are more visible than male streetwalkers are, though middle- and upper-class female prostitutes may outnumber their male counterparts while operating with much greater concealment from exposure.

Modern sociology theories have focused on the social structure and cultural transmission in understanding prostitution. According to Charles Winick and Paul Kinsie in *The Lively Commerce*, prostitution threatened the social structure because "people tend to equate sexual activity with stable relationships, typified by the family."[17] In Kingsley Davis's functionalist theory on prostitution, he argued that "the function served by prostitution is the protection of the family unit, maintenance of the chastity and purity of 'respectable' citizenry."[18] He contended that most women do not become prostitutes because morality outweighs the financial incentives of the sex trade industry, and that prostitution is a creation of the system of morality in society "by defining the sex drive in terms of a meaningful social relationship and denouncing prostitution as a meaningless sexual relationship."[19]

In Edwin Lemert's social pathology theory of prostitution, he advanced that prostitution is a "formal extension of more generalized social pathology in our culture, of which sexual promiscuity and thinly disguised commercial exploitation of sex in informal context plays a large and important part."[20] Prostitution is regarded as situational from this point of view, with the act of prostitution reflecting the conflicts and strains that exist in society.

According to cultural transmission theorists, prostitution results from a "weakening of family and neighborhood control and the persistence and transmission from person to person of traditional delinquent activities."[21] Though some studies have shown that many prostitutes are introduced to the business by other prostitutes, relatives, neighbors, associates, and others who may be homeless;[22] other studies have found that prostitution is less associated with environmental factors and is present across socioeconomic and occupational lines as a result of urban anonymity and lessening moral and traditional values.[23]

Economic Theories

Economic theories on prostitution argue that the opportunity to make money to survive or thrive is the greatest motivation to enter the sex trade and remain in the profession of prostitution. Winick and Kinsie posited that one's decision to go into prostitution is by and large a reflection of few other employment opportunities for many and the potential income prostitution offers.[24] Lemert held that women's lack of power and control where it concerns material gains in society makes the sex trade industry a practical way to achieve some balance in societal status.[25]

According to James, there are five features of the socioeconomic structure that draws women into selling their bodies:[26]

1. There are no comparable occupations for unskilled or low-skilled women to make the same amount of money.
2. Virtually no other occupations exist for unskilled or low-skilled women that provide the type of independence and adventurous lifestyle as prostitution.
3. The woman's traditional role is nearly synonymous with the female sex role as traditionally defined, which is based on physical appearance, sexuality, and service.
4. The importance of wealth and material items culturally causes some women to desire things they would not normally be afforded as a result of their socioeconomic place in society.
5. A discrepancy between accepted sex roles for men and women creates a "Madonna-whore" view of female sexuality that causes women who are sexually active beyond their normal sex role expectations to be labeled deviant, affecting their social status.

Within the economic context of prostitution, there can be a considerable difference in the earnings potential between a streetwalking prostitute and a high-class call girl. However, the financial incentive to enter into prostitution is still relative across prostitution class lines. This includes male prostitutes who may enter the business without the same limitations in the general society as females, but are nonetheless driven by similar needs for survival on the streets or building a comfortable nest egg while operating as a high-class male prostitute.

Though teenage prostitutes generally occupy the lower rung of the prostitution hierarchy, their need to make money while often living on the streets or engage in survival sex may be the greatest. This, however, makes the lure of money and what it can do no less addictive for juvenile prostitutes. In a study of teen prostitution, Joan Johnson wrote: "Money becomes a symbol of love. Just as they could never get enough love as children, prostitutes can never seem to get enough money as teenagers. . . . This hunger for money helps to explain why some adolescents began turning tricks."[27]

Correlates of Prostitution

In addition to theories on prostitution, a number of correlates of involvement in the sex trade industry have been established. These include sexual abuse, substance abuse, sexual orientation/gender identity, survival sex, sexual slavery, and sexual adventure and promiscuity.

Sexual Abuse

One of the most common themes of prostitution involvement is childhood sexual abuse. The correlation between being a prostitute and having been sexually abused prior to leaving home is a strong one. In the book *Street Kids,* prevalence rates for sexual abuse of runaways are reported to be as high as 70 percent.[28] According to a study by Mimi Silbert, two in three prostituted runaways were incest and abuse victims.[29] One report indicated that "sex abuse appears to indirectly increase the chance of prostitution by increasing the risk of running away."[30]

Prostitution-involved youth who are homeless may be even more likely to be victims of child sexual abuse, including rape and incestuous relations. Stephen Gaetz found that homeless youth were five times as likely as non-homeless youth to have been sexually abused when living at home.[31]

Lesbian, gay, bisexual, and transgender (LGBT) teenage prostitute youth, in particular, have a high rate of child sexual abuse victimization. In studies, the majority of prostituted LGBT youths were found to have run away from or were thrown out of the home because of sexual or physical abuse.[32]

One such case of a sexually abused child prostitute was described by researcher Christina Hoag:

> By the time she was eight, Amanda had been sexually abused by her father's friend for four years. At 12, she was peddling crack. At 14, she was selling sex on the sidewalk. Her pimp beat her weekly to keep her working, stitching up her wounds himself to avoid questions at a hospital. Her average earnings of $600 for a 13-hour day of turning tricks bought him a car. . . .[33]

Substance Abuse

The relationship between substance abuse before and after entering prostitution has been shown to be significant. Many street youth were already drug or alcohol users or dependent prior to leaving home. One study found that up to 7 in 10 runaway youth used drugs when living at home.[34] Another study reported that nearly half of runaway prostitutes were users of alcohol before entering the sex trade.[35] According to a 2002 National Survey on Drug Use and Health finding, persons between 12 and 17 years of age who had run away from home within the past year were more likely than minors who had not left home to have drunk alcohol, smoked marijuana, used other illicit drugs such as crack, cocaine, inhalants, heroin, or hallucinogens, or abused prescription drugs.[36]

For homeless prostitutes, there is a strong likelihood of substance abuse problems. A study by Shelly Mallett and colleagues of 302 homeless youth found that 38 percent had become street kids because of alcohol and drug use.[37] Nearly one in five of the homeless youth had begun using drugs after becoming homeless. In a study of 432 street youth in Los Angeles, more than 7 in 10 suffered from substance abuse disorders.[38] Alcohol and marijuana are the most commonly used drugs by the prostituted homeless, although a high percentage also use amphetamines, cocaine, or crack, and abuse prescription drugs.[39] One study found that three out of four teenage prostitutes were substance abusers.[40]

Sexual Orientation/Gender Identity

Youth who experience sexual orientation/gender identity issues at home are at high risk for running away or being thrown away from home and consequently becoming prostituted homeless youth. In a study conducted by the National Gay and Lesbian Task Force and National Coalition for the Homeless, it was found that as many as 42 percent of homeless youth in the United States identify themselves as lesbian or gay, with a disproportionate percentage identified as bisexual or transgender.[41] In Michael Clatts and colleagues' study, up to half the street youth identified themselves as LGBT.[42]

It is debatable whether LGBT youth are more likely to run away or be thrown out of the home. In one study, more than one-fourth of lesbian or gay youth were forced out of the home because of sexual orientation or gender identity issues.[43] However, a survey of 775 homeless gay teenagers in San Francisco, New York, and Denver found that nearly 8 in 10 left home voluntarily.[44]

It is clear that there is a strong correlation between homeless LGBT youth and involvement in prostitution. One study found that LGBT homeless youth were three times more likely than heterosexual homeless youth to prostitute themselves for survival.[45] Another study reported that for many

LGBT street kids, prostitution is seen as a last resort when all other options have been exhausted in surviving while homeless.[46]

Survival Sex

Many homeless persons find themselves engaging in *survival sex*, defined as "the commercial sexual activity of young people as a way of obtaining the necessities of life, including food, drugs, clothing, transport, or money to purchase these goods and services."[47] It has been estimated that anywhere from one-third to over half of homeless youth participate in survival sex, with the actual figures likely being much higher. Researcher Jody Greene and colleagues noted that the dangers "inherent in survival sex make it among the most damaging repercussions of homelessness among youths."[48]

The term *survival sex* tends to often be considered synonymous with prostitution, particularly that involving teenage runaways or thrownaways. However, studies reveal that "many youth involved in the exchange of sex for money or other considerations . . . do not perceive themselves as engaging in prostitution, but rather as doing 'whatever is necessary' to ensure their survival."[49] Moreover, for some homeless youth survival sex relates more to their freedom, previous sexual experiences, promiscuity, and peers than forced sexual relations. Writer Nicholas Ray describes survival sex as "a desperate and risky behavior borne out of isolation and the lack of any tangible resources."[50]

Sexual Slavery

Sexual slavery is a form of sexual exploitation involving the enslavement of individuals, usually women and children, for sexual practices, including domestic servitude and forced prostitution.[51] Human trafficking for purposes of commercial sexual exploitation as prostitutes, participants in pornography, sex tourism, and related coerced sexual activities is considered a modern day form of sexual slavery. Hundreds of thousands of sex slaves are trafficked across international borders into the United States or within U.S. borders between states every year and forced to prostitute themselves.

Perpetrators of sexual slavery include international and domestic pimps, organized syndicates, and gang members. In Asian communities, for instance, thousands of female teenagers are smuggled into this country annually by Asian gangs, where gang rapes and drug addiction are used to force them into prostitution as indentured servants.[52] Some homeless and teenage prostituted crack addicts find temporary shelter in crack houses where they, effectively, become "little more than indentured servants, if not outright slaves," in selling their bodies for drugs and housing.[53]

Sexual Adventure and Promiscuity

Although most persons who enter prostitution, especially on the low end, do so under circumstances of stress and strain or are otherwise forced into the sex-for-sale industry, some turn to prostitution for sexual adventure and freedom, making extra cash, or as a reflection of being promiscuous. In one study of runaways, their initial objectives were found to be acquiring "a place to sleep and then look for adventure—get a crash pad and some kicks."[54] An expert on runaway youth found that "the rule for runaway girls everywhere is often 'ball for bed'—meaning that implicit in an offer of lodging is the expectation of sexual intercourse."[55]

Researchers have found that for a growing number of young individuals, sexual independence, experimentation, money-making opportunity, promiscuity, open-mindedness, and being influenced by like minds, are as likely to result in prostituting themselves as running away from unstable environments or becoming homeless. Dorothy Bracey reported that many prostituted girls enter the business because they have friends offering sexual favors for pay.[56] Group sex was found to be a common practice among runaway teenagers, according to a survey of runaways in New York and San Francisco.[57] In a study of street kids by Pamela Miller and associates, independence was identified as an important element in the decision to become homeless.[58]

A social worker who counsels female prostitutes described the state of prostitution for all too many today: "Sex is no longer for love and procreation, but solely for enjoyment. But this leads to fleeting sexual contacts, which turn out to be meaningless. What gives them meaning is the profit."[59] This position appears to be particularly reflected in call girl prostitution, where many of those involved enter the business for both pleasure and profit.[60]

PART III

Females Plying Sexual Services

Chapter 4

Legal Prostitution

Prostitution is legal in one form or another in many countries throughout the world, including the Netherlands, Hungary, Germany, England, Denmark, Australia, New Zealand, Canada, Venezuela, and Brazil, among others. In the United States, where each state is empowered to determine the legality or illegality of prostitution and to what degree, prostitution (whether selling or buying) is illegal in every state except Nevada. Licensed brothels for prostitution exist in a number of rural counties in Nevada, but prostitution services are banned elsewhere in the state, including Las Vegas and Reno. Nevertheless, illegal prostitution is flourishing in Nevada, including a high incidence of teenage prostitution. Although legal prostitutes in Nevada are predominantly female, in 2010 the first legal male sex worker began prostituting for a brothel. Much controversy exists on the effectiveness and harm of legal prostitution in Nevada, as well as whether or not prostitution should be legalized or decriminalized in other states.

Brothel prostitutes appear to operate in safer conditions than street-walkers (with an apparently much lower rate of sexually transmitted diseases (STDs) such as HIV); however, substance abuse among brothel sex workers is a problem they have in common with illegal prostitutes, as well as the need or desire to make money as their primary motivation for entering the legal sex trade. Polls indicate that the majority of Nevadans tend to favor the status quo of regulated rural legal brothels while opposing legalization of prostitution in larger counties, such as Clark County where Las Vegas is.[1]

Legal Prostitution in Other Countries

Prostitution or receiving payment for sexual favors is illegal in most countries, with penalties varying from as little as a fine to being punishable by death.[2] However, prostitution activities including in some instances pimping, is legal in a number of countries outside the United States.[3] In many such cases, the solicitation, pimping, or housing of prostitutes for sexual services is illegal.[4] The legalizing/regulating, decriminalizing, or condoning prostitution generally pertains to four areas: "victimhood (including potential victimhood), ethics and morality, freedom of the individual, and general benefit or harm to society (including harm arising indirectly from matters connected to prostitution)."[5] Some countries, including the United States in Nevada, have chosen to permit legal prostitution under certain circumstances, in either deciding it was ungovernable or siding with the prostitutes' right to sell their bodies to earn a living. In most such countries, illegal prostitution is present as well, including the prostitution of minors, trafficked prostitutes, pimp-controlled prostitution, and related commercial sexual exploitation such as child pornography, sex tourism, and pedophilia.

With respect to legal prostitution abroad, there are essentially two types: (1) legal prostitution that is regulated and (2) legal prostitution that bans procurement. In the former, such typical sex trade involvement as child prostitution, street prostitution, and pimping are usually excluded. Regulations tend to vary from country to country. For instance, the "prostitutes may be registered . . . hired by a brothel . . . organize trade unions . . . covered by worker protection laws, their proceeds may be taxable . . . [and] not all countries require mandatory health checks (because such checks are seen as too intrusive, a violation of human rights and discriminatory, since the clients aren't subjected to them)."[6] In the second type of legal prostitution, along with procuring, most such countries have laws that ban "soliciting in a public place (e.g., a street) or advertising prostitution," which makes it all but impossible to participate in prostitution without violating applicable laws.[7]

Other countries where prostitution is legal and regulated include Austria, Australia, Bolivia, Ecuador, Germany, Greece, Mexico, the Netherlands, New Zealand, Panama, Peru, Senegal, Switzerland, Turkey, and Uruguay. Perhaps the best example of a country where prostitution is legal and regulated, including the operation of brothels, is the Netherlands. It is estimated that there are 20,000 to 25,000 full-time prostitutes plying their trade there, with some experts suggesting the number would double were part-time prostitutes included.[8]

De Wallen is Amsterdam's largest and most well-known red light district and a prime place for sex tourists from around the world to visit. It consists of a network of alleys containing [hundreds of] tiny one-room cabins rented by prostitutes who offer their services from behind a window or glass door, typically illuminated with red lights. The area also has a number of sex shops, sex theatres, peep shows, [and] a sex museum.[9]

According to city data, in 2008 there were "142 licensed brothels in Amsterdam, with about 500 window displays."[10] The legal sex trade industry in Amsterdam generates around $100 million in American currency a year.[11]

In spite of the success of legal prostitution in the Netherlands, similar to other countries with a legal sex trade industry, it is in strong competition with illegal prostitution within its borders, including streetwalkers, sex trafficking, and "kerb-crawling cars," along with related drug activity.[12] The legalization of prostitution by the government was supposed to "protect the women by giving them work permits."[13] Dutch authorities have since come to believe the business has gotten out of hand, as indicated by the ex-mayor of Amsterdam, Job Cohen: "We've realized this is no longer about small-scale entrepreneurs, but that big crime organizations are involved here in trafficking women, drugs, killings, and other criminal activities."[14]

Countries where prostitution is legal, but procuring is not, include Australia, Argentina, Brazil, Canada, Cuba, Czech Republic, Denmark, Dominican Republic, Ethiopia, France, Finland, Guatemala, Hong Kong, India, Israel, Spain, and United Kingdom. In Canada, for example, though prostitution is not a crime in and of itself, it is illegal to:

> live "off the avails" of prostitution (this law is intended to outlaw pimping) and it is illegal (for both parties) to negotiate a sex-for-money deal in a public place (which includes bars). To maintain a veneer of legality, escort agencies arrange a meeting between the escort and the client. A Canadian Supreme Court ruling in 1978 required that to be convicted of soliciting, a prostitute's activities must be "pressing and persistent."[15]

Similarly, in the United Kingdom, offering sexual relations for monetary payment is legal, but prohibited are such related actions as "soliciting in a public place, kerb crawling, keeping a brothel, pimping, and pandering."[16] According to the Policing and Crime Act 2009, it is "illegal to pay for sex with a prostitute who has been 'subjected to force' and this is a *strict liability offense* (clients can be prosecuted even if they didn't know the prostitute was forced)."[17]

An estimated 2 million or more females are thought to be active in prostitution or have sold their bodies in Great Britain, through legal and illegal avenues.[18] Most of these are prostitutes working in brothels, massage parlors, private health clubs, or saunas "in practically every reasonably-sized town and city across the country, whether in the guise of a private flat or house, or run on more commercial and professional lines."[19] Studies show that there is a high incidence of HIV infection, physical assaults, and homicides among United Kingdom prostitutes.[20] Other research has yielded comparable findings with respect to prostitution-involved individuals practicing their trade in countries with legal prostitution but illegal procurement, as well as illegal prostitution.[21]

Legal Prostitution in Nevada

Prostitutes can operate legally in the United States in regulated brothels inside the state of Nevada, with prostitution banned in the rest of the country.[22] The brothels are all located in rural counties with populations of less than 400,000. Currently there are 28 legal brothels in the state with names such as Angel's Ladies, Moonlite BunnyRanch, Sue's Fantasy Club, Shady Lady Ranch, and the World Famous Mustang Ranch. These brothels are spread out over eight counties, with four other counties legally able to issue licenses.[23] This does not include Clark County where Las Vegas is located, or Washoe County where Reno is located.

Legal brothel prostitution in Nevada is a lucrative enterprise, bringing in about $75 million in revenue annually.[24] However, the illegal sex-for-sale business in Las Vegas alone brings in an estimated $5 billion each year.[25] According to an investigation of female sex workers in America by ABC News, there are around 1,000 women working as independent contractors at legal brothels in Nevada, but only about 300 are active in the legal sex trade at any given time.[26] By comparison, an estimated 10,000 females ply the trade illegally in Las Vegas.[27] Licensed brothel prostitution-engaged women "work a legally mandated minimum of nine days for each work period."[28]

Perhaps the most well-known legal brothel in Nevada is the World Famous Mustang Ranch.[29] First called the Mustang Bridge Ranch, in 1971 it was Nevada's first brothel to be licensed, paving the way for legal prostitution in the state. Spread out over 166 acres in Storey County and yielding the most profits among brothels, the Mustang Ranch was "forfeited to the federal government in 1999 following [the owner Joe] Conforte's convictions for tax fraud, racketeering, and other crimes. It was auctioned off and reopened five miles to the east under the same name but different ownership."[30]

Today the World Famous Mustang Ranch is a multimillion dollar enterprise that's "run with sophistication and a keen eye on the profit margin."[31] Described as being "like a small compound, tucked away off the highway and surrounded by mountains," the brothel has its own Web site with an "erotic menu," to "feed your desires and fantasies," with such entrees as "Straight Lay," "Two Girl Show," and "Menage a Trois."[32] *Love Ranch*, a 2010 motion picture starring Academy Award winner Helen Mirren, was based somewhat on the Mustang Ranch and the lives of Joe Conforte and his wife Sally.[33]

Another well-known Nevada legal brothel is the Moonlite BunnyRanch, which first opened its doors in Carson City in 1955 as the Moonlight Ranch.[34] The brothel, owned by Dennis Hof, was the basis of two HBO America Undercover documentaries, *Cathouse* and *Cathouse 2: Back in the Saddle*, as well as the reality show *Cathouse: The Series*.[35]

The Dynamics of Legal Prostitution

Brothel prostitutes in Nevada must be licensed, which requires the person to be 21 years of age or older, with the exception of Lyon County and Storey County, with 18 as the minimum age. The brothel's license fees to operate are anywhere from $200 a year in Lander County to $100,000 yearly in Storey County.[36] Licensed brothel prostitutes ply their trade as independent contractors and, as such, do not qualify for health benefits, unemployment, or retirement. Legal prostitutes usually tend to "work for a period of several weeks, during which time they live in the brothel and hardly ever leave it. They then take some time off."[37]

The health of legal prostitutes and customers is a big concern for state officials. According to Nevada law, registered brothel sex workers are required to be tested every week "(by a cervical specimen) for gonorrhea and Chlamydia trachomatis, and monthly for HIV and syphilis."[38] Moreover, use of condoms is mandatory for sexual intercourse and oral copulation. Brothel owners can be held liable if customers contract HIV after a licensed prostituted has tested HIV-positive. Apparently, this has not been a problem with regulated legal brothel prostitution in Nevada. The state's brothel industry has not reported a single case of HIV for one of its licensed prostitutes since mandatory testing started in the mid-1980s.[39] In a study of two legal brothels, it was found that "condom use in the brothels was consistent and sexually transmitted diseases were accordingly absent."[40] Most of the prostitutes reportedly did not use condoms in their sexual relationships outside the sex trade.

In spite of the low rate of STDs and the generally healthier conditions in which legal brothel prostitutes work as compared to prostituted females working the streets, drug abuse appears to be as much a problem for licensed sex workers as their street-level counterparts. A prostitute for the BunnyRanch noted to this effect: "A lot of the girls here do drugs. Whether it's illegal drugs on the street, coke, and ecstasy kind of stuff, or whether its prescription drugs, three or four Xanax to get through the day, most of them are on something."[41]

Earnings of Legal Brothel Prostitutes

Legal prostitutes' earnings vary, depending on the brothel, location, services offered, experience, and demand. In general, licensed sex workers tend to make more the closer the bordello is to Las Vegas.[42] For the most part, brothels do not operate with preset fees for service. Whatever their take amounts to, as independent contractors, it is the prostitute's responsibility to pay federal income taxes (there is no Nevada state income tax). Income is reported to the IRS on form 1099-MISC. According to Wikipedia, with respect to the process of prostitute-customer business:

> All but the smallest brothels operate as follows: as the customer is buzzed in and sits down in the parlor, the available women appear in a line-up and introduce themselves. If the customer chooses a woman, the price negotiations take place in the woman's room, which are often overheard by management. The house normally gets half of the negotiated amount. If the customer arrives by cab, the driver will receive some 30% of whatever the customer spends; this is subtracted from the woman's earnings.[43]

Prices for sexual services typically begin at $200 per 15 minutes, but can go higher. According to one sex worker at the Moonlite BunnyRanch, "My rate is $2,000 an hour for everything, $1,000 for half an hour, $500 for 15 minutes."[44] Another claimed to make as much as $3,000 a day at the same brothel, staying "at the ranch for weeks at a time before going home . . . in order to make ends meet and provide for her young daughter."[45]

Susan Austin, the World Famous Mustang Ranch madam, indicated that some of her prostitutes offered their services for between $10,000 and $15,000 a night or for two days of prostituting.[46] Other legal brothel sex workers "may charge up to $10,000 an hour for 'parties' with well-known or novelty women, or more for parties with multiple women."[47]

According to Austin, the older licensed prostitutes with more experience at her brothels tend to "command the higher rates:"

A woman with a little age under her belt has a lot more patience. She's more versed in the business. The young girl a lot of times just starting out doesn't have all the necessary tools. That comes with age, and it comes with practice. It's like taking a rookie baseball player versus a seasoned baseball player, if you know what I mean.[48]

The madam noted that the "girls at the brothel love to brag about making big money; thousands a week in some cases. But the women are willing to accept less."[49]

I have more ladies coming in now than I ever did before because of the economic times. They're all coming in. [It's] the only way to make some decent money in this time and age. Jobs are not that many available because of the economic times and they can make more money doing this than they can flipping burgers at McDonald's.[50]

According to researcher Elizabeth Joseph, based on a two-year investigation of the commercial sex trade industry, many men these days pay out a great deal of money for not just high-class sexual relations, but to enjoy what is known as the Girlfriend Experience or GFE, in which the prostitute plays the part of a well-paid girlfriend.[51] The prostitutes are urged to offer the GFE, as the brothel owner pimps and/or madams benefit by keeping the customers happy and the money pouring in. Hof reportedly directed his brothel sex workers to "fulfill those fantasies. Be the fantasy experience you know and create them;" while promising, "you'll be rewarded handsomely, have six figures and live happily ever after."[52]

One sex worker at the Moonlite BunnyRanch recently recalled being told by her employer: "I could make a good living out here and that I'd be happy. I'd never go without a roof over my head. I'd never go hungry. I'd never go without money."[53]

In today's times, using the Internet is a popular way to promote oneself as a licensed legal prostitute. During an ABC News examination of prostitution in the United States, journalist Diane Sawyer spoke with a high-paid sex worker at the Moonlite BunnyRanch whose Web site drew nearly 300,000 hits per month.[54] Similarly, illegal prostituted women in Nevada and elsewhere routinely "advertise themselves in the online red-light district under various aliases," creating stiff competition for their licensed and regulated counterparts in the sex trade.[55]

Male Legal Brothel Workers

With the licensed legal brothel workers in Nevada entirely female for decades, a gender equality breakthrough of sorts occurred in 2010, when the state allowed the Shady Lady Ranch legal brothel and its owner/madam, Bobbi Davis, to hire male prostitutes. Davis had argued that Nevada's "prostitution regulations were outdated and discriminatory."[56] She received support from the ACLU on the controversial move with opposition from the Nevada Brothel Owners Association, believing the move "could invite unwanted scrutiny and hurt the industry."[57]

The one-time waiver granted to the Shady Lady Ranch on U.S. Highway 95, about two and a half hours from Las Vegas, required that male prostitutes undergo weekly urethral examinations in lieu of cervical exams, use condoms entirely as required by male customers, and submit to blood tests every month.

Davis advertised on the Internet in search of male prostitute prospects, similar to female prostitute recruits, with requirements that included: "Have a Good Work Ethic. Must Be Service Oriented. Have a Willingness to Please. Have a Positive Attitude."[58] However, unlike the female prostitutes in her employ who were in "their mid-30s to mid-40s, based on her clientele of older gentlemen," she sought male sex workers between 21 and 40 years of age.[59]

The Shady Lady Ranch hired its first male sex worker in January 2010. Though Davis anticipated that her male prostitutes would "primarily serve women and couples, the men [were] welcome to take on male clients, just as her women sometimes [did] with other women."[60] However, former upper-level sex worker Tracy Quan believed that for Nevada's licensed males in the sex trade, in terms of supporting themselves through prostitution, offering gay sexual services may well be

the inevitable next step: very few male prostitutes earn a living servicing women exclusively. In every income bracket, men are more capable and determined consumers of professional sex. Women have less experience— and less inclination as well. We aren't 50% of the customer base and I doubt we ever will be.[61]

Rates at the Shady Lady Ranch brothel for legal male prostitute sexual services were set at $200 for 40 minutes of work, $300 to be serviced for an hour, and $500 to spend two hours with him.[62] By comparison, female sex workers at the bordello also commanded $500 per two hours of prostituting, with couple's parties beginning at $700 an hour, and overnight sexual servicing priced at $2,000.[63]

According to Davis, with respect to her pioneering role as a madam and pimp for legal male prostitutes, "The world is changing and you've got to change or you'll die. The eyes of the industry are on us. I don't think anybody's going to do anything until they see how I do."[64]

After reportedly having fewer than 10 customers over several weeks, the first legal male brothel prostitute quit the job and was replaced by another male sex worker, who supposedly charged less money while averaging five clients daily.[65]

With licensed male sex workers just getting started in Nevada, it is too early to know what, if any, implications it will have with regard to health and safety issues, gender-based legal prostitution, or the state or national illegal commercial sex trade industry.

Arguments Against Legal Prostitution

There have been a number of criticisms directed at the existence of legal brothel prostitution in Nevada, particularly as it relates to prostitute safety, exploitation and restrictions, pimping, and illegal prostitution. Although brothel prostitutes are routinely tested for STDs, the same is not true for their customers. Since johns are not restricted from having sex with unlicensed, illegal prostitutes, it is not inconceivable that they could contract an STD, including HIV, pass it along to a licensed brothel sex worker who, if tested positive for an STD, could lose her job and become a street prostitute.[66]

Also, brothel sex workers are not immune to violence on the job. There have been reports of physical and sexual assaults against brothel prostitutes by customers. Julie Bindel reflected on this in an article that appeared in the *Guardian*: "If you believe their PR, Nevada's legal brothels are safe, healthy—even fun—places in which to work . . . why do so many prostitutes tell such horrific tales of abuse?"[67]

Nor does regulated legal brothel prostitution protect its workers from outside violence. In a recent example, Brooke Phillips, a pregnant Nevada brothel prostitute starring in the *Cathouse* reality series, was shot to death in Oklahoma City.[68]

Legal brothels have been further attacked for the restrictive measures placed on their stable of prostitutes. One article suggested that "behind the façade of a regulated industry, brothel prostitutes in Nevada are captive in conditions analogous to slavery."[69] Some legally prostituted women are said to ply the trade for up to 12 hours daily, "even when ill, menstruating, or pregnant," without the option of refusing to work.[70] According to one former prostitute who sold her body at four legal Nevada brothels: "Under this system, prostitutes give up too much autonomy, control, and choice over their work and lives."[71]

There are experts who believe that these limits on brothel prostitutes' freedoms may, in part, account for the high number of illegal prostitutes working in and around Nevada casinos, hotels, and conventions, as many prostitution-involved women prefer "to avoid the isolation and control of the legal brothels," in favor of independent prostituting where one could make hundreds or even thousands of dollars an hour, while rejecting "a customer for any reason without risking management displeasure, and come and go as she pleases."[72]

The prevailing notion that brothel prostitution is absent of street pimps (though controlled by legal pimps and madams) has also been called into question by authorities on prostitution. Some have accused legal brothels of "paying finder's fees to procurers and pimps to bring in a steady supply of fresh prostitutes."[73] *New York Times* columnist Bob Herbert wrote: "Despite the fiction that they are 'independent contractors,' most so-called legal prostitutes have pimps—the state-sanctioned pimps who run the brothels and, in many cases, a second pimp who controls all other aspects of their lives (and takes the bulk of their legal earnings)."[74]

In *Brothel: Mustang Ranch and Its Women*, author and Harvard medical student Alexa Albert suggested that legal brothel owners once required sex workers to have pimps outside the brothel to make them put out that much more effort in selling their bodies: "The involvement of pimps enabled brothel owners to leave discipline to men who wouldn't hesitate to keep their women in line."[75]

Though legal brothel prostitutes are by and large of adult age, there have been at least some occasions where underage females have sold their bodies as regulated sex workers while under the control of pimps. In one instance, Oregon pimps were able to successfully coerce four teenage prostitutes into prostituting themselves as Nevada legal prostitutes, before it was uncovered. The pimps were brought to justice.[76]

Arguments for Legalized/Decriminalized Prostitution

There are some who support Nevada's legal prostitution industry in specific and the legalization or decriminalization of prostitution in general, such as the sex workers rights' organizations, COYOTE (Call Off Your Old Tired Ethics) and PONY (Prostitutes of New York).[77] The term *sex work* was coined by Carol Leigh, a COYOTE member and prostitute, to reflect the "freedom of choice" in selling sexual favors as opposed to prostituting as a necessary means of survival or a victim of sexual exploitation.[78] Another prostitute and member of the National Organization of Women expressed this view: "Sex work certainly isn't for everyone, but you have to give people the choice when it comes to their own bodies. Sex work can be dignified, honest, and honorable."[79]

Such advocates favor decriminalization of prostitution as a means to encourage prostitutes to report crime victimization—particularly sexual assaults. According to one study, only about 4 percent of female prostitute rape victims ever report the crime—with many prostitutes' reluctance being due to the belief that law enforcement and prosecutors will take them less seriously (or reject their claim altogether stereotypically) than if they were seen as more "respectable" women.[80] Decriminalization of prostitution is also seen by supporters as making the sex trade industry "subject to standard labor and occupational safety regulations, and it would be easier to fight the abuses and crimes that accompany their work."[81]

There appears to be stronger support among prostitutes' rights groups and many self-employed sex workers for decriminalization than legalization of prostitution, as "*legalization* is understood to mean decriminalization accompanied by strict municipal regulation of prostitution."[82] One independent sex worker summed up this concern:

> Legalization—unlike decriminalization—would probably mean that prostitutes could not act like independent business people. We'd have to work in a specific district, kick back part of our fees to the city or state, and register as prostitutes—which could go on a woman's public record and affect her ability to travel, get health insurance or an apartment, and keep custody of her children. A lot of us would worry that the city would do a lousy job of running these establishments and we'd be faced with a "sex factory" situation.[83]

Opposition advocacy organizations to legalization or decriminalization of prostitution, such as Standing Against Global Exploitation and Coalition Against Trafficking in Women, argue that groups like COYOTE and their "happy hooker" philosophy and "white, middle-class privilege" are unrepresentative of the greater number of decidedly underprivileged and underage sex workers and their more stressed, and often dangerous, work environment.[84] Most of these prostituted women and teenagers are seen as being highly susceptible to and "least able to resist recruitment" into the sex trade by pimps, traffickers, gangs, and pornographers; while being overly represented with lower- and working-class women, racial and ethnic minorities, refugees and illegal aliens, and teen runaways and thrownaways with nowhere else to go but the streets and into survival sex, prostitution, and other forms of sexual exploitation.[85]

Chapter 5

High-Priced Sex Workers

Call girls are considered the cream of the crop in the commercial sex trade industry, often glamorized in Hollywood and fiction, as well as the media. Some well-known call girls include Xaviera Hollander, Sherry Rowlands, Norma Jean Almodovar, Tracy Quan, Natalie "Natalia" McLennan, and Ashley Dupré. Recent call girl scandals have made headlines, such as that which forced the resignation of New York Governor Eliot Spitzer. Unlike streetwalkers and massage parlor or brothel sex workers, call girl prostitutes have considerably more independence to ply their trade and choose their clients, though some work for madams. They are also less likely to face danger and arrest as high-end prostitutes than lower-level prostitutes, or enter the business with the same emotional baggage, dysfunctional families, or abusive backgrounds. Within the call girl subculture, there are different levels, ranging from the super-elite to middle-class to even lower-level call girls. Some can make enormous amounts of money from high-powered clients, while others can enjoy the flexibility of full- or part-time work without the pressure of street-level prostitution and pimping. The Internet may play an even bigger role in call girl prostitution than other types of prostitution by giving those involved a wide platform for doing business while remaining relatively secretive in their dealings.

Profiling the Call Girl

What is a call girl? The dictionary defines the *call girl* as "a prostitute with whom an appointment may be made by telephone," or by calling the girl or prostitute to arrange for services as opposed to simply picking her up on a street corner, in a strip club, or massage parlor.[1] Call girls are generally considered classy sex workers who offer all kinds of sexual services much more discreetly than the streetwalker prostitute. They are usually in their twenties and thirties, attractive, sharply dressed, and often college-educated and business savvy in taking advantage of a marketplace where they are in great demand and their overhead is relatively low. Whereas racial and ethnic minorities make up a high percentage of lower-level prostitutes, call girls are predominantly white and hidden in plain view and, as such, less likely to be targeted for prostitution busts.

According to writer Linda Lee, in differentiating call girl sex workers from those at the street level, "What distinguishes call girls from street-walkers is appearance, money, and class. . . . An appropriately dressed call girl can walk into a good hotel or drive into a residential neighborhood without attracting police attention. The gear of street prostitution—revealing clothes, excessive makeup, a garish hairstyle—is not for her."[2]

Though most call girls are single (though not necessarily unattached), others are married and bored or looking for a way to make extra money or otherwise exert some independence in their sexuality and lifestyle. The operator of a New York escort service noted: "Some of our escorts are married women. Their husbands think they're working as hostesses. One of our girls is the daughter of a diplomat; she has two art galleries, but she's bored with her life, and she wants to meet executives."[3] In her study of call girls, Karen Rosenblum found that the primary motivations for being in high-level prostitution were a strong need for independence from men and to earn as much money as the profession will allow.[4]

Call girls work both independently and for madams or escort agencies. Although some call girls, particularly teenagers, have pimps, most operate without the domination of a pimp or "boyfriend" controlling every aspect of their prostitution. Call girls promote themselves and their services through the Internet, magazines, escort agencies, and clientele. They work through *incall* sex work, where the client arranges to meet them at the place of the call girl's choosing, as well as *outcall* services, where the prostitute goes to meet the customer at his hotel, residence, or elsewhere. The cost for the sexual services performed is usually agreed on in advance and collected before sexual acts commence.

It is unclear just how many women sell sex as call girls, given the surreptitious nature of the business. Some experts believe that call girls constitute around 25 percent of the total females prostituting themselves in the United States.[5] Others estimate that there are at least as many call girls as streetwalkers plying the trade, and likely comprise the majority of prostitution-involved persons when considering those working full- and part-time in the business, including college students, married women, and teenagers, as well as others who have entered the market as a response to tough economic times in recent years.[6]

The image of the gorgeous, successful, and free-spirited call girl and her entertaining, hilarious, and seemingly stress-free life in the high-end sex trade has been exploited by Hollywood in such movies as *Pretty Woman* starring Julia Roberts, who went from streetwalker to kept woman, and recent television series such as *Secret Diary of a Call Girl* and *Satisfaction*, often to a captive audience.

Madams

Madams are often at the center of well-run and profitable call girl operations such as escort services and brothels, which they manage and often own, procuring clientele, or a list of affluent clients for their girls to work from, at least initially. They usually get a substantial cut of the fees their prostitutes earn for services performed. Many madams have been as infamous, colorful, and controversial as their prostitutes and johns over the years. Some recent well-known madams include Hollywood madams Heidi Fleiss and Jody Gibson; Sydney Biddle Barrows, known as the Mayflower Madam; Washington, D.C., madam Deborah Jeane Palfrey; Pittsburgh madam Paula Cherish; New Orleans madam Jeanette Maier; and Susan Austin, a madam at two brothels in Nevada, including the legendary Mustang Ranch.[7]

Not all call girls work for madams, some of whom were also prostitutes themselves. Some call girls may start off working for a madam before establishing their own independent list of clients. Most madams who understand the business and know how to evade the law can earn untold amounts of money with no shortage of women interested in employment as call girls. The operation run by Fleiss charged a flat fee of $1,500 an hour. Fleiss considered it relative to a client's net worth. She suggested that her wealthy clients "often paid more than the flat rate, partly because their ultra deep pockets wouldn't feel the pinch."[8] Even more was generated by the Emperor's Club, the high-priced escort service that allegedly supplied the call girl, Ashley Dupré, used by former New York Governor Eliot Spitzer, charging clients up to $5,500 an hour.[9]

Other operations, such as the Shadyside brothel, formerly run by Cherish as part of a nationwide prostitution network organized by ex-prostitutes called "The Circuit," charged considerably less at $300 an hour for a prostitute's services within the brothel, while charging clients $400 an hour for out-of-town prostitution activities. The network reportedly grossed

millions of dollars, while bringing in hundreds of thousands a year for the madams and for brothel prostitutes with whom profits were split 50/50.[10]

Most madams seemingly take pride in the professionalism of their organization and the prostitutes in their employ. "The girls didn't hang out at clubs," Cherish said, claiming she didn't allow drugs or drunkenness of her sex workers. "They didn't hustle. They didn't have to. We ran a very clean house. The girls had to follow rules. There were rules like any business."[11]

Former madam Sydney Barrows saw her stable of high-class call girls as intelligent and goal-oriented, once boasting: "Most of my girls were college grads . . . good, nice people with serious goals in life—the kind mothers would be proud to have as daughters."[12]

Brothel Prostitutes

High-end prostitutes often sell their services working in brothels. A *brothel* "also known as a bordello, cathouse, whorehouse, sporting house, [and] gentleman's club," among other names, "is an establishment specifically dedicated to prostitution, providing the prostitutes a place to meet and to have sexual intercourse with clients."[13] Brothels are illegal in the United States except for Nevada, where licensed brothels are operating in a number of rural counties. Illegal and legal brothels are run primarily by madams (although some may also be owned, co-owned, or operated by men or pimps), who can take a cut of up to half or more of a prostitute's earnings. Some madams are ex-prostitutes who worked for pimps, escort services, massage parlors, or other sexual exploiters.

Brothel prostitutes are predominantly attractive women in their late teens, twenties, and thirties with a male clientele. Recently a Nevada legal brothel began employing male prostitutes for heterosexual customers.[14] Some brothel sex workers can earn as much as $15,000 a night, though it is often less. Most brothels charge between $300 and $400 an hour. A typical week's work could net a prostitute $5,000 or more, or hundreds of thousands a year.[15]

Recently a well-organized brothel prostitution ring described by prosecutors as a "business-school model for economies of scale," came under federal investigation.[16] Known as The Circuit, it included as many as 100 brothels and hundreds of high-class prostitutes "who traveled a national prostitution circuit from New York to Boston, Pittsburgh, and Atlanta," as well as such cites as Washington, D.C.; Chicago; Los Angeles; and San Francisco.[17] After working at one location for "a few weeks, the hookers jetted to another brothel and were replaced by new women. Because they moved on quickly, the women couldn't steal a madam's best clients or set up competing brothels."[18]

Circuit call girls paid around $350 a week to rent rooms in the brothels for the privilege of high-end prostituting. In one instance, a Miami brothel in the Circuit located in a "$7,495-a-month Murray Hill penthouse," with possible ties to Asian organized crime, allegedly enticed women to prostitute themselves "from as far away as Mexico, Trinidad and Tobago, and Milan."[19]

> One high-class American prostitute spoke candidly of the lure into the business: It was so simple, so natural, I got right into it. . . . I had a need for security—you know, problems with self-hatred, lack of confidence, and all that stuff—and sex made me feel worthwhile. . . . I decided, if I'm going to be obsessive about sex, I might as well get paid for it. You know, why give it away?[20]

Though high-end brothels offer big money to its madams and elegant prostitutes through its wealthy clientele, there are also middle-class, low-end, and teenage brothels operating in the United States with a decidedly lower level of clients and seedier surroundings. In one such example, a former lower-level brothel sex worker described the method used at her brothel to conduct business with customers:

> There's two ways that it would work. Either . . . we picked up a john on the street, or a john picked us up, and we brought them back there. Or a john would call the building or the house, and they'd set up an appointment.[21]

Escort Service Call Girls

Many of the upper-class prostitutes plying their trade as call girls work for escort services or agencies that offer escorts for their clientele. According to Wikipedia,

> The agency typically arranges a meeting between one of its escorts and the client at the customer's house or hotel room ("outcall"), or at the escort's residence ("incall"). Some agencies also provide escorts for longer durations, who may stay with the client or travel along on a holiday or business trip. While the escort agency is paid a fee for this booking and dispatch service, the customer must usually negotiate an additional fee for any sex work service.[22]

Escort agencies advertise liberally on the Internet, Yellow Pages, and regional listings, usually with provocative ads in seeking out both potential escorts and clients. Though technically and for legal purposes escort services operate under the guise of a legitimate agency providing women for companionship and socializing, most such agencies are actually fronts for prostitution.

The women who work for escort agencies are usually young and attractive, polished, and professional in offering their services. However, some agencies exist that cater to clients who seek lesbian, gay, or bisexual escorts. Agencies typically charge escorts a flat fee per client or take a percentage of the rate established—anywhere from 20 percent to as much as 50 percent of an escort's earnings, less any gratuities. Escort agencies in New York City usually charge between $200 and $1,500 an hour, but it is not uncommon for some agencies or independent call girls to charge more than $5,000 per hour, depending on the services offered, demand of the escort, and other factors.[23]

Like many high-end prostitutes, Natalie McLennan, a former escort service sex worker once billed as "New York's No. 1 escort," was drawn to the money upper-class prostitution offered, after being stressed to make ends meet:

> I was struggling, a starving actress, living in Manhattan, trying to succeed. The option was presented to me. I weighed the pros and the cons. I decided to try it once to see if it was something I could handle. It was, so I continued until it wasn't right for me anymore. . . . An escort makes as much money as she can possibly make for herself. The average escort in New York City I would estimate makes between $600 and $1,200 an hour. It can be a great living for a certain amount of time. It's like Wall Street; you have to go in, make your money, and get out. The most money I personally ever made as an escort was either $2,000 an hour with a two-hour minimum, or $29,000 for one weekend.[24]

Similarly, former call girl turned sex counselor Veronica Monet was enticed by the money the business afforded her. According to an ABCNews.com article, "What Makes a Woman Become an Escort":

> She went from earning $25,000 in her previous job to earning six figures as an escort, charging up to $1,350 an hour. . . . Monet says that she could make over $5,000 a day and that one wealthy client once flew her first-class to New York, put her up in an expensive hotel and wrote her a check for $16,000.[25]

Monet offered advice to others seeking to become an escort, suggesting they educate themselves: "Do a 'My Fair Lady.' You won't get the high-end escorting gigs unless you're able to use the right fork, know how to cross your legs. You have to have a wardrobe."[26]

One such woman who recently found success as a $4,300-an-hour high-class call girl and unwanted notoriety for paid sex with a powerful politician was former prostitute Ashley Dupré. In an interview with ABC's Diane Sawyer, the 23-year-old spoke of being a runaway, abusing drugs, relationship issues with men; then described how she got into the escort service business under the alias "Kristen" after moving to New York with dreams of becoming a singer:

> You don't mean to make those choices but you're put in a situation and, you know, you have an opportunity to do it. I really didn't see the difference between going on a date with someone in New York, taking you to dinner and expecting something in return. I really thought it was more of a trade-off. He's expecting something in return when you date, whereas, you know, being an escort, it was a formal transaction.[27]

Dupré claimed to have "worked on and off for the escort service and, after being left by a boyfriend with a $3,600 apartment lease to pay off, medical bills, and a heavy load of credit card debt, she returned to the agency," that arranged for her to go to Washington, for a "date" with a governor.[28]

While Dupré's circumstances in the escort business may have been a bit unusual given the fallout, they also aptly reflect the world of high-end call girls and the wealthy, risk-taking clientele they often attract and advertise themselves to target.

Perhaps the most popular service escorts offer currently is the Girlfriend Experience, or the GFE, which involves mimicking a real romantic relationship. A typical GFE session was described in an online chat forum:

> A GFE session might proceed much more like a non-paid encounter between lovers. That may include a lengthy period of foreplay . . . [and] also activities where the customer works as hard to stimulate the escort [as vice versa]. Finally [the] session usually has a period of cuddling and closeness at the end [as opposed to quickly dressing and leaving once the sex has concluded].[29]

According to Wikipedia, "A call girl advertising the provision of a 'girlfriend experience' is implying that she provides deep French kissing (DFK), 'full service' (intercourse) usually with protection, and fellatio and cunnilingus, both with or without protection."[30] Call girls today often use the GFE angle to attract clientele on Web sites and through other advertising. "He wants you to be his girlfriend for however long he booked you for," one call girl prostitute revealed about customers and GFE. "Whether that's 10 minutes or 10 hours, kissing, holding hands, cuddling."[31]

An escort service sex worker recently described the lush and leisurely life her work as a high-class prostitute afforded her:

> I live a pampered kind of life: get up around noon, work out for a couple of hours with my personal trainer, spend the rest of the day shopping, or having a manicure, pedicure, and facial. Around five in the afternoon, I go for a three-mile jog, then return to my sumptuously furnished apartment that's been meticulously cleaned by my housekeeper. I hop into the tub for a refreshing bubble bath, dress in one of my designer suits, apply makeup, and style my hair.
>
> Then I call the escort service. "This is Olivia," I tell my supervisor. "I'm ready for work."[32]

Though the crime victimization rate within call girl prostitution is fairly low compared to streetwalker prostitution, the risks of becoming a victim as an escort are real nevertheless, as one prostitute made all too clear: "Even on the escort service, I saw women who were stabbed multiple times trying to escape. I saw women walking into hotel rooms to be raped, to be beaten, to be robbed, and they justified all of this by the amount of money they were getting."[33]

The glamour façade of escort service prostitution was dispelled by another former upper-class call girl: "Escort agencies aren't that glamorous. It's very dangerous for an escort, and one reason they charge so much is that everyone's taking a big risk. . . . [We] were always being hassled by the police; they were always being closed down or shaken down. I was just so horrified."[34]

Super-Elite Sex Workers

Among the upper echelon of the sex trade industry, there is an even more secretive super-elite group of sex workers. These women sexually service the very rich and are rewarded accordingly. Some can command up to $100,000 a day and make as much as half a million dollars a year.[35] Powerful clients are willing to pay thousands of dollars in hourly rates to spend time with an elite call girl, in sessions that could last for hours or even days. Recently, former New York Governor Eliot Spitzer was alleged to have spent $4,300 for a date with a prostitute he met in a hotel room in Washington, D.C., and reportedly spent more than $80,000 for high-end call girl prostitution in a year.[36] Although a significant amount, some experts believe this to be on the low end of what many wealthy men are willing to pay for sex these days.

Top-level call girls are often the beneficiaries of what is referred to in the high-end sex trade as "The Brick"—described as "$40,000 in hundred-dollar bills in a package, payment for a long weekend on a yacht in the Caribbean with a super-wealthy 'date' or a week-long trip to Europe to keep company with a sheik."[37]

According to one expert on super-elite call girls: "They're not full-time, they don't consider themselves hookers, they don't have pimps, and they don't talk about money. 'The Brick' is understood and it's paid at the end. They never have to ask."[38] Another source knowledgeable on this class of prostitute noted: "You have to live at that level and have a referral, otherwise you'll never meet them."[39] Such referrals typically come from other upper-level sex workers, their affluent clients, or other well-connected individuals.

Prostitution-involved women belonging to "The Brick" are often beautiful models, lesser-known actresses, and high-class call girls seeking to make lots of money "on the side." They tend to be articulate and college-educated, while possessing "all the social graces" necessary to achieve success at this level of the sex trade.[40]

What separates upper high-end prostitutes from brothel and streetwalking prostitutes to command such enormous amounts for their services? According to the CNBC special *Dirty Money: The Business of High-End Prostitution*, wealthy men "are willing to pay a premium for someone they can trust to be entirely discreet. Many also want compatibility . . . and some new selling points are not just bust size but education and interest."[41] In a recent survey of the wealthiest men in America, more than one in three admitted to paying for sex within the past five years.[42]

In the article "The Economics of High-End Prostitution," another perspective was given on the high earnings of elite call girls:

> The most obvious reason why high-end prostitutes can charge so much is that they are doing something illegal. Being arrested for prostitution will certainly hinder future earnings prospects in other industries (unless one manages to write a juicy tell-all about the experience; still, how many such books can the market support?). A premium fee is justified by the risks involved in

working in an illegal industry, as well as the related stigma of being paid for sex.[43]

Experts believe that the existence of an elite upper crust of prostitution is a reflection of a wave of upscale sex-for-pay offerings established in the digital era between opportunistic, intelligent, business-oriented women and a growing crop of very wealthy men who have the means to pay for the sex and short-term companionship offered to them for the right price. Anthropologist Katherine Frank referred to this as "intensified focus on the creation of 'atmosphere' and luxury."[44]

According to Elizabeth Bernstein, an Assistant Professor of Women's Studies and Sociology at Barnard College and author of the book *Temporarily Yours*, "Over the last two decades, 'gentleman's clubs' and commercial sexual services with names like 'Platinum Crown Escorts,' 'Prestige Escorts,' 'The Gold Club,' and 'VIP Massage' have proliferated to cater to clients' fantasies of consumptive class mobility."[45]

One former high-priced call girl, Dmitry Ekmektsis, who worked for International Escorts, one of Manhattan's top escort agencies, opened up about some of her experiences in a *New York Daily News* interview:

> I would try to postpone the sex in order to make more money. But I enjoyed the entertaining conversations with these rich, smart guys. Many were lawyers, doctors, or CEOs of big corporations. They'd take me for dinner at places like the Four Seasons, Le Cirque and Mr Chow. One client was an Arab prince from Oman who paid me $4,000 a day to join him in Las Vegas for the weekend. I flew there from Teterboro on his private jet.[46]

Although some super-elite call girls work for madams and high-priced escort agencies as the aforementioned, many working the sex trade are independent entrepreneurs, smart, and very driven to succeed by supplying sexual services that are in great demand by high-end clients, in spite of the economy's recent downturn or perhaps because of it. As *Vanity Fair* writer Vicki Ward pointed out,

> Ironically, when the market is down, men go to high-end prostitutes, because they need to feel better about themselves. And who better to make them feel good about themselves than a stranger that they're paying to listen to them, to listen to their problems. They don't want to tell their wives, they're too proud.[47]

Some well-established super-elite level sex workers are able to ply their trade without the need for advertising online or off, or working for a prostitution service. However, most successful ultra high-class prostitutes take advantage of the benefits and potential clientele of the super rich that the Internet offers in advertising their services and connecting with those successful men who will pay handsomely for them. According to an article titled, "Inside the World of High-Priced Hookers":

> Premier high-priced hooker sites are well organized. They're easy to navigate and customers can pick and choose women from photos, according to ethnicity, size, hair color, intimate physical details and age. For example, on one Web site, prostitutes offer a menu of sexual acts they will—or won't— perform, state when they are available and how to contact them. Abbreviations or acronyms are used to describe services.[48]

There are numerous such online Web sites, social networks, chat rooms, and bulletin boards that upper elite sex workers use to target specifically well-off and powerful men, using both traditional business practices and seductive techniques to get their interest, while promoting themselves as beautiful, intelligent, sophisticated, and sexy women the men can talk to about anything, as well as being able to fulfill their sexual needs.

Former high-priced prostitute and author of *Diary of a Manhattan Call Girl*, Tracy Quan described what it takes to be a successful elite prostitute:

> You have to project glamour and self-confidence, enormous levels of pride and narcissism, and at the same time be a little humble internally . . . When you're with your customer, you have to be thinking about his needs, how to keep him happy, how he feels. You have to be able to empathize with. . . . You need to keep the person physically happy, emotionally happy, and also stay very much within your own mental and emotional kind of cocoon. And that's a huge balancing act.[49]

High-End Internet Prostitution

Prostitution in general, and high-class sex worker prostitution in specific, has benefited greatly from going digital in recent years, particularly the Internet. Doing a search on Yahoo.com for "call girls" produced more than 328 million results, with 66 million results for "high-class call girls." Nearly 41 million results come up for "escort services" and 39 million for "prostitutes." A study found that in San Francisco alone, online advertising for escorts had more than doubled between 2000 and 2005, indicative of the explosion in Internet use by upper-class prostitutes and prostitution services.[50]

The Emperors Club V.I.P. is an example of a former high-class prostitution ring soliciting wealthy and powerful clients largely through its Web site, reportedly raking in more than $1 million before being shut down in 2008. It operated in Brooklyn, but was international in scope with 50 call girls whom the site rated by diamonds on a scale, with hourly fees ranging from $1,000 to $5,500 that "could be paid for with cash, credit card, wire transfers or money orders."[51] A prostitute that rated seven diamonds, the highest level, could have cost customers up to $31,000 a day.

The Emperors Club V.I.P. Web site promotion of its prostitutes and their services included the following:

> Our meticulous standards of beauty, intelligence, and charm ensure that you always encounter the quality you've come to expect in a woman, when with an Emperors' Club VIP model. Each of our companions is a product of an exceptionally fine background and a success in her right. All rendezvous are individually crafted to suit the needs of your specific occasion. Note that each model has a place in her schedule for a select number of appointments per month, so your date will be a special one for both of you.[52]

Craigslist is one of the Web sites that features online advertising for high-end prostitution services. Based in San Francisco, in 2009 the popular but controversial site under pressure replaced its "erotic section" with "adult services," in response to charges that it was operating as an "Internet brothel," while also under investigation in relation to crimes that involved women advertising erotic services.[53]

The demand for high-class prostitutes and the great deal of money that can be made for those in the business makes the Internet with its far-reaching capabilities through Web sites, chat rooms, bulletin boards, instant messaging, and e-mail, the perfect tool for bringing together call girls and customers through both prostitution services and independent prostitutes. The anonymous nature of online advertising of prostitution, relative safety, greater difficulty in law enforcement detection, and earnings potential makes it all the more tempting for all parties involved—encouraging longtime professionals, college students, part-time prostitutes, and newcomers to get involved in the lucrative high-end sex trade.

Bernstein further put this in some context:

The Internet has indeed reshaped predominant patterns of sexual commerce. For many indoor sex workers, it has become easier to work without third-party management, to conduct one's business with minimal interference from the criminal justice system, and to reap greater profits by honing one's sales pitch to a more elite and specialized audience.[54]

One former brothel sex worker recalled how she turned to the Internet and became an independent high-class call girl:

I started realizing that there was a large pool of frustrated men out there, earning good money. . . . So I placed an ad with some pictures of myself in a garter belt, stockings, and lingerie. . . . Now I advertise only on the Internet. It ensures me of a reliable pool of well-educated professional men with predictable manners.[55]

Another upper-class sex worker described what prompted her to sell sexual favors to a high-end clientele:

I came across somebody called "The Educated Escort" and I just thought it was brilliant. She had a two-day minimum and it was $12,000 a day. I set up my Web site and that's when I started garnering a clientele. And I saw there really was a huge market for educated women in this industry.[56]

The Internet boom in erotic dating has recently spawned a new group of high-class prostituted women known as "sugar babies." These women, mostly young and attractive, seek out wealthy men or "sugar daddies," through Web sites such as SeekingArrangement.com, and can allegedly make tens of thousands of dollars each month. One 23-year-old advertiser's profile read that she was seeking a "playful, open relationship with financial benefits."[57] Referring to herself as a model/actress, she told an interviewer for *20/20*: "I'm dating four sugar daddies right now."[58]

Millions of women advertise on these sugar daddy "dating" sites, offering themselves to willing men in exchange for money and other material comforts, which authorities believe constitutes high-end prostitution.

Call Girls and Psychological Conditions

Unlike streetwalking sex workers, some researchers have found relatively few psychological issues exist within the call girl subculture. In a study of white-collar prostitutes, Coramae Mann found no indication of pathology among them or any hostility toward men.[59] An examination by John Exner and associates of the psychological characteristics of prostitutes found full-time call girls to be "probably as mature and well-adjusted as demographically similar females engaging in other occupations. In fact, if financial success is added to any criteria of successful adjustment, these kinds of prostitutes have a clear edge."[60]

In the book *Sisters in Crime*, author Freda Adler found that:

> At the upper level, among the full-time call girls and part-time housewives who appear to lead economically secure, stable, arrest-free lives, there is no evidence of special pathologies. At the lower level, inhabited by streetwalkers, drug addicts, juvenile runaways, and deviants of many different stripes, the population is so prone to psychological pathology that it is difficult to know what part, if any, prostitution contributes to their many difficulties.[61]

Another study of call girls found that they were not "self-destructive, frigid, nymphomaniacal, or desperate."[62]

Other researchers, however, have found that there are some pathologies among women involved in high-class prostitution. In *The Elegant Prostitute*, psychotherapist Harold Greenwald identified severe personality disorders in his patients who were call girls, although unsure if these developed before entering the sex trade or afterward.[63] He suggested that upper-level prostitution was "not necessarily more degrading than working at a job one hated or being married to a man one found physically repulsive."[64] Greenwald felt that there was a fairly simple means to keep women from engaging in high-class prostitution, as he had "never known a call girl who had strong bonds of love and affection with her family."[65]

Call Girls as Therapists

Beyond their primary role as well-paid prostitutes, many call girls see themselves as therapists to the men they service sexually. In his study of occupational ideologies and call girls' attitudes, James Bryan supported this contention, finding that high-class prostitutes believed their services were greatly needed by their clients as sex therapists, counselors, and social workers.[66] After a four-year study of call girls and their customers, an actual social worker found that the women were, in fact, "paraprofessional therapists" or functioned as an "underground sexual health service," and should receive training in "mental health principles."[67] She observed that these women "met their clients' needs for crisis intervention, venting of problems, and sexual counseling, as well as raised self-esteem and restored confidence 'in their own sexuality.'"[68]

Concurring with this point of view is former call girl Delores French, "There aren't many careers where your job is to renew people's self-esteem. That's really what this job is all about—renewing people's self-esteem."[69]

Call Girls and Arrests

Upper-class call girl prostitutes are much less likely to be arrested for prostitution activities than their middle- and lower-class counterparts. Nevertheless, even with the secret world in which most operate and the relative safety of online advertising, they are not immune to being targeted by law enforcement. Some of the most well-known call girls and prostitutes have been arrested or served time. These include:[70]

- Heidi Fleiss, the former Hollywood prostitute and madam, who served time in federal prison on prostitution-related charges of income tax evasion.
- Natalie McLennan, a high-priced call girl known as "Natalia," worked for NY Confidential, the largest escort service in New York.
- Deborah Jeane Palfrey, the so-called D.C. Madam, convicted on racketeering and money laundering charges.
- Norma Jean Almodovar, a cop turned call girl, arrested and incarcerated on pandering charges.
- Kristin Davis, dubbed the Manhattan Madam, served time on Rikers Island for promoting prostitution.
- Jeanette Maier, a New Orleans madam and member of The Circuit brothel prostitution ring, pled guilty to charges of conspiracy.

Recent crackdowns have broken up major high-end prostitution businesses, including The Circuit, an escort service in Sarasota County, Florida, an East Coast brothel organization, and the largest prostitution ring in Houston.[71]

Chapter 6

Streetwalkers

Images of Julia Roberts as a streetwalker in the hit movie *Pretty Woman*, or Nancy Kwan as a beautiful lower-class prostitute in *The World of Suzie Wong* often come to mind as Hollywood's fanciful portrayals of women working in the sex trade industry. In reality, the streetwalker prostitute, or one who sells sex by soliciting customers on the streets, typically occupies the bottom rung of the prostitution pecking order. Street prostitutes do not have the safety and health benefits of regulated legal prostitutes nor do they enjoy the independence and earning capacity of upper-class sex workers. Those who operate on the streets are often the most desperate to sell their bodies as underage prostitutes, for survival or drug dependency, to escape homelessness, work under the direction of pimps or pornographers, victims of sex traffickers, and other means of commercial sexual exploitation. Streetwalkers are also most vulnerable to sexually transmitted diseases (STDs), other various mental and physical health problems, street crime, serial killers, and arrest compared to other prostitutes or persons involved in the sex trade industry. Few streetwalking prostitutes ever make the jump to high-class prostitution, as most lack the business acumen and support group to do so, or find themselves trapped in the cycle of scarred backgrounds, survival sex, substance abuse, dominating pimps, and other facets of street life and its gripping elements.

Profiling the Streetwalker

Streetwalkers, often referred to as "hookers," "whores," "hos," "kerb crawlers," and other colorful terms, are defined as a prostitute "who solicits customers along the streets," or sex workers, "especially [those] who solicit in the streets."[1] A social scientist defined the *streetwalker* as a female "who overtly solicits men on the street and offers sexual favors for payment."[2] Street prostitution, therefore is considered a

> form of prostitution in which a sex worker solicits customers from a public place, most commonly a street, while waiting at street corners or walking alongside a street, but also other public places such as parks, beaches, etc. The street prostitute is often dressed in a provocative manner. The sex act may be performed in the customer's car, or in a nearby, secluded street location, or at the prostitute's apartment or in a rented room.[3]

Street prostitution typically takes place in and around *red-light districts* (defined as areas or neighborhoods where activity and establishments involving the adult entertainment and commercial sex-trade industry exists, such as strip clubs, bars, adult porn theaters, and sex shops). But streetwalkers also ply their trade anywhere they can find willing customers, including on busy urban or suburban streets, in park settings, and around popular resorts, hotels, and stadiums.

Streetwalker sex workers are often distinguished by their overtly sexual and over-the-top hairstyle, makeup, and attire. One article described street-walkers as wearing "ankle-length coyote and raccoon coats over Victoria's Secret-type chemises of shimmering satin, black stockings, and five-inch red heels or boots," or "G-strings with sparkling pasties on their nipples, or in lace panties and bras."[4] Some younger streetwalkers dress more appropriate to their age and contemporary clothing, while wearing little to no makeup, as their pimps target customers who prefer this.[5]

Many streetwalkers are caught in a convergence of dysfunctional backgrounds, substance abuse, impoverishment, violence, and despair, and have no easy out. In a *Seventeen* article, "I'm a Shadow," writer Adrian LeB-lanc gave us a reality check on the glamour of the Hollywood streetwalker versus those who typically sell street sex in real life:

> The Cinderella experience of Julia Roberts' character in the movie *Pretty Woman* is a fantasy far away from any real world. No one is coming to rescue Trina, and although she's tried to escape the street and quit the drugs, she, like most of the girls who inhabit this dark world, has been unable to break the cycle herself. . . . Many young streetwalkers are born and raised in an environment of poverty, drugs, and violent crimes.[6]

Many streetwalkers today fit the profile and circumstances of Estella Marie Thompson. The 24-year-old African American Hollywood street-walker, known as Divine Brown, gained national attention in the mid-1990s after being arrested for performing oral sex on British actor Hugh Grant in his BMW on Sunset Boulevard.[7] Thompson was charged with lewd conduct and received a sentence of 180 days behind bars. Her john, Grant, was fined a small amount and given two years' probation.

Thompson was a single mother of two daughters and began prostituting herself in San Francisco when she was unable to pay an electric bill totaling $133, pulling in $1,000 one day after selling her body for five hours of work. She explained her rationale for entering the business:

> I just wanted the best for my children and I didn't want them to struggle as hard as I had, so I did what I had to do. I wanted to make money, you know, do the right thing . . . go home and raise my children and just have a good life, a good quiet positive life.[8]

It is estimated that streetwalking prostitutes constitute anywhere from 10 to 25 percent of sex workers in the United States, which in total could top 2 million prostitution-engaged persons and even more when part-time sex workers are included.[9] In New York City alone, an estimated 5,000 to 8,000 females sell sexual favors as streetwalking prostitutes.[10] The vast majority of teenage prostitutes are streetwalkers, most of whom are runaways, thrownaways, drug-involved, and homeless, while controlled by pimps.[11]

Whereas most upper-class prostitutes are white, street-level sex workers are more likely to be persons of color, though prostituted white females are still well represented among streetwalkers.[12] Studies have shown that in inner city red-light districts and other spots with a high level of streetwalking prostitution, racial and ethnic minorities may represent half or more of the prostitution-involved females.[13] In a three-year study of New York City streetwalkers, Joyce Wallace, the executive director of the Foundation for Research on Sexually Transmitted Diseases, Inc., found that half the street prostitutes were African American and 25 percent Latino, with the other 25 percent white.[14] According to Rachel Lloyd, who mentors teenage and young adult females at risk for commercial sexual exploitation, more than 80 percent of those she was involved with were African American and 15 percent Latina.[15] Only around 2 percent were white, though Lloyd suggested that white prostituted women were underrepresented in the figures due to an overrepresentation of prostitution-engaged minority women experiencing arrest compared to their white counterparts.[16]

Other research has shown teenage streetwalkers to be predominantly white. In Minneapolis and San Francisco studies, 8 out of 10 prostituted girls were found to be white,[17] with further studies indicating the proportion of African American teen streetwalkers ranging from 10 to 50 percent of the sample groups.[18] Other minority group girl streetwalker representation, such as Latina and Asian, fall between 2 and 11 percent of teenage girl sex workers.[19]

Although a high percentage of streetwalkers come from lower-class and usually dysfunctional families, many entered the sex trade with middle- and upper middle-class backgrounds and no apparent traumatic upbringing. As one writer pointed out, prostitution-involved persons operating on the streets come "from a range of backgrounds: rich or poor; well-educated or illiterate; urban, suburban, or rural."[20] A sociologist with the Centers for Disease Control and Prevention noted that many streetwalking prostitutes "have lived the typical All-American family life. They grew up in the suburbs, went to ballet school—the whole thing."[21] Sex workers who operate on the street tend to reflect their personal situation (such as runaways, drug addicts, survival sex, need for money, and recruitment into the business by pimps or other prostitutes) rather than their socioeconomic, class, and familial determinants.

Similar to legal prostitutes and high-class call girls, some streetwalkers (and their pimps) have turned to the Internet in blogs, chat rooms, social networks, and personal ads to promote themselves and solicit clients.[22] Although few of these street prostitutes move indoors or online permanently to do business, the Internet does offer them a new and less conspicuous means in this digital era to gain greater exposure and potentially bring in more paying customers.

Types of Streetwalkers

Streetwalkers have been broken down into various categories by criminologists and researchers. In terms of control over their functioning as prostitutes, there are essentially two types of streetwalkers: those who are independent sex workers and those who operate under the control of a pimp or boyfriend/manager. These are not mutually exclusive, as some streetwalkers may gravitate toward one or the other depending on their circumstances or perceived need for management or protection.

The streetwalkers' "strolls" or "tracks" have been mentioned by some researchers with regard to their street movements in soliciting customers.

In a study of street-based prostitutes, Celia Williamson and Lynda Baker identified three types of sex workers: pimp-controlled prostitutes, renegade prostitutes (working as self-employed entrepreneurs), and outlaw prostitutes (who "hustle, manipulate, and exploit" johns).[23]

Prostitution expert Jennifer James divided streetwalkers into two broad groups: true prostitutes and part-timers.[24] She broke these down into 13 roles. True prostitutes include the following:

- *Outlaws:* prostitutes who ply the trade without pimps.
- *Rip-off artists:* thieves under the guise of prostitutes; prostitution is not their primary source of income.
- *Hypes:* prostitutes who sell their bodies to support drug dependency.
- *Ladies:* sex workers identified by their carriage, class, finesse, and professionalism.
- *Old-timers:* seasoned prostitutes lacking the class of ladies.
- *Thoroughbreds:* young, professional sex workers.

Part-timers include prostitutes who have "no style and amateurs or 'hos.' "[25] Streetwalkers can fit into more than one role. The roles relate to "different behavioral dimensions . . . as opposed to complete behavioral types," per se, "each having elements from all streetwalker modes of behavior."[26]

Researcher Elizabeth Bernstein divided San Francisco streetwalking prostitutes into upper-class, middle-class and lower-class sex workers—designated by the street corners they plied their trade on within the Tenderloin and Mission districts in the city, along with hourly rates, and physical characteristics or "bodily capital."[27] The upper-class streetwalkers were described as mostly white, Asian, and light-skinned African American "circuit girls" who traveled from one city to the next as street prostitutes.[28] Middle-class streetwalkers were less sharply dressed and composed more of racial and ethnic minorities. Lower-class streetwalkers included older prostitutes, teenage runaways, and drug-addicted sex workers who were not necessarily concerned with dressing the part to indicate "sexual availability."[29]

Streetwalkers have also been categorized as *career prostitutes* and *crack prostitutes*, or "cash-for-sex" versus "drugs-for-sex."[30] The former tended to more clearly separate their private and public lives, including different living and working places.

In a study of female juvenile streetwalkers, pimps that were interviewed described one type as "housewife prostitutes," or women who "freelanced and came into the city from the suburbs one or two nights a week 'to make money.' "[31] These sex workers were portrayed as bored and in need of excitement. They were often given plum jobs in servicing upper-middle class johns.

Streetwalkers and Pimps

Many adult streetwalkers—representing perhaps as many as 80 percent of all streetwalker prostitutes in the United States—operate without pimps or boyfriend managers.[32] These mostly independent prostitutes may have had prior involvement with a pimp and chose to work for themselves or work primarily to feed drug habits. They can also work in direct competition with prostitutes who have pimps, ply their trade around other independent sex workers, or establish their own territory to solicit customers. However, some adult-aged prostitutes do have pimps for various reasons, including carryover from underage prostituting, drug dependency, intimidation, management, and protection.

Pimps play a much bigger role in prostituting teenage girls. An estimated 75 to 95 percent of prostitution-involved underage females were initiated into the sex trade or remained there under the direction of pimps.[33] The vast majority sell their bodies as streetwalkers. Many are troubled runaways or thrownaways turned into street kids or drug addicts who pimps can easily exploit as the need for survival sex or prostitution mounts with each day of homelessness or loss of direction.[34] One such tragic and all too common example of a thrownaway teen streetwalker's convergence with the often dangerous world of pimps was described by researchers Richard Estes and Neil Weiner:

> Sandy, a 16-year-old Caucasian from upper New York State was thrown out of her house after her mother found marijuana in her book bag. Shocked, confused, unsure where to go, she went to the area bus terminal. She was quickly picked up by a couple of pimps who trafficked her to New York City where they sold her to another pimp for $2,500—Sandy received none of the money. Sandy was prostituted on the streets of New York City. . . . Two years after her mother threw her out, a john—customer—murdered Sandy.[35]

According to *The Prostitution of Women and Girls*, virtually all streetwalking sex workers, regardless of age or degree of independence, have had some contact or involvement with pimps, panderers, pornographers, and related sexual exploiters.[36] Bernstein found that approximately two-thirds of the upper- and middle-class streetwalkers in her research had pimps, which she suggested reflected more on the pimps' charms and power of persuasion in recruiting women to sell themselves sexually than the prostituted females' "need for outside management."[37] She pointed out that in the process the pimp "commodifies his own sexuality" and goes to "great lengths" as a smooth talker and in dressing sharply to achieve his objective in turning out females onto the street, including promoting his position in the sex trade industry through "business cards with original motifs."[38]

Although the assumption is that streetwalker prostitutes with pimps are less likely to experience violence with customers or others than independent street sex workers are, studies have indicated the opposite. Prostituted women with pimps have been found to more often sell their services on the streets in areas with a higher crime rate as well as engage in more risk taking in plying the trade as a result of pressure put on by their pimps to reach their quota from day to day.[39] See further discussion on the pimp's role in the lives of streetwalkers and prostituted teenagers in Chapters 7 and 10.

Earnings of Streetwalkers

The amount earned by streetwalkers for selling sex varies depending on location, age, motivation, experience, ability to negotiate, drug dependency, whether or not a pimp is in control, and other factors. In their research on street prostitution, Michael Scott and Kelly Dedel found that the typical amount streetwalkers charged was $20 to $50 for oral copulation and $50 to $100 to have sexual intercourse; with prostituted crack addicts willing to sell sexual favors for as little as "a single rock of crack cocaine."[40]

In New York City, the cost of doing business with streetwalker prostitutes includes between $40 and $50 for oral sex, $75 for sexual intercourse, and around $150 for outcalls. One expert contended that an attractive young streetwalker might be able to generate as much as $1,500 singlehandedly on a weekend night.[41]

According to Bernstein, San Francisco streetwalkers' earnings differed in relation to whether they were upper, middle, or lower-class sex workers. Those who did the "upper class stroll" could make between $100 and $400 for a 15-minute "date;" while some could bring in $800 to $900 for a night's work, if "brave enough," in terms of their willingness to get in cars with anonymous johns.[42] Middle-class streetwalkers could command $20 to

$100 per "date," depending on such variables as location and appearance, whereas many lower-class street prostitutes such as older ones and runaways could expect to earn a "few bucks" for survival sex, drugs, or shelter.[43]

Bernstein found that drug-addicted streetwalkers would often "sell pussy" for $20 to be used to buy crack, heroin, or speedballs, while pointing out that "in the standardized economy of the streets, the $20 was the ubiquitous note of exchange, good for a blow job, or a hand job, a hotel room, or drugs."[44] It was not uncommon for some drug-dependent streetwalkers to explicitly "turn tricks for rocks," forgoing the solicitation of johns to receive cash for sexual services.[45]

In 2007, the Cook County, Illinois, sheriff's office reported that street prostitutes there tended to charge anywhere from $10 to $50 per sexual encounter, compared to prostitutes who used the Internet to solicit clients at $150 to $300 for a sexual interaction.[46] According to economists Steven Levitt and Sudhir Venkatesh, based on a study of Chicago streetwalkers in 2008, independent prostitutes serviced customers for around $25 an hour on average, with prostitutes who worked for pimps earning about 50 percent more—or four times what they would make from nonprostitution work.[47]

Although independent street sex workers pocket all of their earnings or apply it to their needs—food, shelter, or drugs—streetwalkers who work for pimps often have to give up around 60 to 70 percent of what they earn to them, according to some studies.[48] Some street prostitutes—many of whom can work up to six to eight hours daily, five or six days per week, while servicing on average three to five customers every night—may be forced or coerced into giving pimps all of their earnings to achieve daily quotas, as punishment for showing disrespect or otherwise not deserving the money, to pay for drugs, food, shelter, or protection, or as an illustration of love for their pimp boyfriends.

Dynamics of Streetwalking Prostitution

Most streetwalkers have been the victims of sexual and/or physical abuse or sexual assaults prior to entering prostitution. According to the Huckleberry House Project, 90 percent of teenage streetwalkers had been sexually molested.[49] It has been reported that almost 8 out of 10 prostituted girls were victims of child sexual abuse and 9 in 10 had been physically abused before becoming prostitutes. Similarly, two-thirds of girl prostitutes in Mimi Silbert's research had been victims of incest or physical abuse;[50] while

Ronald Simons and Les Whitbeck found sexual abuse to be a precursor to prostitution among homeless women and teenage girls.[51] The relationship between streetwalking prostitution and child sexual and physical abuse are interlinked with running away, low self-esteem, promiscuity, substance abuse, and vulnerability to sexual exploitation.[52]

The motivation to become a streetwalker prostitute includes independence, financial need, rebellion, drug dependency, homelessness, and pimp influence. Researcher Claire Elifson contended that the "driving force" behind most prostitution is drug use, abuse of drugs, and drug addiction.[53] Jennifer James broke down streetwalkers' motivations for selling sexual favors into three categories: conscious, situational, and psychoanalytic, describing them as follows:[54]

1. *Conscious:* economics, working conditions, adventure, and a convincing pimp.
2. *Situational:* early life experiences, child abuse and/or child neglect, experience.
3. *Psychoanalytic:* general experiences, oedipal fixation, latent homosexuality, and retardation.

The motivating factors or circumstances leading to involvement in prostitution notwithstanding, streetwalkers "are not equally committed to" the sex trade, according to Scott and Dedel.[55] They point to those who are "deeply committed" as result of economics or lifestyle, with others committed because of drug addiction, and those whose commitment is seen as weak due to it being the simplest way to earn money. Research has found that most prostitutes turn to selling sex on the streets because they are unable to secure employment that pays comparable wages. Although some streetwalkers seek to leave the business, most find themselves unable to for reasons that include threats by and fear of their pimps, no other viable alternatives for making money, substance abuse, being too ensconced in street life, sexual addiction, and no marketable skills or educational requirements for finding work in the job market.

Streetwalkers tend to ply their trade in areas that are under one square mile, which may often be multiple places in big cities including failing neighborhoods, bus and train stations, near restaurants, coffee shops, motels, hotels, convention centers, under bridges or in tunnels, in industrial areas, and areas where gang or drug activity is common.[56] Within these locations, street prostitutes or their pimps also choose spots to do business that "allow drivers to slow down or stop, ideally where the driver's side of the vehicle is closest to the curb;" as well as "places offering escape avenues from the police and dangerous clients."[57]

Prostitution at the street level has been found to have a higher prevalence in poor and dilapidated parts of the city, as well as areas with a large number of single men as opposed to neighborhoods filled with women, the elderly, and families. For the street sex trade to prosper, "the surrounding neighborhood cannot be too crime-ridden or appear too threatening to potential clients."[58] As such, street prostitution tends to exist in "areas that are marginal or in transition, rather than in thoroughly blighted areas."[59] Yet, the appearance of streetwalkers and their johns and pimps can often lead to deterioration and lowering property values in a neighborhood, which often results in fierce public opposition to prostitution and increased pressure on law enforcement personnel to deal with street prostitution.

Substance Abuse

Substance abuse plays a big role in the life and times of streetwalkers. Many enter the business with alcohol or drug dependency. Others become hooked after entering the sex trade through addiction as part of the risky environment they are in, to try and cope with the harsh realities of selling their bodies on the street, and through pimps who may use drugs to keep prostitutes dependent and in their stable.

Numerous studies support the correlation between streetwalkers and alcohol and/or drug use (including intravenous [IV] drug use). For example, a 2005 study by Amanda Roxburgh and colleagues showed a strong drug dependence among street sex workers, involvement in paid sex, and related risk behaviors.[60] Another study found alcohol use to be prevalent among streetwalkers and other prostituted women and associated it with self-medication, illegal drug use, mental health issues, and sexual victimization.[61]

Crack cocaine use by streetwalkers is a serious concern among health workers and social scientists. Describing crack as "the new pimp," according to the National Center for Missing and Exploited Children's publication, *Prostitution of Children and Child–Sex Tourism*, "Younger girls who get crack from their pimps are seen as willing to do anything to feed their habits."[62] In an Australian study of streetwalkers and cocaine use, it was found that an increase in sex work among this group was associated with increased use of cocaine and IV drug use by prostituted heroin addicts.[63] Another study of African American crack-addicted streetwalking prostitutes related the heavy use of crack to selling sexual favors, childhood abuse, homelessness, and unemployment.[64]

In their research on street prostitution, Scott and Dedel indicated that "crack cocaine markets drive down the price of street prostitution," with some drug-dependent streetwalkers willing to offer their bodies below market value and without condom protection from STDs in the desperation to get drugs.[65] This, in turn, can cause friction with other streetwalkers or pimps, while increasing the chances for customer violence, prostitutes robbing their johns, or otherwise erratic behavior among drug-addicted street-based sex workers.

Teenage homeless streetwalkers have a particularly high risk for substance abuse-related issues, based on a history of substance abuse and current problems with alcohol or drug dependency. One study found a relationship between prostituted female juveniles and higher child abuse and neglect rates, negative peer associations, and school problems.[66] In an article on teenage prostitution, Adrian LeBlanc profiled a 19-year-old typical streetwalker drug addict:

> Tina's childhood was tumultuous. By nine, she started to use drugs, mostly pills. When she was 11, she once had to be hospitalized after drinking until she passed out. . . . Whether the drug use led to prostituting or the prostituting inspired more use of the drugs isn't wholly clear. Whatever the case, drugs— and the mission to do what she needed to get them—became routine.[67]

In an examination of the overall correlation between female street sex workers, crack use, and other drug abuse appearing in *Drugs: Education, Prevention, and Policy*, the authors concluded that "there is a vicious circle between sex working and taking drugs—sex work generat[ing] funds [while] drugs facilitate continuation of work."[68]

Sexually Transmitted Diseases

Streetwalkers have a high rate of STDs, although there are conflicting data on the incidence of HIV infection among these sex workers. Caught in the current of a high-risk lifestyle of multiple and varied sex acts with multiple anonymous sex partners, a high number of teenagers' inconsistent use of condoms, substance abuse, IV drug use and addiction, sexual assaults, and other risk factors within the street subculture, streetwalking sex workers are more likely than other prostitutes to contract one or more STDs.

With their still-developing bodies and immune system, along with their often dire or desperate circumstances, teenage and young-adult streetwalkers are especially at risk for becoming infected with an STD. To get more money from johns, many such prostitutes may have "raw sex," or sex without the use of a condom to offer some protection from diseases.[69] Alcohol and drug use by streetwalkers can further reduce their ability to resist having unprotected sex. Police sweeps tend to cut down the time street-level sex workers have to evaluate customers and negotiate conditions of the sexual interaction, which increases the risk of involvement with a john unwilling to use a condom and resorting to rape or other violence.[70]

Researcher Nancy Walker reported that from selling sex, more than 8 in 10 prostitution-involved teenagers in the United States have contracted an STD such as herpes, genital warts, gonorrhea, syphilis, and hepatitis B.[71] Similarly, Clare Tattersall in *Drugs, Runaways, and Teen Prostitution* estimated that as many as two-thirds of teenage prostitutes become infected with at least one STD.[72] Data on homeless, underage streetwalkers are consistent in the connection between high-risk activities such as survival sex, unprotected sex, prostitution, and IV drug use, and exposure to STDs.[73]

The extent of HIV infection among streetwalkers is debatable. According to Scott and Dedel, for example, prostitution "has not been demonstrated to be a primary means of HIV transmission" in the United States.[74] The researchers ascribe this to streetwalkers mostly participating in oral sex rather than sexual intercourse where the risk for infection is lower and suggest that the majority of sex workers—excluding drug-addicted prostitutes—plying their trade on the street make their johns wear condoms. They cite other research to argue that prostitutes are more likely to become HIV infected through contaminated needles by IV drug use.[75]

However, there is much evidence to indicate that street prostitution by itself, as well as in combination with sharing dirty needles among drug-addicted prostitutes, continues to place streetwalkers at high risk for HIV infection as a precursor to AIDS. In Wallace's HIV testing of more than 3,000 streetwalkers in New York City, 35 percent were HIV-positive.[76] Another study reported that 61 percent of the streetwalkers sampled tested HIV-positive.[77] In a comparison of HIV among streetwalkers and call girls, it was found that while 41 percent of the former group tested positive for the virus, none of the call girls had been infected.[78]

Unprotected sex and sex with multiple partners may put teenage streetwalkers, in particular, at the greatest risk for HIV infection, although adult streetwalkers also remain vulnerable to the disease. As teenage prostitutes may be more amenable to or coerced into having sex without protection than older street prostitutes, their risk for exposure to the AIDS virus may be higher as well, along with their propensity for frequent drug use. According to a study by the San Diego Association of Governments on female teenage prostitution, 81 percent of professionals working with prostitution-involved girls believed that safe sex was only practiced "some of the time."[79] One study found that 84 percent of street youth were involved in one or more HIV-related sexual or drug situations.[80] Other studies in New York City and Cleveland found that the risk for developing AIDS increased among prostitution-involved street youth who had unprotected sex with multiple partners.[81] Homeless teens, most of whom engage in survival sex and prostitution, are 7 times as likely to die from AIDS and 16 times more likely to contract HIV as youth in the general population.[82]

Concerned with becoming infected with an STD passed along through unprotected sexual intercourse, some streetwalkers turn to safer kinds of sexual activity—or those that do not require vaginal or anal penetration. These include *mammary intercourse*, defined as a sex act in which a female's breasts and cleavage are used to stimulate the male's penis. In a study of condom practices among New Zealand prostitutes, mammary intercourse was found to be an acceptable substitute to intercourse for some customers who were unwilling to use a condom, as when "performed by a woman with large breasts[, it] felt to the client like penetrative vaginal sex."[83]

Though oral sex is considered a safer form of sexual activity and is performed routinely by most streetwalking prostitutes—mainly as their clients' preference—this sex act without a condom still carries the danger of transmitting an STD, including HIV, human papillomavirus, herpes, and multiple strains of hepatitis. As noted by Wikipedia:

> Any kind of direct contact with body fluids of a person infected with HIV (the virus that causes AIDS) poses a risk of infection. . . . If the receiving partner has wounds or open sores on their genitals, or if the giving partner has wounds or open sores on or in their mouth, or bleeding gums, [the] risk of STD transmission [increases]. Brushing the teeth, flossing, undergoing dental work, or eating crunchy foods such as chips relatively soon before or after giving oral sex can also increase the risk of transmission, because all of these activities can cause small scratches in the lining of the mouth. These wounds, even when they are microscopic, increase the chances of contracting STDs that can be transmitted orally under these conditions.[84]

Crack-using streetwalkers who service their customers through oral sex may face an even higher risk for exposure to HIV. As one writer put it, fellatio or a "blow job" obviously "puts [the female street prostitute at] more at risk than a man: common sense tells us that the AIDS virus gains easy entry through mouth lacerations from crack smoking."[85]

General use of crack cocaine and other injectable drugs has also been shown to be a key means for HIV infection among streetwalkers. In a study of 110 former IV drug-using streetwalkers, 46 percent tested positive for HIV.[86] Thirty-seven percent of female street sex workers who were IV drug users in another study had the AIDS virus.[87] An even stronger relationship has been shown among racial and ethnic minority streetwalkers, IV drug use, and HIV infection. For example, in a sample of Baltimore HIV-infected streetwalkers, the exposure rate was found to be highest among African American prostitutes.[88]

Other Health Issues

Streetwalkers are at risk for a range of additional health problems while plying the trade and living the dangerous and unstable street life. These include concussions, broken bones, genital mutilation, pelvic inflammatory disease, nutritional deficiencies, infertility, cervical cancer, irritable bowel syndrome, eating and sleeping disorders, and a shorter life span than nonprostitutes.[89] The mortality rate for prostitutes is 40 times the national average.[90]

There is a high incidence of pregnancy and miscarriage among prostitutes working the streets. A 1996 survey of nearly 2,000 women streetwalkers revealed that more than two-thirds had one or more children, with two offspring on average.[91] One-fifth of these children lived with the mother as she plied her trade, with 9 percent living in foster homes. In another study of Minneapolis/St. Paul prostitution-involved women, more than two-thirds averaged three pregnancies while prostituting, "which they attempted to bring to term."[92]

Teenage prostitutes also have a high pregnancy rate. According to one study of homeless female runaways, 50 percent of those living on the street and 40 percent of runaways staying in a shelter had been pregnant.[93] Around 1 in 10 of the street and shelter runaways were pregnant at the time the study was carried out. Less than one in four female runaways used birth control. Some studies have found that many homeless female youth participate in "risk clustering," or multiple risky sexual involvements concurrently, putting them at even greater risk to become pregnant, contract STDs or HIV, or encounter other circumstances harmful to their health.[94]

Aside from unwanted pregnancies through unprotected sex with johns, many female street sex workers became mothers after having sex with their pimps, being sexually molested, or sexually assaulted.[95] A high percentage of these prostitute mothers become sterile as a result of infections brought on by STDs.[96]

Streetwalkers also experience a high rate of mental health issues, such as severe depression, anxiety, schizophrenia, suicidal ideation, attempted suicide, and psychosomatic disorders.[97] In many instances, prostitutes enter the sex trade with mental problems that are exacerbated by the psychological toll it can take when offering your body to strangers for pay.

Streetwalkers and Violence

Violence, including rape, assault, mugging, and verbal threats, is an everyday reality for streetwalkers, who are the most prone to victimization among the various classes of prostitutes. In a study by Melissa Farley of 854 streetwalkers in nine countries including the United States, 95 percent of the prostituted females had been the victims of physical assaults and 75 percent had been raped.[98] *The Prostitution of Women and Girls* cites a study that estimated that 70 percent are raped repeatedly by customers for an average of 31 sexual assaults per year, with 65 percent physically assaulted by johns.[99] The percentage of assaults by pimps was estimated to be even higher. Wallace's research supported this contention in finding that the majority of streetwalkers she interviewed had been sexually or physically assaulted.[100]

Many street prostitutes have been found to be victims of kidnapping. Lloyd pointed out that the majority of the prostituted girls she counseled had been kidnapped at some point by the johns they sexually serviced, asserting that if a teen prostitute has "been on the streets [selling her body] six months to a year, it's almost guaranteed she's been kidnapped."[101] Street prostitutes have also been "branded with irons, burned with acid, or beaten to the point that they needed hospitalization."[102]

Streetwalkers are also vulnerable to becoming homicide victims with offenders including pimps, customers, gang members, and serial killers.[103] Homeless, young, and drug-addicted street prostitutes have long since been targeted by murderers and serial killers for their easy access, susceptibility, and often their hatred of prostitutes. Such infamous serial killers as Gary Ridgway (Green River Killer), William Suff (Riverside Prostitute Killer), and perhaps the most well-known of all, Jack the Ripper, set their sights mainly on runaways and streetwalkers, who continue to capture the attention of these types of homicidal sociopaths.[104]

Many streetwalking sex workers, aware of such potential dangers, often seek to lower their risk of victimization by conducting their business with customers in locations close to where the solicitation occurred. Though the sex is usually not in view of persons walking or driving by, or employees at a lodging facility, the proximity is such that prostitutes can make noise or break away for assistance, if necessary. Unfortunately, more often than not, streetwalkers remain at a high risk to be victimized as part of the dangerous environment they occupy.

Streetwalkers and Arrest

Although the relatively rare arrest of upper-class prostitutes tends to be high profile and capture the public's imagination, streetwalking sex workers are much more likely to be arrested on a regular basis and otherwise put into the criminal justice system. According to the Federal Bureau of Investigation's annual publication, *Crime in the United States*, there were 40,772 arrests of females for prostitution and commercialized vice in 2008.[105] Of these, 39,894 arrests were of persons age 18 and over. The majority of these arrests were of the more observable lower-class women prostitutes plying their trade on and around street corners in metropolitan areas and red-light districts, with police stings often focused on streetwalkers rather than high-class sex workers, or even those working in such establishments as massage parlors and illegal brothels. One source reported that a street prostitute is arrested one time per "450 encounters" with law enforcement, of which "every tenth arrest [leads to] jail time. Once every 30 encounters, a prostitute gives free sex to an on-duty police officer to avoid arrest."[106]

Racial and ethnic minority streetwalkers have a higher rate of arrest than white streetwalkers do, especially African Americans. Studies show that they are seven times as likely to be arrested for prostitution and commercialized vice as street sex workers of other races.[107] These arrests tend to occur most often in predominantly poor areas of inner cities with high levels of depression and police bias widespread.

Female streetwalkers are arrested far more often than male streetwalkers, the prostitution-engaged women and teenage girls' clients, or the pimps and other commercial sexual exploiters that control many of the street prostitutes.[108] Recent years have seen law enforcement step up efforts in arresting and prosecuting pimps and johns and related sexual exploiters of women and children.[109]

However, female prostitutes, particularly those plying their trade on the streets, continue to be targeted most often by authorities. A recent article in the *Los Angeles Times* explored the tragic case of a crack-addicted, HIV-positive longtime streetwalker, Panchita Hall, who had been arrested and convicted multiple times on prostitution charges and had violated a state law by continuing to solicit customers for sex in spite of knowingly being infected with HIV.

> Hall got as far as a diploma from Manual Arts High, then became a fixture on Figueroa Street—a career prostitute with an addiction to crack cocaine. [The 46-year-old] has a rap sheet that stretches back to 1984. She was found to be HIV-positive after a court-ordered test in 1995, but continued soliciting and was convicted of prostitution six more times. After her most recent arrest on April 28, Hall's thick file landed on [the deputy district attorney's] desk in the Compton courthouse. . . .
>
> Prostitution is usually tried as a misdemeanor. But in Hall's case, [the prosecutor] filed felony charges, using a 1988 state law that requires prostitutes who [tested] HIV-positive . . . to be charged with a felony [if arrested a second time]. Conviction carries a maximum three-year sentence. [The prosecutor planned to] ask for three times that much because the criminal justice system has failed to sufficiently punish Hall during her string of arrests for soliciting while infected.[110]

A plea bargain was eventually worked out, where Panchita Hall received a prison sentence of four years for violating probation on a previous conviction. Hall's example is indicative of the often high-risk lifestyle streetwalking prostitutes engage in with respect to not only serious health issues and victimization, but also susceptibility for arrest and incarceration.

Chapter 7

Prostituted Teenage Girls

If call girls represent the upper echelon of female prostitution, teenage girl prostitutes occupy the lowest rung. Most research shows that girls comprise the majority of juvenile prostitutes. Many of these prostituted girls are runaways and thrownaways, and have been sexually, physically, or mentally abused. There are some, however, that strike out on their own for independence, due to behavioral problems, or sexual orientation/gender identity issues. Almost all girl prostitutes work for a pimp and are streetwalkers, though some are prostituted in brothels, massage parlors, or escort services. As with most others involved in the sex trade, the Internet plays a big role in the commercial sexual exploitation of prostituted girls, who are advertised by pimps and pornographers, and even self-promoted to reach a wider audience of sexual exploiters.

Girl prostitution often involves substance abuse, survival sex, pornography, sexual assaults, and other crimes of violence and victimization. Sexually transmitted diseases (STDs) such as HIV and genital warts are common among prostitution-involved girls, as are a range of other health problems. Prostitution-involved girls are often the most likely among prostitutes and others involved in the sex trade industry to be arrested, as their highest visibility and, perhaps, gender partiality makes them a likely target for law enforcement focus. Many of these prostituted girls become prostituted women and carry the same baggage along with the inherent risks associated with the sex-for-sale business.

The Extent of Prostitution-Involved Teenage Girls

Just how many teenage girls are active in the sex trade industry? Reliable figures are difficult to come by. Though teenage prostitution is flourishing by most accounts, it is an ephemeral business with girl prostitutes being moved from city to city or different parts of town by pimps and sex traffickers to avoid losing them to other pimps or traffickers, or arrest and protection by law enforcement. According to one report, prostitution-involved female teens are "often trafficked from state to state, and moved off the streets by pagers and cell phones, make[ing] it even harder to illuminate the shadows of the underground child sex network."[1]

There are also indications that prostituted girls are underrepresented in official data. In an article on teenage prostitution in New York City, writer Mia Spangenberg noted of prostitution-involved girls: "many are identified as adults when arrested. They often have phony identification and stolen social security numbers. [There were] a few girls who all had the same photocopied birth certificate and identification card their pimp had given them."[2] Then there is the fact that beyond streetwalking girl prostitutes, prostitution-involved girls are increasingly being placed "underground into brothels and other incall places and [relying] on the Internet and paging services, it becomes virtually impossible to know how many under-age youth are [out there]."[3]

This notwithstanding, some experts estimate that there are anywhere from 300,000 to as many as 3 million teenage prostitutes working in the sex trade, of which as many as two-thirds may be female.[4] Most girl prostitutes are believed to be runaways, many of whom end up home-less. The National Runaway Switchboard estimated that between 1.6 and 2.8 million youth leave home by running away or being thrown out every year.[5] The Research Triangle Institute reported that about 2.8 million persons between the ages of 12 and 17 have at least one epi-sode of homelessness due to running away.[6] Research show that more than two-thirds of runaway girls who do not return home will become involved in prostitution.[7]

Characterizing the Girl Prostitute

Girl prostitution is a major part of the U.S. sex trade industry, affecting potentially millions of underage females with often devastating conse-quences for many, such as HIV infection. They work full- and part-time, often depending on the whims of pimps or so-called "boyfriends," and how much money they are required to bring in daily. Although most work as streetwalkers, teenage girls also sell their bodies as call girls and through escort services, massage parlors, strip clubs, brothels, hotels, and even out of private residences. Services can include sexual intercourse, "oral sex, anal sex, homosexual activities, multiple partner sex, sadomasochistic activities, urination or defecation, and obscenity related sexual performances."[8]

Most prostitution-involved girls are white, with studies showing that they represent as many as 80 percent of the total, including those trafficked into the United States from Eastern Europe and elsewhere.[9] However, African American girl prostitutes are overrepresented as teenage prostitutes, constituting between 10 and 50 percent of those plying the trade.[10] Other racial and ethnic minority teenage females are also active in the sex trade, with Latino and Native American girls accounting for anywhere from 2 to 11 percent of those sampled.[11] There has been an increase in Asian prostituted girls in recent years as Asian gangs and sex traffickers from the Philippines, Vietnam, and other parts of Asia have stepped up efforts to recruit and lure young females into the United States as sex slaves (see Chapter 8).[12]

Prostituted girls enter the sex trade from lower-class, middle-class, and even upper-class backgrounds, contrary to popular belief that most come from underprivileged environments. Although small sample groups of girl prostitutes have shown a greater percentage come from lower or working classes, studies with larger samples have found that middle- and upper-class backgrounds were more represented among prostitution-involved girls. In a study by Mimi Silbert, 7 in 10 prostituted girls came from families where the income level was average or greater.[13] Anthropologist Jennifer James reported finding a "phenomenal" rise in the number of "affluent and overindulged" prostitute-engaged girls.[14] Many of these female teens drift into prostitution out of boredom, need for excitement, keeping pace with friends in the sex trade, or making extra money. According to researchers at the University of Pennsylvania, "Wealthier teens sell sex often to their own peers as a way to get more expensive clothes or other consumer goods."[15]

Girl prostitutes tend to come from families beset by dysfunctional dynamics such as marital discord, divorce, and separation. In Maura Crowley's study, 85 percent of prostituted girls reported the absence of at least one parent.[16] Seventy percent of the prostitution-involved girls in the Huckleberry House Project were from broken homes, with a high percentage having a negative, unloving relationship with parents or guardians.[17] Three in four of the girl prostitutes in Diana Gray's study reported relationships with their parents as being "poor" or "very bad."[18]

Prostituted Girls and Sexual Abuse

One of the strongest predictors of involvement in prostitution by girls is a history of child sexual abuse. Nine out of 10 girl prostitutes in the Huckleberry House Project reported being sexually molested, while another study found that 8 in 10 prostituted girls had been victims of child sexual abuse.[19] Similarly, teen prostitution researcher D. Kelly Weisberg reported a high percentage of girl prostitutes had been victims of intrafamilial sexual abuse.[20] Other research has pointed toward sexual abuse by a father, stepfather, or other male father figure such as the mother's lover, as a precursor to girls becoming involved in the commercial sex trade.[21]

According to *Runaway Kids and Teenage Prostitution*, "Children who are sexually abused are at increased risk to run away from home; in turn, most long-term runaways will become prostituted youth. Girls who are sexually abused are more likely than boys to leave home as a direct consequence and engage in a prostitution lifestyle."[22] This sentiment was echoed by Susan McClanahan and colleagues, who posited that childhood sexual abuse victims who were runaways were much more likely than child sexual abuse victims who remained home to have ever become prostituted or were currently active in the sex-for-sale business.[23]

The sad correlation between child sexual abuse and underage prostitution and the vicious cycle many prostituted girls must endure is highlighted in the National Center for Missing and Exploited Children publication, *Female Juvenile Prostitution*, in a case study of a former prostitute named "Cheryl":

> Cheryl's stepfather began sexually abusing her when she was 10 years old. . . . The abuse stopped, when at age 14, she left home. . . . After beginning to prostitute at age 14, Cheryl dropped out of school. She was picked up by law enforcement for prostitution and returned to her biological father. . . . During this period of time, her father brought home his best friend who sexually abused her. . . . She returned to the street where she was exploited by her pimp.[24]

The Runaway Girl

Statistics show that the number of girls who run away from home or foster care or are thrown out of the home by parents or caretakers could reach into the hundreds of thousands or more each year. The Office of Juvenile Justice and Delinquency Prevention reported that females comprise 6 out of every 10 runaway youth.[25] Some believe the number is even higher. According to the National Runaway Switchboard, in 2008, crisis callers were female 72 percent of the time.[26] Many flee sexually abusive environments. The National Network of Runaway and Youth Services reported that 7 in 10 runaways in youth shelters have been the victims of sexual molestation or abuse.[27] Ann Hayman, creator of the Mary Magdalene Project in Los Angeles, argued that runaway girls in particular were regularly subjected to "lots of incest . . . [and] lots of sexual battery."[28] A recent study in Wisconsin of juvenile female offenders found that of girls who had run away from home three times or more, 93 percent had been sexually abused or assaulted.[29]

Other girls leave home due to physical abuse. In one study of runaway youth, 90 percent or more were found to have been victimized by "severe" child abuse.[30] In another study more than three out of four teenage runaways had been victims of physical abuse prior to leaving home.[31] Child physical abuse of runaways often goes hand in hand with child sexual abuse. One study of abused runaways reported 84 percent of the girl runaways had been sexually and physically abused.[32] Further research supports this strong correlation between runaways and child physical and/or sexual abuse.[33]

Substance abuse often plays a big role in the lives of girls who leave home. Many are alcohol or drug dependent, leading to their inability to live at home, or are asked to leave by parents because they are out of control. A typical example of a runaway prostitute addict can be seen in the Myrna Kostash's "Surviving the Streets":

> At 9, Diane ran away from home. . . . By age 12, she was smoking pot. . . . By 16, she was a hooker and a junkie, sleeping under benches on the streets. . . . Everything had become incidental to the drugs—sex, friendships, plans, promises, security. . . . The first thing on her mind when she woke up was how long she would have to work for her first fix. On cocaine, she could turn tricks for 12- or 14-hour days, the most intense part of the high lasting 15 or 20 seconds.[34]

Girls also leave home for various other reasons or in conjunction with sexual or physical abuse, such as the need for independence, disciplinary issues, and mental illness. The *Las Vegas City Life* article, "On the Run," reported: "Some kids run away from home after ordinary family conflicts, which can be exacerbated by other circumstances, like financial crises. Some want to get out of abusive situations. Some are kicked out by parents after becoming pregnant—or after telling parents about their sexual orientation."[35]

Though many runaway girls return home, many others do not and find themselves facing new and dangerous challenges while trying to make it on their own. Journalist Dotson Rader gives a frightening example of this from his research on prostituted runaways:

> I went to Los Angeles and talked to runaways cruising Hollywood Boulevard and Santa Monica. I interviewed a girl who said she had fled Milwaukee when she was 12 because her father and uncle raped her. Now, at 14, she lived in an abandoned bathhouse on Venice Beach with several other kids and pushes drugs. She was four months pregnant and didn't know by whom.[36]

Homeless Girls

Girls who leave home as runaways or thrownaways often end up homeless or living as street kids. According to researchers, running away or being forced to leave home "are among the pathways most commonly identified by public policy and research as leading to youth homelessness."[37] It is estimated that anywhere from several hundred thousand to as many as 2 million teenagers become homeless every year. Studies indicate that at least as many, if not more, girls as boys experience homelessness at some point in their lives.[38]

Homeless girls enter a world where frightening scenarios exist around every corner. Although they tend to find common ground with other homeless youth, most will find that they are ultimately alone in the journey from homes to homelessness and must often fend for themselves with few weapons at their disposal for survival and safety. A recent report from the U.S. Department of Health and Human Services puts in perspective what the typical homeless girl faces: "Once on the street, young people lack support and guidance in dealing with the negative feelings resulting from their family experiences and in obtaining and retaining a job. With no source of income, many cannot acquire basic necessities like food, clothing, and shelter."[39]

Those who may offer homeless girls such essential items for living often have ulterior motives that can lead to prostitution, pornography, forcible rape, STDs, substance abuse, drug dealing, and various other forms of victimization, violence, and health issues. Given the bleak reality of street life, many homeless girls still feel that returning to abusive or dysfunctional homes is not an option. Neither is any expectation of an easy avenue for existing as a homeless person.

Survival Sex

As part of the street culture and need for basic necessities, friendship, independence, sexual experimentation, and support, many homeless girls find themselves engaging in *survival sex*, defined as "the commercial sexual activity of young people as a way of obtaining the necessities of life, including food, drugs, clothing, transport, or money to purchase these goods and services."[40]

Unlike prostitution, which by definition requires the exchange of money for sex, survival sex does not always involve giving or receiving cash payment. Often desperate, homeless teenage females engaging in street sex may accept anything offered in order to survive from day to day, including food, clothing, drugs, or even pointing in the right direction. Moreover, researchers have found that "many youth involved in the exchange of sex for money or other considerations . . . do not perceive themselves as engaging in prostitution, but rather as doing 'whatever is necessary' to ensure their survival."[41]

Other homeless girls participate in survival or recreational sex as part of the exploration and experience of sexual freedom and promiscuity often found among the homeless and, as such, is more about choice than a requirement for survival. Teen prostitution researcher Pam Oliver spoke of the mindset for some street girls in their decision to engage in sexual relations in a homeless environment: "The term 'sex for favors' suggests that sex may also be carried out to make life more enjoyable or tolerable in terms of material goods or accommodation, or for emotional security, approval, attention, or affection."[42]

Studies indicate that anywhere from 10 to 50 percent of homeless youth get involved in survival sex, which can be a form of prostitution or a prelude to offering their bodies for monetary payment. In a study of homeless teens in New York City, more than one in three participated in sexual relations as a mechanism for survival.[43] A similar proportion engaged in survival sex in a San Francisco study.[44] One expert on juvenile prostitution referred to survival sex as "a desperate and risky behavior borne out of isolation and the lack of any tangible resources."[45]

Entry into Prostitution

For many homeless girls, prostitution becomes an inevitable consequence of life on the streets and the need to survive from day to day with the one thing of value they have: their bodies. Studies indicate that within 36 to 48 hours, and often much sooner, of a girl becoming homeless, she will be solicited for sex, or "persuaded, coerced, recruited, or abducted into prostitution and/or pornography by pimps, customers, gangs, pedophiles, or pornographers. . . . Most newly homeless youth, away on their own for the first time and frightened, are easy marks for those who would take advantage of their desperation and vulnerability."[46]

Studies have shown that the longer a runaway or thrownaway girl is away from a secure environment, the greater the chances she will become prostitution-engaged or a victim of other commercial exploitation. Remaining homeless for 30 days has been found to be perhaps the single greatest determinant in a street youth turning to prostitution.[47] Many homeless youth become prostituted much sooner. In one study, it was found that after being homeless for two weeks, 75 percent of runaways will have entered the sex trade as a prostitute, in child pornography, or some other form of commercial sexual exploitation.[48]

Prostitution-involved girls typically began selling sexual favors between the ages of 12 and 14, according to researchers such as Ayala Pines and Susan Hunter.[49] According to a longtime New York City street prostitute, "Half of the girls in the renowned child prostitute tracks in East New York and Long Island City, Queens, are between the ages of 13 to 15."[50]

However, a number of experts believe that many girls are entering the sex trade at even earlier ages. Marcia Cohen found in a study that females began selling sex between 9 and 12 years of age; whereas one in four prostituted girls came into the business under the age of 14 based on research by Miriam Saphira.[51] One in 10 were age 12 and younger. In New York, the average age of girls entering prostitution is 12. According to Spangenberg, with respect to girl prostitutes and initiation into the sex trade, "Many girls physically mature between the ages of 12 and 13 and are prime candidates for the sex trade. . . . Since the *average* age for starting out is between 12 and 13, there are youth that start even younger."[52]

The attraction of young prostitutes in East New York, Brooklyn, was noted by reporter Laura Italiano: "The youngest girls are so popular, their customers cause traffic jams."[53] The stereotypical image of teenage streetwalkers in heavy makeup, very provocative attire, and high-heeled stilettos does not always apply to younger prostitutes, according to Holly Joshi, an undercover police officer in Oakland, California, who works with the Vice and Child Exploitation Unit. She stressed that pimps tend to "make sure the very young girls look like the very young girls. . . . They just send them out there with no makeup, looking young. That's what the customers [want]."[54]

The mental and physical toll a girl endures in starting prostitution in adolescence was put in context in a literature review of the commercial sexual exploitation of children:

> A girl who begins prostitution at 14 will have submitted to the sexual demands of 4,000 men before she is old enough to drive a car, 8,000 men before she is old enough to vote, and 12,000 men before she is deemed mature enough to buy a single beer in most states.[55]

Most girls enter prostitution as part-time sex workers, hoping to earn enough to pay for food, cigarettes, drugs, clothes, shelter, and pocket money. For many, their needs and circumstances, including involvement with pimps, turns their part-time status as prostitutes to full-time sex work. Studies reveal that, typically, a teenage girl prostitute will "be turning tricks as a full-time way of life within eight months to a year after her initial experience as a prostitute."[56]

The process of a girl becoming a full-time prostitute is described in *The Prostitution of Women and Girls*:

> Girl prostitutes undergo a change in self-image. . . . Adapting to the reality of being prostitutes, along with the negative self-image this brings, adolescent prostitutes become, in effect, what they are labeled by society: sluts, whores, or hookers. The more they become a part of the prostitution subculture . . . the more they come to regard themselves as prostitutes and the more committed they become to working the streets, selling their bodies full-time.[57]

Prostituted Girls and Pimps

Virtually all prostitution-engaged girls are recruited into the sex trade by a pimp or become involved with one over the course of her prostituting. An estimated 75 to 95 percent of all prostituted girls have been turned out by pimps who use a mixture of charm, affection, romance, street smarts, intimidation, dependency, drugs, and violence to control and manipulate the girls in their stable.[58] In one survey of teenage streetwalkers, there were hardly any who did not report an association with a pimp to one degree or another.[59] According to the book *Street Kids*, for most prostituted girls, pimps "play a major role in everything from recruitment to where they ply their trade to how much customers are charged for sexual favors."[60]

Though most pimps are older males who begin as strangers to prostituted girls, some are not much older than the teenage girl recruits, or are romantically involved with the girls before coercing them into prostitution.[61] Many are pimp-pornographers, pedophiles, or drug dealers, men who seduce and exploit these girls as a relatively easy way to make money and satisfy sexual urges for themselves or clientele. There are also some female pimps or madams, many of whom are ex-prostitutes, who bring underage girls into the business to work in brothels, escort services, or on the streets. Around one in five girl prostitutes enter the sex trade after being recruited by other prostitution-involved girls.[62] Many of these are recruiters or runners working for pimps, as another technique to lure naive and vulnerable girls into the world of commercial sexual exploitation.

Gang pimping of teenage girls is on the rise. They set their sights on runaways, thrownaways, substance abusers, school dropouts, and girls who are promiscuous. According to an article on teenage prostitution:

> These girls are under the control of more than one gang member, which places greater restrictions on their freedom. They are also subject to more violence, including sexual assault and rape, and may be at greater risk for STDs and AIDS, since they will likely have more than one gang member as a sexual partner.[63]

Experts contend that as the recruitment of new members to the gang increases, the likelihood that vulnerable female teens will continue being targeted for commercial sexual exploitation is high.

In some instances, girls are actually pimped by a member of their own families, such as the father, stepfather, brother, or even mother. Parry Aftab, who works for an Internet safety group, noted that when parents turn out to be the pimps, "there is almost a 100 percent chance that these kids are already being molested and will continue to be abused."[64] Child pornography is also often involved when parents or other family members recruit underage girls into prostitution.

Runaway and thrownaway girls are especially targeted by pimps and their cohorts, taking advantage of their dire straits and susceptibility to being "offered a helping hand." An expert on the sexual exploitation of teenagers observed: "Pimps lurk in cars in the shadows, calculating the night's take. But not all pimps are gangsters. Often it is the father who sits in the backup car or mother who negotiates the deal for her daughter."[65]

These newly homeless girls are typically found at "bus and train stations, shopping malls, coffee shops, arcades, street corners, and anywhere that runaway, wayward, and lost kids hang out or end up [such as youth shelters]."[66] Pimps have no trouble identifying targets for their prostitute stable as the girls are often "disheveled, look hungry, alone, disoriented, frightened, under the influence of alcohol or drugs, and in need of comfort and friendship."[67] Pimps take full advantage of these vulnerabilities by "coming to the rescue," under the guise of flattery, camaraderie, or romancing. According to the author of a *Psychology Today* article on teen prostitution titled "Coming of Age on City Streets," these pimps offer the unsuspecting girls "a roof over their heads, a 'caring adult,' clothes, makeup, and promises of love and belonging."[68] The girl recruit is often unaware of the one-way path into the commercial sex trade industry she is being led down until it is too late to turn back.

Writer Deborah Jones's article "Pimped," portrayed the typical scenario of seduction used by pimps in gaining a girl's confidence:

> It often starts out with romance. Seduced at malls and in schoolyards, courted with restaurant meals and expensive gifts, the girls eventually find themselves cut off from their families and being asked to "return a favor." They are all, after all, very young. But the pimps also choose their targets well—girls from broken homes, girls living on the streets, girls who are just somehow troubled.[69]

The Internet, cell phones, and other digital technology have made it easier than ever for pimps, pornographers, and other sexual exploiters to prey on vulnerable youth while often keeping authorities at arm's length. Popular culture is also seen by sociologists as an important factor in the success of the sex trade industry and recruitment of teenagers. According to an article on teen prostitution, "the glorification of sex and pimping in music and fashion sends a message that the lifestyle is OK."[70]

The vast majority of pimp-controlled prostituted girls are streetwalkers. An estimated one out of every five streetwalker prostitutes is a teenage girl.[71] Some believe an even higher proportion of streetwalkers are underage females. Pimps also prostitute girls through massage parlors, sex clubs, escort services, topless bars, sex rings, and the Internet, which is perhaps the fastest growing means in the digital age for pimps to promote girl prostitutes to a wider audience of johns, pedophiles, pornographers, and other sexual exploiters of minors, while reducing their risk of exposure and apprehension.

Prostitution-involved girls are physically and sexually assaulted by pimps (and customers) on a regular basis, including "being hit with closed fists, slapped, kicked, burned, and beaten with 'coat hangers to lashings with a six-foot bull whip.'"[72] A self-report survey revealed that more than two-thirds of streetwalkers had been beaten up by their pimps on more than one occasion as part of the pimp's strategy for respect, cooperation, and intimidation. Some prostitutes have accused their pimps of "severe violence, torture, and attempted murder."[73]

According to Rachel Lloyd, an ex-prostitute and now executive director of a education and mentoring program for prostituted girls in New York City, pimp violence comes with the territory for teenage girls in the sex-for-sale industry:

> Sometimes I meet a girl who says, "I have a really good pimp—he beats me only with an open hand." . . . Many of the girls see the pimps as boyfriends, but violence is integral to everything that happens in the sex industry.[74]

Prostituted girls who attempt to leave a pimp's stable may be at the greatest risk for bodily harm. This was underscored by an Oakland, California, police officer, "If the girls express any desire in leaving, a lot of them do, but when they do, the pimps resort to physical violence, threats, beating, rape, pistol whipping, torture, withholding food."[75]

One girl prostitute recalled what happened when she tried to get out of the prostitution business: "He told me to take my clothes off. I wouldn't so he punched me so hard he lifted me off the ground. . . . My skin split. Blood was spraying and it was like a horror movie."[76] (See further discussion on pimps in Chapter 10.)

Cost of Services Offered by Prostituted Girls

Prostitution-involved girls are, by and large, at the low end of the prostitution hierarchy in earnings for their services. They also tend to keep the least amount of what they earn while often putting in the most hours on the job. The actual cost of services performed by girl prostitutes varies depending on the service, location, experience, and even the familiarity between prostitute and client. Generally speaking, prostitutes charge between $20 and $50 for oral sex, and can earn between $50 and $100 for sexual intercourse.[77] In New York City, the price for oral sex is $40 to $50, $75 for intercourse, and $150 for outcalls.

Oral sex is the most common type of sexual service that prostituted girls perform. According to one study, three-quarters of streetwalkers' sex work involves fellatio, or oral copulation only.[78] An expert on girl prostitution noted that the prostituted girl's primary sexual contact is oral sex because "it is what her customers want and the most practical for working in cars. It's also quick, which is a concern, because street prostitution is illegal, and when the cops show up, it is sometimes necessary to run."[79]

Pimps can make more money from girl prostitutes who are younger, more attractive, and in good health. According to the authorities in Oakland, California, for example, "Girls aged 11 and 12 can earn as much as $500 a day for their pimps."[80] In New York, an attractive prostituted girl servicing 10 johns on a Saturday or Sunday night could bring in as much as $1,500 on her own.[81]

Conversely, for a teenage prostitute addict, the price for sex could be "as low as the market price for a single rock of crack cocaine."[82] Such was the case of a girl prostitute and crack addict as depicted in a *Time* magazine article:

> "Eva" is a 16-year-old patient at New York City's Phoenix House drug rehabilitation center who got hooked on crack two years ago. The product of a troubled middle-class family, she was already a heavy drinker and pot smoker when she was introduced to coke by her older brother, a young dope pusher. "When you take the first toke on a crack pipe, you get on top of the world," she says.
>
> She started stealing from family and friends to support her habit. She soon turned to prostitution and went through two abortions before she was 16. "I just wanted to get high," she says. "Fear of pregnancy didn't even cross my mind when I hit the sack with someone for drugs."[83]

Some crack houses also serve as "sex-for-drugs" centers. A study on drugs and teen prostitution found that teenage use of crack in poor neighborhoods in the inner city has increased the incidence of street-level teenage prostitution.[84]

Girl prostitutes who work for pimps more often than not receive only a fraction of what they actually bring in, and sometimes nothing at all, while still being expected to work long hours. Once part of a pimp's stable, prostituted girls are typically "subject to his rules, regulations, and manipulation which include falling in love, working for him, believing him, [and] giving him much of her earnings."[85] In her study of child commercial sexual exploitation, Anne Rasmusson spoke of the tremendous burden and pressure to make money placed on prostitution-involved girls by their pimps:

> Pimps usually impose quotas of earnings on their girls, give them little money, beat them if they fail to meet their quotas, and often have a "stable" of girls who work for them. Pimps most frequently beat them for not making enough money, being disrespectful to the pimp, violating some rules, or leaving, or threatening to leave.[86]

Sexually Transmitted Diseases

Girl prostitutes face a high risk for contracting STDs, such as HIV, "as a result of the combination of unsafe survival sex, multiple anonymous sex partners, lack of condom use, and intravenous drug use along with sharing tainted needles."[87] According to Nancy Walker, Associate Director for the Institute for Children, Youth, and Families, more than 85 percent of teenage prostitutes in the sex trade industry have contracted an STD, such as genital warts, gonorrhea, herpes, hepatitis B, and syphilis.[88] It was reported by the National Center for Missing and Exploited Children that almost 84 percent of homeless youth have engaged in one or more high-risk behaviors for AIDS.[89] In *Drugs, Runaways, and Teen Prostitution*, author Clare Tattersall estimated that between one-half and two-thirds of teenage prostitutes get infected with an STD.[90]

Prostitution-involved girls are particularly vulnerable to STDs "because of their youth, immaturity, and inability to resist customers who engage in unsafe, high-risk, sexual practices."[91] Covenant House, the largest New York City shelter for runaways estimated that girls who sold their bodies on regular basis could have a rate of HIV infection exceeding 50 percent.[92] In a study of prostituted youth, Pam Oliver described the internal consequences for sexually active girls and the dangers of STDs:

> Most children and young adolescents are not sufficiently developed physically to engage in penetrative sex. The physiologically immature reproductive tract in pre-menarchal girls is much less capable of resisting invasion and subsequent damage by sexually transmitted microorganisms. The sexual activity is often violent, and this can cause internal damage, destroying the

normal vagina and infection barriers, and putting children at greater risk than adults for contracting sexually transmitted disease.[93]

Girl Prostitutes and Arrests

As the most visible and lowest type of prostitute in the sex trade industry, female streetwalker prostitutes are more likely to be arrested, rearrested, or otherwise in contact with the criminal justice system than other prostitutes are, although some believe male streetwalkers may be equally prone to arrest. Prostitution-involved girls are arrested more often than prostitution-involved boys, according to recent official data. The U.S. Department of Justice's *Crime in the United States* reported that in 2008, females under the age of 18 were arrested more than three times as often for prostitution and commercialized vice as males younger than 18.[94] Girls were also more likely to be arrested as runaways than boys, as this is often seen as the precursor to involvement in prostitution. Additionally, prostituted girls face arrest on prostitution-related charges, such as alcohol and drug offenses, curfew and loitering law violations, and vagrancy.

Evidence suggests that prostitution-involved girls may be viewed by law enforcement more as victims than offenders and are sometimes referred to social services or other child welfare agencies in lieu of arrest.[95] Studies have found that three-fourths of girl prostitutes have had contact at some point with police officers, juvenile courts, or other parts of the juvenile and criminal justice systems.[96] However, even when prostituted girls are arrested, most spend relatively little time in custody. According to Lois Lee, founder of Children of the Night, a Van Nuys, California, shelter for homeless teenage prostitutes: "Juvenile authorities turn these kids back onto the streets almost as fast as they are brought in," further suggesting that "social service agencies want little to do with street prostitutes."[97] As a result, many prostitution-involved girls wind up back on the streets offering their bodies for cash, food, drugs, and a place to stay, along with participating in other risky activities until they are rearrested, become ill, or get out of the business, if fortunate enough to do so.

Recently authorities have begun to crack down on pimps and johns in an effort to focus more on those controlling the sex trade industry rather than the sexually exploited. However, prosecutors have found many prostitutes reluctant to testify against their pimps, due to intimidation, loyalty, misguided love, and even self-incrimination.[98]

Chapter 8

Trafficked Prostitutes

Human trafficking for purposes of forced prostitution and other types of commercial sexual exploitation is a global problem of epidemic proportions. Around 1 million women and children from South and Southeast Asia, Eastern Europe, South and Central America, and other undeveloped regions are estimated to be victims of sex trafficking every year, brought across borders to developed regions such as Western Europe, the Middle East, Asia, and North America. Tens of thousands of these children and women are trafficked into the United States and prostituted or otherwise turned into sexual slaves. Most of the victims are impoverished, uneducated, and vulnerable, making them easy targets for human and sex traffickers to manipulate, deceive, and sexually exploit. Recent theatrical movies and television miniseries such as *Sex Traffic, Human Trafficking, Trade*, and *Taken* and documentaries including *Cargo: Innocence Lost, Red Light*, and Frontline's *Sex Slaves*, have shed light on this serious international plight of human and sex trafficking.

Domestic sex trafficking has proven to be an even bigger issue within the United States with hundreds of thousands of youth at risk annually for this type of commercial sexual exploitation by pimps, pornographers, organized criminals, and gangs who transport victims around the country to sell their bodies to johns, pedophiles, and other sexual exploiters. Although there are laws against sex trafficking, much as there are outlawing other forms of sexual exploitation and prostitution, perpetrators continue to circumvent and victimize their targeted group, aided in part by the Internet and other digital applications in the modern age that open up the marketplace considerably while making it more difficult for law enforcement authorities to detect and apprehend them.

Human Trafficking

What is human trafficking and how does it relate to the prostituting of individuals? In *Sex Crimes*, it is defined as "the recruiting and transporting of persons through deception, coercion, or other means of manipulation for purposes of forced labor, involuntary servitude, sexual abuse and exploitation, and/or enslavement."[1] Wikipedia defines *human trafficking* as "the illegal trade in human beings for the purposes of commercial sexual exploitation or forced labor; a modern-day form of slavery."[2] Human trafficking is the "fastest growing criminal industry in the world, tied with the illegal arms industry as the second largest, after the drug-trade."[3]

According to the United Nations Protocol to Prevent, Suppress, and Punish Trafficking in Persons, human trafficking involves the:

> recruitment, transportation, transfer, harboring or receipt of persons, by means of threat or use of force or other forms of coercion, of abduction, or fraud, of deception, of the abuse of power or of a position of vulnerability or of the giving or receiving of payments or benefits to achieve the consent of a person having control over another person, for the purpose of exploitation. Exploitation shall include, at a minimum, the exploitation of the prostitution of others or other forms of sexual exploitation, forced labor or services, slavery or practices similar to slavery, servitude, or the removal of organs.[4]

In the United States, "severe forms of trafficking in persons" has been defined by the federal government through the Victims of Trafficking and Violence Protection Act of 2000 and again its reauthorization in 2003, as

> (a) sex trafficking in which a commercial sex act is induced by force, fraud, or coercion, or in which the person induced to perform such act has not attained 18 years of age; or
> (b) the recruitment, harboring, transportation, provision, or obtaining of a person for labor or services, through the use of force, fraud, or coercion for the purpose of subjection to involuntary servitude, peonage, debt bondage, or slavery.[5]

Human traffickers or slave traders typically target the most vulnerable—especially young women and children—and exploit their often dire circumstances in life, including impoverishment, discrimination, political instability, corruption, and even terrorism.

In hoping to find a better life and a higher standard of living, many victims may leave home voluntarily (albeit due to difficult circumstances) before realizing too late that they were deceived, only to find themselves forced into domestic servitude, labor in sweatshops or agriculture, prostitution, pornography, and other forms of slavery. A victim's consent to the initial trafficking is seen "as irrelevant in defining as a victim of human trafficking because of the deception, coercion, sexual exploitation, violence, and solution that typically occurs as a result of trafficking."[6]

The Global Reach of Human Trafficking

How widespread is trafficking in persons? As a result of the often hidden or underreported human trafficking and inconsistencies in definitions and estimates, it is impossible to assess its true dimensions on a global scale. However, the available figures give some perspective on its enormity as a social issue.

According to UNICEF, an estimated 1.75 million women and children are trafficked across international borders each year, with children alone accounting for 1.2 million trafficked persons.[7] An estimated 2.5 million people from a minimum of 127 countries are being bought and sold and otherwise victimized by human traffickers annually, according to the United Nations.[8] This is lower than their previous estimate of 4 million but considerable nevertheless.[9] Approximately 50,000 people are believed to be trafficked into the United States from Mexico every year, one in three of whom are Latin Americans.[10]

A U.S. Department of Justice estimate put the number of persons who are bought, sold, or forced into the world of human traffickers at around 800,000 to 900,000 annually.[11] The U.S. State Department's *Trafficking in Persons* (TIP) *Report* estimates that approximately 600,000 to 820,000 children, women, and men are trafficked involuntarily or through deceptive practices across international borders each year; with there being an estimated 12.3 million children and adult victims of human trafficking worldwide, according to the 2010 TIP.[12] Around sixty percent of those trafficked are female and at least half are children—with the majority of victims forced or coerced into involvement in prostitution or other forms of commercial sexual exploitation and sexual abuse.

It is conservatively estimated by the Justice Department that some 14,500 to 17,500 foreign nationals are brought into the United States annually as victims of human trafficking.[13] The State Department has estimated that 45,000 to 50,000 persons are trafficked into this country annually.[14] A recent estimate by an analyst with the Central Intelligence Agency was similar.[15] The number of Americans trafficked each year within the United States is also believed to be significant, with anywhere from 250,000 to more than 300,000 American children estimated to be at risk for sex trafficking victimization each year.[16]

According to the *Assessment of U.S. Government Activities to Combat Trafficking in Persons*, in 2004 the greatest number of human beings trafficked into the United States every year originate from East Asia and the Pacific, with between 5,000 and 7,000 trafficking victims. This is followed by Latin America, Europe, and Eurasia, with between 3,500 and 5,500 victims of trafficking.[17] Within the 2009 TIP Report, Secretary of State Hillary Clinton noted that "the global financial crisis has decreased the global demand for labor and increased the number of people willing to take risks for economic opportunities and will likely increase the prevalence of cases of forced labor and prostitution."[18]

In a disturbing major study of human trafficking in the United States, it was found that the trafficking of women for forced labor, sexual exploitation, and slavery often lasted for years before it was discovered. Forced labor or services tended to last between 4.5 and 6.5 years, while prostitution continued for an estimated 2.5 years, and other kinds of sexual exploitation went on between 10 months and 3 years before discovery. On detection, it took an estimated 1.5 years for completion of an official investigation and prosecution of the human traffickers.[19]

The Business of Human Trafficking

Human trafficking is a multibillion-dollar worldwide industry. An estimated $9.5 billion is generated in yearly revenue from human trafficking.[20] According to the Council of Europe, "people trafficking has reached epidemic proportions over the past decade, with a global annual market of about $42.5 billion."[21] Recent criminal investigations into human trafficking in the United States found that traffickers made between $1 million and $8 million over a period of one to six years of trafficking activities.[22] The supply and demand of female and young trafficking victims makes human trafficking an attractive venture for traffickers, recruiters, pimps, pornographers, and others who profit from the trafficking in persons for purposes of prostitution and other commercial sexual exploitation. This includes the men who pay to sexually exploit youth and women such as customers, sex tourists, molesters, pedophiles, and pornographers through child sex tourism, streetwalkers, escort service sex workers, arranged forced sex acts, and child pornography.[23]

The trafficking of persons is closely associated with organized crime and other criminal activity, often using profits from trafficking for other criminality such as money laundering, pornography, drug trafficking, human smuggling, document forgery, and murder.[24] Human traffickers often "operate through a spectrum of criminal organizations—from major crime syndicates, to gangs, to smuggling rings, to loosely associated networks. Major trafficking organizations are Asian criminal syndicates, Russian crime groups and syndicates, and loosely associated Latin American groups."[25]

With the vast profits resulting from the trafficking in persons, traffickers and related offenders are "willing to engage in any type of psychological manipulation or physical violence to control victims and continue the vicious cycle of deception, slavery, and exploitation."[26]

Entrance for Trafficking Victims into the United States

Trafficked victims generally gain entry into the United States in one of three ways: (1) proper travel documents that are used illegally, (2) fake passports, and (3) by eluding inspection.[27] According to law enforcement authorities, the majority of trafficked women enter the United States by airplane.[28] However, victims of trafficking can also gain entrance into the country by automobile, boat, train, swimming, and on foot.

Traffickers use various points of entry to smuggle children and women into the United States, including primary immigration ports of entry that run along the U.S. and Canadian border as well as such entry points as New York, Miami, Detroit, Los Angeles, and Chicago. Trafficked women have also been reported to enter the country through U.S. military bases.[29]

In a study of sex trafficking of women in the United States by Donna Hughes and colleagues, the process is described as frequently involving:

> the use of many transit nations before [victims] arrive at the country of destination. An Asian crime investigator noted that many Asians might have been in South America before coming over the Mexican border into the United States. . . . These entry points for trafficking, however, are fluid and when the Immigration and Naturalization Service conducts crackdowns in particular areas of the country, the entry points shift to another location.[30]

After successful entry into the United States, the trafficking routes within the country vary "from regional to national to one coast to the other, depending on the traffickers' intentions for victims."[31] For instance, in the Midwest, a recent report found that Russian women were "trafficked from Chicago to the escort services and clubs of Minneapolis; especially after the crackdown of a Latvian-American trafficking ring in Chicago."[32] For women and child victims of sex traffickers, typical destinations for commercial sexual exploitation include Detroit, New York, Houston, Tampa, Denver, Las Vegas, Seattle, and Miami.

A typical example of a trafficked Russian young woman for entry into the United States by way of Mexico for purposes of prostitution was recently described in a *48 Hours* report on the international sex slave trade:

Olga, 25, [was] a survivor of a million-dollar sex slave trafficking ring in Russia. Her ordeal began in 1999 in her hometown of Moscow, a growing supplier of sex slaves to the United States. She was the perfect target for traffickers. Both her father and boyfriend had been murdered by the Russian mob. She was scared and desperate to get out. A friend introduced her to a man . . . who was looking for girls to work in America. [He] offered Olga a chance at a new life: a job as an assistant and transportation to the United States.

After [the man] spent the money on the plane tickets, he made it clear there was no backing out. "If anybody try to run away, he's not going to deal with you," says Olga. "I'm just going to cut your head off."

Olga got on the plane with four other Russian girls. In that instant, they became the personal property of an international slave trader. Olga's plane, however, was headed to Mexico. [The sex trafficker] was planning to smuggle the women across the notoriously unsupervised border between Mexico and the United States.[33]

According to Rebecca Leung, who wrote an article on sexual slavery:

Girls like Olga are sometimes put to work in Mexican strip clubs before heading north. But Mexico is more than just a transit country and training ground for Eastern Europeans. In its own right, Mexico is the No. 1 country providing slaves to the United States, accounting for the majority of federal trafficking cases.[34]

Human traffickers have become adept at finding means to circumvent Immigration and Customs Enforcement agents or deceive them in crossing borders into the United States from Mexico and Canada or other countries with often unsuspecting victims for purposes of commercial sexual exploitation.

Sex Trafficking

Sex trafficking as a subset of the trafficking of persons is defined as "the recruitment, harboring, transportation, provision, or obtaining of a person for the purpose of a commercial sex act in which a commercial sex act is induced by force, fraud, or coercion, or in which the person forced to perform such an act is under 18 years of age."[35]

According to the Department of Justice's (DOJ) Child Exploitation and Obscenity Section (CEOS): "Sex trafficking is nothing less than slavery. When an offender takes a woman or girl against her will and forces her to engage in prostitution, that offender has stolen her freedom and her dignity."[36] One researcher defined sex trafficking as the sexual exploitation of a minor for profit or pleasure.[37] Another, Robert Moossy, who gave a presentation at the DOJ's Fourth National Human Trafficking Conference in September 2008, described sex trafficking as "a hidden crime, perpetrated in alleys, brothels, and illicit massage parlors," while defining it as "a particularly degrading form of human trafficking, defined generally as recruiting, enticing, harboring, transporting, providing, or obtaining" victims for purposes of commercial sexual activity by means of compulsion or fraud.[38]

The U.S. Department of Health and Human Services Administration for Children and Families views sex trafficking as enslavement and bondage involving commercial sex acts that the victims are physically or psychologically coerced into performing, or forced to participate in while younger than 18 years of age.[39] The Trafficking Victims Protection Act of 2000, which makes sex trafficking a federal crime, defines *commercial sex act* as "any sex act on account of which anything of value is given to or received by any person," while defining traffickers' use of any type of *coercion* as including "threats of serious harm to or physical restraint against any person; any scheme, plan, or pattern intended to cause a person to believe that failure to perform an act would result in serious harm to or physical restraint against any person; or the abuse or threatened abuse of the legal process."[40]

According to Anne Rasmusson, an expert on child commercial sexual exploitation, there are two categories of sex trafficking: "one in which the participant is aware of the circumstances and one in which [she or he is] not."[41] The first type consists of "hiring an individual to engage in prostitution in any country, state, or territory other than that in which [the person] live[s]."[42] The second kind of trafficking is "disguised traffic," which pertains to "hiring women or girls to work away from their homes in an industry in which they will likely come into contact with pimps and prostitutes."[43] Trafficking victims are "coerced into prostitution by being forced to repay debts to the employment agency that paid for their ticket to another country and found them employment."[44]

The trafficking of women and children for sexual exploitation, in particular, is a global crisis. Millions of women and children are the victims of sex traffickers through prostitution, white slavery, molestation, rape, child sex tourism, military prostitution, pornography, live sex shows, and related sex offenses. The gravity of sex trafficking as a problem can be seen in the following data:[45]

- The trafficking of people is third only to drug and arms trafficking in worldwide revenue.
- As many as 2 to 4 million women may be actively involved in the sex-for-sale business in the United States.
- An estimated 30 million women have been sold into prostitution since the mid-1970s.
- No less than $4 billion is estimated to be generated annually from brothels across the globe.
- At least half a million women have been trafficked from developing countries and forced into prostitution.
- Two million or more youth in Asia alone are actively being sexually exploited in the commercial sex trade.
- Between 50 and 60 percent of underage victims of sex traffickers are younger than 16 years of age.
- Child pornography brings in an estimated $1 billion a year.
- One quarter of child sex tourists internationally are American citizens.

Sex trafficking has unified nations throughout the world "in its expansion and victimization of women and children by recruiters, traffickers, pimps, and customers who have crisscrossed international borders, often with impunity or indifference."[46]

Victims of International Sex Trafficking

International sex trafficking victims are predominantly women and girls, but can be men or boys as well. As noted in Wikipedia, they are

generally found in dire circumstances and easily targeted by traffickers. Individuals, circumstances, and situations vulnerable to traffickers include homeless individuals, runaway teens, displaced homemakers, refugees, and drug addicts. While it may seem like trafficked people are the most vulnerable and powerless minorities in a region, victims are consistently exploited from any ethnic and social background.[47]

Victims of sex trafficking come from well more than 100 nations, both poor and wealthy, with some countries in particular notorious for trafficking including Russia, Ukraine, Romania, Bulgaria, Philippines, Thailand, Vietnam, Columbia, Nigeria, Iraq, and Nepal. But even such prosperous nations as Japan, England, Germany, Canada, and the United States have experienced victims of sex trafficking being taken abroad for commercial exploitation. Popular destinations for sex trafficking include Western Europe, the Middle East, and North America. The United States, in particular, with its many entry points and large expanse for doing business is attractive to traffickers.

Victims of sex trafficking are typically "conditioned" by their abductors through such means as "starvation, confinement, beatings, physical abuse, rape, gang rape, threats of violence to the victims and the victims' families, forced drug use, and the threat of shaming their victims by revealing their activities to their family and their families' friends."[48] They are at risk for numerous physical and psychological perils from being sex slaves, such as traumatic brain injuries, broken bones, tearing of the vagina or anus, sexually transmitted diseases such as HIV infection, menstrual issues, miscarriages, substance abuse, depression, suicidal ideation, insomnia, and post-traumatic stress disorder. Some victims can also experience traumatic bonding, which is "a form of coercive control in which the perpetrator instills in the victim fear as well as gratitude for being allowed to live."[49]

Sex trafficking victims from abroad forced into the sex trade in the United States face many challenges in terms of their ordeal and seeking to escape, and their distrust toward the police. This was put in perspective by Moossy:

> Unlike many crime victims, sex trafficking victims may be afraid they have committed the crime of prostitution, and thus they may be wary of law enforcement. Victims may be aliens from countries with systemically corrupt law enforcement officials who work for the sex traffickers. These victims are often highly traumatized, having lived through months or even years of brutality, sexual assaults by the traffickers and clients, false promises, and fear. In some instances, victims develop survival or coping mechanisms that manifest as distrust, deceptiveness, and an unwillingness to accept assistance. Sometimes they express love for their traffickers.[50]

Virtually all victims of sex trafficking are forced into prostitution by traffickers and sex slave traders. As noted by a group of researchers, "Trafficking for sexual exploitation is, for the most part, trafficking for prostitution. Domestic trafficking is, for the most part, trafficking for prostitution. . . . Traffickers rely on local and existing sex industries, whether women are trafficked domestically or internationally."[51]

In a study of females trafficked from Mexico to the United States, Marisa Ugarte and colleagues contended that victims tend to be taken by traffickers to any destination with a demand for prostitution services.[52] Dorchen Leidholdt described this "global prostitution" from a study of prostitution and the trafficking in women with the more common type of prostitution as "domestic trafficking."[53]

Studies show that few trafficked women and girls wish to prostitute themselves. According to a 2003 study in the *Journal of Trauma Practice*, 89 percent of prostituted females sought to escape the sex trade. The study found that between 65 and 75 percent of the prostitutes had been raped; 70 to 95 percent physically assaulted; and 68 percent of those prostitution-involved suffered from post-traumatic stress disorder.[54]

Traffickers and Trafficking Victims Brought into the United States

A high percentage of human trafficking victims entering the United States are prostituted by their traffickers. The Justice Department reported that between January 2007 and September 2008, 83 percent of human trafficking cases in the United States involved sex trafficking.[55]

An article in the *Portland Alliance* on sex trafficking estimated that 75 percent of trafficked females are victims of sexual exploitation commercially as prostitutes.[56]

According to Elizabeth Salett, who wrote an article on human trafficking and sex slavery:

> While it may be difficult to believe that modern-day slavery and human trafficking exist in the United States in the 21st century, the fact is that it is present in every state, in both our urban and rural areas. Traffickers exploit the migration process, using legal or forged documents, often making use of visas like the temporary guest worker visas, fiancés visas, domestic workers, or others to bring in women and children for prostitution.[57]

International sex traffickers who take, buy, and sell women and children and bring them into this country run the gamut in terms of their appearance, nationality, and background. They originate from and operate out of places where sex slave abductions flourish, such as former Eastern bloc nations, Southeast Asia, and South America; as well as points of transit or destination, including Mexico, Israel, the Netherlands, Japan, Turkey, and the United States. Some traffickers run their operations in countries where they have no direct association aside from the lucrative market for victims of sex trafficking.

For foreign traffickers who bring trafficked persons into the United States for purposes of commercial sexual exploitation or forced labor, studies have shown that many were "recently naturalized U.S. citizens who maintained close ties to their country of origin."[58] In a report conducted by the Human Rights Center, such sex traffickers were typically found to be Russian-Americans, Mexican-Americans, and Chinese-Americans.[59] The State Department found that a high percentage of trafficking victims migrate to this country voluntarily, whether through legal or illegal means, as a result of "false promises of employment."[60]

The following is an example of a successful operation by traffickers who lured underage females from Veracruz into the United States and turned them into trafficked prostitutes:

> Their traffickers met the demand for cheap sex by targeting their services toward migrant workers who were already there that worked on remote farms. Law enforcement and inspectors from the Department of Labor were unlikely to visit. Neither the girls nor the men were likely to contact authorities as most of the workers there were in the country illegally.[61]

Traffickers are often members of organized crime syndicates, gangs, drug dealers, child sexual abusers, white-collar criminals, and other criminal elements. In the Hughes and associates' study of sex trafficking, it was found that 60 percent of international women and 40 percent of American women in the sex-for-sale industry were recruited and controlled by people representing organized criminal enterprises, such as the mafia, gangs, brothels, and escort services.[62] Some sex traffickers may have a legitimate front as businessmen or women, diplomats, investors, tourists, or co-workers, while operating secretly as traffickers.

Traffickers and slave traders oftentimes are family members of victims, intimates, friends, and associates, many of whom may double as traffickers, recruiters, pimps, pornographers, pedophiles, or even customers. According to one study, 20 percent of international prostitutes and 28 percent of American prostitutes reported having a husband or boyfriend as their pimp, while a low percentage said that drug addiction was the primary reason for entering the sex trade.[63]

A strong relationship has been found between members of the U.S. armed forces and the trafficking and pimping of females.[64] Many servicemen have married or promised to marry foreign or American women who were previously involved in the sex trade, only to force or coerce them into prostitution on the streets, in massage parlors, or elsewhere in the United States. Such women are often susceptible to their pimp lover's demands that they sell their bodies because of such issues as displacement, language barriers, substance abuse, domestic violence, fears of being returned to impoverished or politically unstable native lands, or threats of bodily harm or death.

Domestic Sex Trafficking

Aside from the tens of thousands of women and children trafficked into the United States and prostituted, there are perhaps hundreds of thousands of American teenage girls being trafficked from state to state across the country yearly for purposes of prostitution and other commercial sexual exploitation by domestic traffickers, including pimps, pornographers, gangs, and organized criminals. According to the CEOS:

> The interstate sex trafficking of minors is a growing problem, [where] young people are recruited into prostitution through forced abduction, pressure from parents, or through deceptive agreements between parents and traffickers. . . . Once these children become involved in prostitution they are often forced to travel far from their homes and as a result are isolated from their friends and family. Few children in this situation are able to develop new relationships with peers or adults other than the person who is victimizing them. The lifestyle of such children revolves around violence, forced drug use, and constant threats.[65]

Although precise figures on domestic trafficked prostitutes are difficult to establish as a result of the underground world in which it operates, along with the common grouping with overall national and local prostitution data, a 2001 study by the University of Pennsylvania estimated that anywhere from 244,000 to 325,000 youth in the United States were presently in jeopardy of being sexually exploited commercially yearly through such means as trafficked prostitution, other teenage prostitution, and child pornography.[66]

In a review of the literature on human trafficking in this country, Heather Clawson and colleagues cited arrest, runaway, and homeless youth data that further illustrated the national problem of prostitution-involved teenage girls and sex trafficking.[67]

Writer Bridgette Carr noted bleakly on the extent of domestic trafficking for purposes of child sexual exploitation: "The grim reality of child sex trafficking in the United States is this: Human traffickers are selling sex with children in big cities and small towns throughout America."[68] According to a recent study on human trafficking in Ohio alone, it was found that around 1,000 children born in this country were victims of forced prostitution every year.[69]

In the Department of State's 2010 TIP Report, the United States was included for the first time, acknowledging the problem of human and sex trafficking domestically. The report indicated: "the United States is a source, transit, and destination country for men, women, and children subjected to trafficking in persons, specifically forced labor, debt bondage, and forced prostitution. . . . More investigations and prosecutions have taken place for sex trafficking offenses than for labor trafficking offenses."[70] In one such example, in April 2010 federal authorities announced that sex trafficking charges, among others, had been filed against 14 members of the reputed Gambino organized crime syndicate, including use of the Internet to advertise teenage prostitution.[71]

In a recent CBS News investigation into sex trafficking, a typical case of domestic sex trafficking was described:

> In Shauna's case, she made friends with a new girl at school. Shauna described the girl's so-called "father" as a guy who hired Shauna and her new "friend" to clean condos. He always gave them money for the mall. He was always very attentive to Shauna. She says she could never have predicted that the man would hurt her. The "father" turned out to be a trafficker and the new "friend" was his recruiter. How could a high school "girlfriend" be part of such a terrible plot? The "father" or one of his cohorts slipped Shauna a date rape drug in a glass of water. She was beaten and raped repeatedly by a group of men. She remembers talk of money changing hands and a conversation about going to Texas.[72]

Runaway and thrownaway teens in particular are targeted by sex traffickers, just as they are by other pimps and sexual exploiters since such youth are most vulnerable for sexual exploitation as they are often afraid, hungry, homeless, dealing with substance abuse or mental issues, and even looking for love or parent figures. In a recent ABC News article, such a 12-year-old runaway trafficked girl was profiled:

> For four years, M.S. was forced into child prostitution with four different pimps. She was taken from city to city, forced to have sex with random men against her will. She rarely got to keep any of the $1,500 she made every day. Instead, she was abused mentally and physically by both her pimps and other girls who he housed. . . . M.S. was scared to run away, afraid that her pimps would turn their threats of hurting her family into reality. Even when, two years after being sold into sex, M.S. found out that her grandmother and sister had put out fliers looking for her and had even put her name on the missing persons list, she didn't contact them.[73]

The Internet plays a big part in the proliferation of prostituted teenage girls and domestic sex trafficking. This was reflected on by the president of The Rebecca Project for Human Rights, Malika Saada Saar, who noted that a:

> cyber slave market is being built up by Craigslist and other Web sites. . . . This is a new and emerging phenomenon. Ten years ago, there were not the same disturbing stories of traffickers seeking out and preying on girl runaways within 48 hours after they have left home. Why is this happening? There is the Internet, which has created an easy and accessible venue for the commercial sexual exploitation. As a result, young girls are the new commodities that traffickers and gangs are selling. And, there isn't a culture of crime and punishment for selling girls as there is for selling illegal drugs.[74]

Trafficking Victims Protection Act

To combat sex trafficking in the United States and abroad, in 2006 the Trafficking Victims Protection Reauthorization Act of 2005 was signed into law.[75] It reauthorized and strengthened the Trafficking Victims Protection Act of 2000, the first comprehensive federal statute aimed at prosecuting sex traffickers and reducing the trafficking of persons in this country for purposes of prostitution and other commercial sexual exploitation. New funding was included for investigating and prosecuting domestic trafficking and related criminality, along with battling international human trafficking.

Other government tools used to fight sex trafficking and child sexual exploitation in the United States include the PROTECT Act, new and tougher anti-trafficking laws at state and local levels, initiatives for battling trafficking in persons internationally, and aggressive prosecution of traffickers and other sexual exploiters of trafficking victims.[76] A number of high-profile cases involving sex trafficking have been brought to light and successfully prosecuted. According to U.S. Immigration and Customs Enforcement (ICE), in "fiscal year 2009, ICE initiated 566 human trafficking investigations, a 31 percent increase over the previous fiscal year. ICE trafficking investigations in FY09 led to 388 arrests, 148 indictments, and 165 convictions."[77]

According to Erik Breitzke, who heads ICE's Human Smuggling and Trafficking Unit, with respect to human and sexual slavery in the 21st century:

> One of the most disturbing trends in recent years has been the increasing sophistication of criminal networks when it comes to trafficking in human beings. This requires a sophisticated law enforcement response, and no other agency has ICE's combined authorities for enforcing immigration and customs laws, which gives us a set of powerful tools for attacking these organizations.[78]

Human rights organizations such as the Arizona League to End Regional Trafficking and the Los Angeles-based Coalition to Abolish Slavery and Trafficking have also been established to battle human traffickers and assist victims.

PART IV

Males Involved in the Sex Trade Industry

Chapter 9

Male Hustlers

Though prostituted females garner much of the attention from the media, social scientists, and criminologists when exploring the commercial sex trade industry, prostituted males may be equally represented in selling sexual favors. Where it concerns male prostitution, many people tend to think of the movie *American Gigolo* with Richard Gere playing a high-priced Beverly Hills escort to beautiful women. Although males do work as escorts (and recently, Nevada had its first legal brothel male prostitute) in servicing females as clients, much more often their sex work involves prostitution with male clientele. Male sex workers, often known as hustlers, operate in many of the same environments as their female counterparts, including on the streets, hotels, and male brothels, as well as gay bathhouses, bars, and sex clubs. Working independently, they service male, female, and bisexual customers, depending on the prostitute's occupational circumstances, opportunities, needs, and personal preferences.

Male prostitutes' sexual orientation/gender identity does not always reflect their sex work, which is based primarily on what clients want and will pay for. Prostitution-involved males generally make less than female prostitutes make and are less likely to be arrested for selling sex. The male prostitution subculture places sex workers at high risk for sexually transmitted diseases (STDs) such as HIV infection, drug involvement, violent victimization, and gay bashing. As with female sex workers, a high percentage of prostituted males are victims of child sexual and physical abuse, have histories as runaways or thrownaways, and turn to survival sex when homeless. The Internet has become the primary means for male prostitutes to advertise their availability and reach out to target groups.

The Scope of Male Prostitution

Male prostitution, or the involvement in sexual activity for money and other items such as food and shelter, is wide in scope, though not talked about as often as female prostitution. Many experts believe that the incidence of prostitution-involved males is as great as or greater than that of prostitution-involved females. This notwithstanding, reliable figures on the extent of male prostitutes are difficult to come by with lesser visibility and the transitory nature of prostituted males.

Much of the estimates on male prostitution have focused on youth, specifically underage prostitutes, though most researchers and criminologists think that the vast majority of male prostitutes in this country are 18 years of age and over.[1] The *Encyclopedia of Sex and Sexuality* estimated that the number of male youth prostitutes in the United States runs into the tens of thousands.[2] One study estimated the number of underage male prostitutes nationally was around 35 to 40 percent of all prostitutes.[3]

In his ground-breaking 1976 book *For Money or Love: Boy Prostitution in America*, Robin Lloyd estimated there were approximately 300,000 teenage male prostitutes active in the sex-for-sale industry in the United States.[4] The proportion of prostituted young males appears to be greater in larger cities such as New York and San Francisco.[5] However, boy prostitution has been reported on the rise in smaller cities.[6]

Though there are only limited data on prostitution-involved males who identify as gay, bisexual, or transgender, it is believed that on the whole this group "form[s] a significant minority" of the prostituted teenagers in this country.[7] A study of homeless teenagers, which included street kids who were sexual minorities, found that half reported involvement in survival sex.[8] There was a higher rate of prostituted homeless male youth than their female counterparts.

Profiling the Male Prostitute

Similar to female prostitutes, male prostitutes reflect a range of racial and ethnic backgrounds, as well as other characteristics that include being "delinquent school dropouts to well-educated, refined college students; they come from inner-city projects and middle-class suburbs; from completely disintegrated families and from effective loving families."[9]

Prostitution-involved males include those who hate being in the business but believe they have no other viable choice; those who merely tolerate it as a means to an end, such as for the money or to feed a drug addiction; and those who enjoy the independent lifestyle and multiple sex partners that the sex trade industry affords them. Many male prostitutes have joined the ranks of the homeless while experiencing crime and violence; others are addicted to drugs or infected with HIV; some are incarcerated, often for crimes that related directly to living on the streets. Yet, there are also male prostitutes who have managed to thrive in the world of high-priced, and relatively safer, elite-level prostitution.[10]

In the case of "James," a 43-year-old bisexual streetwalking prostitute who relocated from Galveston to Houston, prostitution was a means to earn money and buy a car:

> Dressed in a woven poncho with the hood pulled up, James paces under the yellow streetlight, waiting for his next trick. A waiter by profession, James came to Houston . . . a few months ago . . . but says he was unable to find a job.
>
> "You have to have a car in Houston," said James. "I am saving up for a car and I'm halfway there. I live by myself and have a nice apartment. As soon as I get enough money for a car, I will quit."
>
> . . . With a diamond-stud nose-ring and no drug habit, James seems better off than his competition down the block. He claims that he makes about $500 a week, charging $10 for a hand-job, $30 for a blow-job, and $50 for anal sex.
>
> "It's a job," said James. "You gotta do what you have to do."[11]

Studies have found many male prostitutes to be self-destructive with high levels of psychopathology, while being unstable and immature.[12] Prostitution-involved males also are prone to being the regular victims of crime and violence, bias offenses, and have a high rate of STDs, alcoholism, and drug addiction.[13]

The majority of prostitution-involved males were victims of child sexual and physical abuse. However, unlike with female prostitutes, broken homes do not appear to be a strong factor in the prostitution of males, though there is evidence to support greater dysfunction such as drug abuse and incest in the families of male prostitutes than nonmale prostitutes.[14]

Among male prostitutes whose first sexual activity was with a male, surveys show that more than half were seduced, while two out of three were paid to have sex.[15] One study found that 9.6 years was the average age of a male prostitute's first homosexual experience. Three-fifths of the respondents reported receiving payment of some sort for their participation.[16]

Most male prostitutes do not identify themselves as homosexual, but rather regard their sexual activity as primarily to earn money. While nearly 75 percent of male prostitutes in one study were labeled as homosexual, only 6 percent identified as gay.[17] In another study, however, two-thirds of prostitution-involved males reported being gay or bisexual.[18]

According to sex therapist Ruth Westheimer:

> Many of these male homosexual prostitutes—often referred to as "hustlers"—do not consider themselves homosexuals because even though they may enjoy the sexual contacts, they limit the activity to being fellated rather than performing fellatio on a customer or engaging in anal intercourse.[19]

Some research has found that male prostitutes and their clients harbor "deep hatred" toward each other. Both find themselves wrestling with "conflicting emotions during their time together, often creating fantasies that are acted out in the course of their sexual encounter."[20]

Earnings of Male Prostitutes

The amount of money made by male prostitutes in general or for specific acts in selling sexual services can vary considerably, depending on a number of dynamics. These include whether the prostitute operates at the upper-, middle-, or lower-level of prostitution; works full- or part-time, the supply and demand, the location, the level of experience and ability to negotiate terms; range of or specific services offered, time spent with the client, and characteristics such as age, appearance, nationality, race, ethnicity, personality, and physical endowment.

Though some high-end male prostitutes can make good money selling sex, few can expect to earn sums equivalent to high-class female prostitutes. Most prostituted males working as full-time professionals in big cities charge anywhere from $200 to $250 an hour.[21] Elite upper-level male prostitutes can charge $400 or more an hour with other high-class male prostitutes charging $150 to $200 an hour, depending on location.[22] Upper-echelon male prostitutes bring in the most money on average in such large urban cities as New York, Los Angeles, and London.

The price of individual services performed by a typical prostituted male such as kissing, hand masturbation, oral sex (including receiving), and anal sex, also varies in relation to time involved, additional requests, going rate in a given city, the needs of the prostituted individual (for example, being forced into survival sex), willingness of the customer to pay, as well as the aforementioned factors.

Use of the Internet has increased avenues for paid sex among male prostitutes on all levels in utilizing such sites as Craigslist, Manhunt.com, and Gay.com to advertise and locate customers. In Nicholas Ray's book on the homeless epidemic, the author noted the routine of a 22-year-old male prostitute in the business for seven years, indicative of many homeless youth and the draw of Internet resources in plying their trade: "Like other sex workers, Brian will often seek shelter in an all-night Internet cafe where he can cruise online for a man to have sex with. . . . New technologies provide new techniques for homeless young sex workers to find their clients."[23]

Types of Male Prostitutes

There are different types of male prostitutes operating in the commercial sex trade industry, categorized by services, sexual orientation, and where they practice their trade. These include *gigolos, hustlers, escorts*, and *rentboys*, described as such:

- *Gigolo:* a paid male escort for women.
- *Hustler:* a prostitute who is "hustling on the side" while having a sexual relationship with someone.
- *Escort:* has paid sexual relations with male clients (referred to as "gay for pay") but does not identify self as gay.
- *Rentboy:* rents out to clients, or pays rent from earnings as a sex worker.

According to Sivan Caukins and Neil Coombs' psychosocial study of male prostitutes, a "gay sex market thrives in every big city. . . . a profit oriented street corner college for the recruiting, training, and selling of boys and men to older, affluent homosexuals."[24] The researchers identified four types of male prostitutes: *street hustlers, bar hustlers, call boys*, and *kept boys*, and described them as follows:[25]

- *Street hustlers:* drifters who sometimes resort to prostitution to support family.
- *Bar hustlers:* drifters who support a wife and/or children through prostitution.
- *Call boys:* escorts for upscale clients for social events, such as dinner, along with offering prostitution services.

- *Kept boys:* houseboys who, aside from selling sexual favors, perform non-sexual household chores.

In their study of prostitution-engaged males and intravenous (IV) drug use, Dan Waldorf and Sheigla Murphy divided male prostitutes into two general categories: *hustlers* and *call men*.[26] Hustlers typically found clients in cruising spots for male prostitution, such as gay bars, adult bookstores, theaters, and parks. They were subdivided into three types: *trade hustlers, drag queen hustlers,* and *youth hustlers,* as follows:

1. *Trade hustlers:* heterosexual or bisexual males who have sex for pay, while rarely acknowledging being gay or enjoying sex with homosexual men.
2. *Drag queen hustlers:* transvestites and transsexuals who specialize in oral sex, usually in gay red-light districts.
3. *Youth hustlers:* admitted young homosexual males who seem naive, but are often well experienced as prostitutes.

Call men reflect the ways in which clients were located along with the types of sexual services offered, rather than erotic style. Waldorf and Murphy subcategorized call men into four groups: *call book men, models and escorts, erotic masseurs,* and *porn industry stars,* describing them as such:

1. *Call book men:* often identify themselves as gay or bisexual, while usually acquiring customers from a call book or keeping a regular clientele. Drag queen call girls are transvestites who work from a call book.
2. *Models and escorts:* find clients by way of advertising on the Internet, or in general or special interest publications. They often develop a network of steady clients and may also own a call book.
3. *Erotic masseurs:* seek new clients through advertising while also maintaining a regular customer list. Many are certified by licensed massage schools and tend to combine massages with sexual services while typically charging less than other call men.
4. *Porn industry stars:* the upper-echelon or highest-earning male prostitutes, such as erotic dancers and porn stars; customers are often propositioned on the job with the sexual activity occurring outside the workplace.

Prostituted Boys

Most male prostitutes began getting paid for sex as preteens and early teens. Studies have found that on average boys, including gays and transgenders, first entered into prostitution between the ages of 11 and 13.[27] The male john in a boy's initial sexual experience has been shown to be an average of five or more years older.[28] One study found that about 6 in 10 boys had been compensated for participating in their first sexual activity.[29]

Many prostitution-involved boys are runaways or thrownaways. According to one study, two-thirds of full-time prostituted boys had left home as runaways.[30] Another study of homeless runaways found that 55 percent were male.[31] Street youth were often thrown out of the home due to sexual orientation or gender identity issues. Teenage homosexuals have been shown to be especially at risk for being told to leave home by "parents or guardians [who] evict them from their homes, most often because they are gay or lesbian . . . or otherwise considered . . . as just too much trouble to deal with."[32] Up to one-half of all prostitution-involved males were "thrown out of their houses because of sexual identity issues."[33]

A typical example of a thrownaway can be seen in the following scenario from an article on street youth:

> Six years ago, Daniel left home. At age 12. His mom and dad . . . verbally abused him and his brother. Sometimes the ugly confrontations got physical. Daniel is gay, which he says his mother had a hard time accepting. So . . . like thousands of children who feel unwanted, unloved, and unsafe at home, [he] took his chances elsewhere, staying at friends' houses or sleeping on San Diego's streets. Daniel describes himself not as a runaway but as a "refugee fighting for his stability."[34]

Most runaway youth turned street kids will be sexually exploited shortly thereafter. Researchers have found that typically a newly homeless youth will be solicited for sex or forced into it within 36 to 48 hours, if not sooner.[35] On living on the streets for two weeks, 75 percent of homeless youth will become involved in some type of commercial sexual exploitation, such as prostitution or pornography.[36] In his study of gay, lesbian, bisexual, and transgender homeless youth, Ray quoted a homeless gay teenager about the necessity to engage in prostitution activities: "I'd go to the library, I'd get on Craigslist, and Manhunt, and Gay.com, just to find somewhere to sleep for the night, not for money. I slept with them so I could have a place to stay."[37]

Studies have found money to be the greatest determining factor for teenage males to enter the sex-for-sale business, with one study reporting as many as 80 percent prostituting themselves for monetary gain.[38] One prostitution-involved boy spoke frankly about this:

> I liked the money and the way it came in, so I just kept with it. I was making more money as time went by. Like, the most I ever made from a trick was $250, and that was for an hour. It's [fast, easy money]. It's all easy 'cause everyone knows how to have sex. The money is good. . . . Money talks. Every man has his price. Like, you flash a $100 bill in somebody's face and they'll say "yes" if they only have 35 cents in their pocket. It's a quick buck.[39]

Profiling Boy Prostitutes

Boy prostitutes are white, African American, Latino, and Asian; and come from the lower, middle, and upper classes, with many experiencing various forms of abuse at home, in the neighborhood, or at school. Though prostitution-involved boys tend to cater largely to homosexual men, their sexual orientation or gender identity may be heterosexual, gay, bisexual, transgender, or undecided. The first national study of teenage male prostitution was conducted by the Urban and Rural Systems Associates of San Francisco.[40] According to its findings:

- Boy prostitutes sell sexual favors primarily for financial reasons, exploring their sexual orientation, and/or as a means to meet gay men.
- Money is the most important motivating factor in teenage boys entering and remaining in the sex trade industry.
- The average age of a prostitution-involved boy is 16.
- The vast majority of boy prostitutes are runaways/thrownaways.
- More often than not, prostitution-engaged boys come from homes that have a single parent or are dysfunctional.
- There is a high rate of sexual, mental, and physical abuse in the backgrounds of prostituted boys.
- Many boy prostitutes are high school dropouts or performed poorly in school.
- Delinquency and criminality are common themes involving boy prostitutes.
- Gay-identified prostituted boys initially find the prostitution lifestyle to be exciting.
- Pimps are extremely rare in the world of teenage male prostitution.

Most prostituted boys are streetwalkers. In a study of adolescent prostitution, *Children of the Night*, D. Kelly Weisberg found that more than 90 percent of boy prostitutes sold sexual services on the streets.[41] However, there are some boy brothels (also known stables), where prostituted boys live and work. These are often run by pimps or madams. According to Joan Johnson, a juvenile prostitution researcher, boy brothel prostitutes occupy the lowest level of the male prostitution hierarchy.[42]

Boy prostitutes have been shown to have high rate of drug addiction, mental illnesses, and STDs; and are at risk for violent victimization, verbal aggression, and involvement with law enforcement and the juvenile justice system.[43]

Types of Boy Prostitutes

Along with general typologies of male prostitutes, researchers have developed subcategories of prostituted boys. Johnson described prostitution-involved boys as *street hustlers* who were gay, bisexual, and heterosexual; and others as transvestite prostitutes and upper-class prostitutes.[44] She identified upper-class boy prostitutes as often better looking and better outfitted, along with greater self-confidence than street hustlers. Many teen prostitutes were seen to be aggressive and drug addicts.

According to Weisberg, there are two distinct types of boy prostitutes: (1) *peer-delinquent subculture* and (2) *gay subculture*.[45] She described these as follows:

> For youth in the [peer-delinquent] subculture, prostitution is an integral aspect of delinquent street life. These adolescents engage indiscriminately in prostitution, drug dealing, panhandling, and petty criminal activity. They sell their sexual favors habitually as a way of making money, viewing prostitution as just one aspect of "hustling"—as the term is used to mean procuring more than one gives.
>
> Youth in the gay subculture engage in prostitution for different reasons. Prostitution is one outlet for their sexuality. They find in the gay male subculture a means for identification, and prostitution satisfies their need for social interaction with gay persons and for sexual partners. Simultaneously, it provides a way of making money, since the purchase and sale of sexual activity is a product of the sexual mores of that community.[46]

These subcultures were further broken down into four types of prostitution-involved boys: *situational, habitual, vocational,* and *avocational* prostitutes:

1. *Situational prostitutes:* participate in prostitution activities only on certain occasions, while viewing it as an irregular activity.

2. *Habitual prostitutes:* engage in urban street life, for which prostitution is an important element, including dealing drugs, robbery, and petty theft.
3. *Vocational prostitutes:* view teenage prostitution as a vocation or leading to such an occupation and regard themselves as professionals.
4. *Avocational prostitutes:* vocational boy prostitutes who look at what they do in the sex-for-sale industry as part-time work.

Chickens and Chicken Hawks

Another type of prostitution-involved boy is known in the child sex trade business as a *chicken*, defined as the young boy or teen preference of older males.[47] They are referred to as *chicken hawks* or *chicken pluckers*. Law enforcement and psychiatrists view the gay men who prey on young prostitution-engaged males as pedophiles and child molesters.[48] Underage male prostitution often tends to occur in cities with a large gay male population. However, prostituted boys can also be found selling their bodies in suburbs and small towns across the United States.[49]

A typical chicken-chicken hawk encounter has been demonstrated by law enforcement as follows:

> The boy will usually find a set of marble steps, sit, and observe passing cars. Eye contact is the key. The "chicken hawk" will stare at the boy he feels could be a "hustler." If a period of eye contact is made between both, the "chicken hawk" will still circle the block several times, making eye contact at each passing. Finally the "chicken hawk" will nod and, if the boy returns the nod, a deal is in the making. At times, the "chickens" would work as teams, usually two together. If the customer wanted two boys, he would use hand signals, indicating how many boys he wanted and how much he was paying.[50]

Though the majority of chicken hawks prefer young boys or teenage prostitutes, many seek out youthful-looking prostitution-involved males, no matter their age. Some pedophiles solicit chickens who fall into a particular age range and "will not pick up any boys who might be older or younger than he desires."[51]

The chicken hawk can be typically characterized as:

- Middle aged.
- Relating to children often better than adults.
- Views the chicken as the sexual aggressor.
- Usually single, but some are married.

- Involved with other chicken hawks, child molesters, and pedophiles.
- Nonviolent.
- A victim of child molestation.
- Acts like a friend to the chicken.
- Tends to have a white-collar occupation.

In "Male and Transsexual Prostitution," Garrett Prestage described further the motivation for targeting boy prostitutes by male clients:

> Some simply like the sensibility and particular appeal of the "trannies;" some are attracted by the "kinkiness" of sex with a transsexual; some are attracted to the idea of sex with another man but are reluctant to choose a partner which is actually a man; and some enjoy particular sexual activities which require that their partner has a penis even though they prefer female partners.[52]

Male Prostitutes and HIV/AIDS

There is a high rate of HIV infection among male prostitutes. Given the intersection between frequent and often unprotected sex on and off the job, multiple gay and bisexual partners, STDs, IV drug use, and other risky behavior that exists in the male prostitution subculture, this is not too surprising. HIV is the precursor to AIDS. Typically, infection is spread two ways: by receiving AIDS-infected bodily fluids, most often through anal intercourse, and sharing dirty needles and tainted blood by IV drug users. Some believe that with the perilous lifestyle common to many prostitution-involved males and their particular vulnerabilities with respect to homosexual relations, they may be at a higher risk for exposure to the AIDS virus than prostitution-involved females.

A number of studies have documented the relationship between HIV/AIDS and male prostitution. For example, in a study of male prostitutes who visited a venereal diseases clinic in New York City, 53 percent of the ones involved in homosexual prostitution tested HIV-seropositive.[53] By comparison, only 10 percent of male prostitutes whose clientele were strictly female tested positive. A high rate of HIV infection among male street prostitutes was also found in a study of clients' sexual patterns by Edward Morse and associates.[54] In a study of prostitution-involved male youth in Manhattan, in which 50 percent were gay, 26 percent bisexual, and 24 percent heterosexual, it was found that the risk of becoming infected with HIV was highest due to "differential condom use" and other high-risk sexual activities.[55]

Male teenage prostitutes may be even more susceptible to having a compromised immune system and contracting the AIDS virus. In a survey in Chicago of self-reported risk factors for exposure to HIV among street youth, nearly 9 in 10 respondents had participated in one or more risk factors, such as having multiple or high-risk sex partners, infrequent use of condoms, engaged in anal sex, prostitution activities, and/or IV drug use.[56] In noting the high rate of STDs among prostituted male youth, A. Markos and colleagues posited this to be a significant risk factor for infection with HIV.[57]

Male Prostitutes and Arrests

Though there are arguably as many male prostitutes as female prostitutes selling sexual favors in this country, there appears to be a disparity in arrest rates. According to Federal Bureau of Investigation (FBI) figures, females were more than twice as likely to be arrested as males for prostitution and commercialized vice in 2008.[58] This pattern has been consistent in arrest data. However, in an examination of teenage prostitution based on the FBI's National Incident-Based Reporting System, David Finkelhor and Richard Ormrod found that male youth were more likely to be arrested for prostitution involvement than female youth, and more likely to be regarded as offenders instead of victims of commercial sexual exploitation.[59] Moreover, in her study of adolescent prostitution, Weisberg found that prostituted boys had a high rate of contact with the juvenile and criminal justice systems, with two out of three teenage male prostitutes having been arrested one or more times for prostitution activities.[60] Prostitution-related offenses accounted for one-third of male juvenile arrests.

The greater visibility of prostitution-involved females and a desire to help get them off the streets may help explain the disparity in official arrest statistics between male and female sex workers, especially for low-end prostitution. Male street prostitutes may be more involved than female prostitutes in related crimes such as drug dealing, property offenses, and crimes of violence that could result in arrest.

In recent times, authorities have placed a greater focus on going after johns and pimps, both of whom are generally less likely to face arrest than male and female prostitutes.[61]

Chapter 10

Pimps

A key figure in the street-level female prostitution subculture is the pimp. Unlike the madam, who is often glamorized by the media for her role in running high-end female prostitution establishments such as escort services and brothels, pimps are typically stereotyped and cast in a negative light and associated with manipulation and violence in controlling the mostly young, sexually abused, undereducated, homeless, susceptible, and lower- and middle-class prostitutes in their stables. However, there is also a certain glamorization of the pimp in popular culture and in urban communities, where pimps are often seen as role models, successful businessmen, and charming. Well-known pimps include Iceberg Slim, Jason Itzler, Don Juan, Dennis Hof, and Al Swearengen.

Many pimps are also involved in pornography, gangs, drug dealing, and other forms of criminality, but are primarily associated with the prostituting of females—especially teenage and runaway girls—in a society where many other female prostitutes work independently or in higher-class prostitution minus a pimp. Though pimps conduct their business largely through streetwalker prostitution, some are also in the commercial sex trade by way of brothels, escort services, massage parlors, strip clubs, and related services. Two 1999 documentaries, *American Pimp* and *Pimps Up, Ho's Down*, as well as Slim's autobiographical book, *Pimp: The Story of My Life*,[1] explore the pimp culture and image through first-person accounts from the men who operate in this world of commercial sexual exploitation. Blaxploitation films such as *The Mack* and *Willie Dynamite*, as well as more recent movies such as *Pimp*, also offer fictional perspectives on pimps and street prostitution. The Internet has become a key tool for pimps in marketing their stable on sites such as Craigslist and Eros.com, as well as procuring prostitutes through such social networks as Twitter, MySpace, and UrbanChat.com.

Identifying the Pimp

The dictionary defines a pimp as "a man who procures clients for a prostitute" or "a man who solicits for a prostitute or brothel and lives off the earnings."[2] In fact, few pimps actually procure customers, per se, for prostituted females, according to the book *Street Prostitution*, "because clients do not typically want to associate with anyone other than the prostitute."[3] Pimps involved with brothels, massage parlors, escort services, or prostitution at private residences are more likely to solicit clients for their stable than those whose prostitutes work the street corners, also referred to by those in the business as "the track."

In most instances, the pimp-prostitute financial arrangement is one-sided—calling for the pimp to take the lion's share of what a street prostitute brings in from selling sexual favors. It has been estimated that pimps may take as much as 70 percent of what a prostitute earns.[4] In some instances, the pimp may take all the money made, while offering prostitutes in his stable drugs, shelter, clothing, and romance. Pimps have also been known to be physically violent toward the women and girls in his stable who come up short in established quotas for a day—sometimes forcing their prostitutes to put in up to 10 working hours a night, six days out of seven.[5]

A popular misconception often portrayed in Hollywood productions is that pimps are predominantly undereducated, urban African American males "wearing flashy clothes, hats, and jewelry and driving a Cadillac or other large status symbol car."[6] The reality is that pimps come from every racial and ethnic background, social class, geographic location, and educational level. In some instances, a prostituted female may be turned out by a family member, including another female. Indeed, there is every reason to believe the majority of pimps in the United States are white males, as they are not only well represented in street-level prostitution, but also tend to own or operate a high percentage of prostitution-involved businesses such as prostitution rings, massage parlors, brothels, escort services, strip clubs, and bars.[7] Asian pimps are also gaining a bigger presence in this country through an increase in sex trafficking of women and children from South and Southeast Asia.[8]

Experts indicate that pimp attire and transportation in modern times also goes against stereotype. According to one source, many pimps favor dressing like businessmen in professional suits or "corporate casual" wear, so as not to stand out for law enforcement to more easily target.[9] And BMWs and other cars less identified with pimps are being driven more often by those in the business rather than Cadillacs.

Many pimps start pimping in their twenties and can still be sexually exploiting females well into their fifties. However, there appears to be a shift toward younger pimps, as noted by Rachel Lloyd, executive director of an education and mentoring service for girls, who estimated the average age of pimps today to be 18 to 20 years of age.[10] This was echoed by a member of the Port Authority Police Department, who contended that "kids are picking up kids and pimping them."[11]

Gang members are playing a bigger role in the pimping of females through recruitment, multiple sexual partnership, sexual assaults, and other violence—all of which places the prostituted girl at further risk of sexually transmitted diseases (STDs) contracted from a member of the gang or other johns.[12]

Types of Pimps

Within the pimp subculture of the sex trade industry, researchers have identified different types of pimps, though none are mutually exclusive of the others. Wikipedia refers to pimps as *jonas pimps*, those who rely on intimidation and violence in controlling their stable, and *finesse pimps* are those who "use psychological trickery to deceive younger prostitutes into becoming hooked into the system."[13]

Based on her review of literature on the commercial sexual exploitation of children, researcher Anne Rasmusson identified two types of pimps. The first is a villain pimp who "lives off [his] victim[s], beats them, and makes false promises to keep them."[14] For the second type of pimp, his relationship with prostitutes "is seen more as a bargained for exchange, where he protects them from police and perverts."[15] Rasmusson described the latter as in actuality a "power relationship in which prostitutes are subject to domination, violence, and torture by their pimps, as well as theft of their earnings."[16]

In *Teen Prostitution*, Joan Johnson broke pimps down into three categories: *the popcorn pimp, the player pimp*, and *the Mack pimp*.[17] Popcorn pimps are least successful or respected among pimps and often the newest. They work mainly with teen prostitutes and have little in the way of roots or money. Popcorn pimps are often very competitive with one another in the recruitment of mostly runaway girls. These pimps are the most violent toward the girls in their stable and tend to have a higher turnover rate than more established and secure pimps.

Player pimps are usually more successful, with a few prostitutes under their control, often including a "special" one whom the pimp lives with.

Players are generally less violent than popcorn pimps are and prefer to rely on psychological means to keep the girls in their stable under control. One expert on the pimp hierarchy estimated that a successful player, or mid-level pimp, could earn upward of $200,000 annually.[18]

Mack pimps are seen as the upper echelon of pimping. They tend to have the largest group of prostitutes in their stable, with one serving as the pimp's "lady." The Mack pimp combines street smarts with savvy business skills, often investing prostitution profits in legitimate ventures. High earnings allow Mack pimps to live well in the suburbs while maintaining a low profile, making it more difficult to put them out of operation.

Another type of pimp was established in the government publication *Female Juvenile Prostitution*, categorized as an *angry pimp*, or one who "has a deep anger and contempt for women and prostitutes."[19] One pimp, in particular, blamed this on the untrustworthiness of women, while arguing: "The hardest thing to get in this business is honesty. It's all about being [as] crooked and dirty as they can be."[20]

According to criminologists, pimping as a business often moves from generation to generation. The "tricks of the trade" can also be acquired from a pimp mentor, other pimps, or even prostitutes. Within the lower-level pimp culture, in particular, there is normally some cooperation and understanding between pimps.[21]

Contrary to popular opinion, most prostituted women are free to switch from one pimp to another as, generally speaking, "pimps respect free enterprise and competition," or adhere to the street rule, "Bros before Ho's."[22] However, it is considered a "professional courtesy" to inform a pimp that someone in his stable has moved on to another pimp. Responding with violence will often cause such a pimp to be labeled as a "Gorilla" or "Godzilla."[23] The prostituted females who shuffle back and forth between pimps regularly are referred to as "choosey Susies." Prostitutes are apparently free to "'bounce' from pimp to pimp without paying the 'pimp moving' tax."[24]

Procuring Prostitutes for a Pimp's Stable

Pimps have developed effective procurement strategies to build a stable of females to work for them as prostitutes. Although these have proven successful with adult female prostitutes, much of their effort is focused on teenage girls who are often homeless runaways and thrownaways and seen as the most susceptible and submissive to their coercion techniques. Up to 90 percent of prostitution-involved girls are believed to have been introduced into the sex trade by pimps, and as many as 95 percent of female teen prostitutes are currently under the control of pimps.[25] Most of these girls are streetwalkers, but some also work in massage parlors, brothels, or as escorts.

Pimps use a combination of street- and technology-savvy methods along with charm, charisma, cunning, and resilience to reel in females that they can turn out for profit. According to Susan Breault, who works for the Paul & Lisa Program, Inc., an all-volunteer, street-based outreach program to assist prostitution-involved and sexually exploited young women: "We greatly underestimate the intellect, the cunning, and entrepreneurship of pimps."[26] Based on a study of pimping, James Hodgson found that pimps used two main ways to procure prostitutes: *seduction* and *stratagem*. The former typically involves seducing young, innocent females into the sex-for-sale industry "through strategic deployment of affection."[27] The latter method focuses on the pimp's "role in facilitating a lifestyle of grandeur and ease."[28] In an example of procurement in which a 26-year-old pimp played on a vulnerable teenage girl's affections:

> "He said, 'I don't have time for little girls,'" she says. "He told me if I wanted to be with him I had to work for him, or just get lost. I was so focused on being with him that I said I would." Soon, Shaquana was going on "dates" he set up for her. He taught her how to perform oral sex, and strung her along, being nice one minute, manipulative the next. Shaquana says she felt completely trapped. "It was so degrading, and I felt like I was the only one my age who could possibly be doing this."[29]

Another instance demonstrates the brazen nature of a pimp when preying on a thrownaway girl in enticing her into prostitution:

> My parents kicked me out when I was 15. . . . One night a pimp approached me at a strip club and offered me $300 more to have sex with a trick in a van. . . . I needed the money, so I agreed to do it.[30]

According to an expert on teenage prostitution and the pimps who prey on them: "The kids that are stable and know what their lives are all about will tell these guys to hit the road. But kids who are vulnerable and hungry take up their offers of food, clothing, and a relationship, and once the girls are with them, they're the pimp's property."[31]

Interviews with pimps and other data by researchers further reveal the use of advertising on the Internet, newspapers, and other publications for secretarial work, models, and dancers to lure unsuspecting victims.[32] Other times, they may get other prostitution-involved females to act as recruiters. In some instances, pimps claimed that needy or ambitious females approached them to enter the business based on the pimp's reputation, charm, and treatment of the girls in his stable.[33]

Pimps will also often hone in on drug-addicted females to turn out, whom they see as willing to do anything for a fix. In the words of one pimp: "A lot of time[s] I'd pick up these junkie girls that I knew I wouldn't have . . . longer than a week, two at the most . . . but I played it 'cause I knew that was money for two weeks."[34]

The Game in Pimping

Although pimping is very much about power, manipulation, and violence, at its core, prostitution is seen by those who earn a living off its proceeds as primarily business. Most pimps understand the business of pimping, marketing their girls, and investing in them as necessary to return a profit. This prostitution underworld is often referred to by the pimping establishment as "The Game." For the men who operate as Macks, players, and pimps in the sex trade, this is described in "The Pimping Game" as follows:

> To these men in power, it is a game in which they control and manipulate the actions of others subordinate to them. The pimping game requires strict adherence to the rules. The idea of a "game" parallels the formal economy in that one can be said to be in a game, e.g., he's in the real estate game. Players and pimps are also said to "have" game. To have game is to possess a certain amount of charisma and smooth-talking, persuasive conversation toward women.[35]

To be a successful pimp, a number of rules must be followed in the game, not the least of which is the pimp must "know his prostitutes inside and out, without letting them completely know him."[36] The most important rule, according to experts in the pimping world, is that "the pimp must get paid," meaning there can be no "shame in your game," or that a pimp "must require and, if necessary, demand the money."[37]

The second rule is that successful pimps must not forget that "the game 'is sold and not told,'" which means a pimp is

> expected to sell it to a prospective prostitute that he wants to occupy his stable without revealing his entire game plan. In order to do this, he has

to develop "his game" or "his rap." These consist of a series of persuasive conversations similar to poetic and rhythmic scats that are philosophical in nature and ideological about life and making money.[38]

The last rule for being successful at pimping is that a pimp must have prostitutes in his stable who wish to

see him on top. He is looking for dedication [and] someone who wants to see her man in fine clothes and driving fine cars. His success or lack of success is a reflection on her. If her man is not looking his best, then she is not a very successful ho. . . . As a committed prostitute, she must work very hard to earn his respect, his love, and to keep him achieving the best in material possessions. He in return invites her into his social network along with the sense of security that it brings.[39]

Researchers have found that although pimps turn out females from all racial and ethnic persuasions, white prostitutes have proven to be the most marketable in the game of pimping. The reasons for this are that white females are still considered the "symbol of beauty" in this country and pimps believe they tend to cause less trouble with law enforcement.[40] Studies do show that racial minority prostituted females, particularly African Americans, are disproportionately (or even in total numbers, depending on the location) more likely to be arrested on prostitution-related charges than white prostitution-engaged females.[41] There is also indication that pimps generally feel that African American women get into more clashes with johns, are more likely to resist arrest, and often become more confrontational than is the case with white females.

The Pimp's Role in Prostitute-Customer Relations

Pimps play a major role in the daily schedule of their stable in the sex trade. Although most prostitutes do much of the work in soliciting potential johns, deciding who to offer their bodies to and who not to, collecting money for their services, and seeking to avoid arrest, pimps are often involved in the particulars of the prostitute-customer relationship.[42] This includes deciding precisely where the prostituted girls in their stable will sell sexual favors (typically on street corners or in pimp-controlled neighborhoods), the amount to charge johns for each particular sexual offering, and what percentage, if any, of earnings the prostitutes get to keep.

The pimp is also responsible for bailing his prostitutes out of jail during frequent arrests on prostitution-related charges, after which he usually sends them back out on the streets to recoup his lost money. Pimps also often use prostitutes to steal from johns. Under a pimp's orders, some prostituted females will rob johns of cash, credit cards, drugs, or other possessions, of which the pimp will take possession without taking the risks of john retaliation.[43] If the prostitute were to deviate from any of her pimp's orders (including allowing herself to be arrested), she risks being beaten, sexually assaulted, losing what little money she earns, or other punishment, including targeting other johns to rob.

Many pimps double as pornographers and take explicit photographs and videos of their prostitutes having intercourse, fellatio, anal sex, and masturbating, as well as other sex acts and perversities such as sadomasochism (or S&M), bondage, urinating, and defecation. These are advertised by the pimp online, in various underground publications, and elsewhere to potential customers, other pornographers, gang members, and pedophiles who then use the pornography for their own sexual gratification or to sell to others, in addition to receiving the prostitution services the pimp offers from his stable.[44]

The tripartite association between pimps, prostitutes, and johns often includes STDs such as HIV. Studies have shown that prostitution-involved women and girls typically have high-risk unprotected sexual relations (or use condoms infrequently) with pimps, who routinely have multiple unprotected sex partners and a high rate of intravenous drug use.[45] These same prostitutes have been found to regularly engage in sexual activity with multiple johns, often without safeguards against STDs and possible exposure to HIV.[46] When customer drug use, including intravenous, and risky sexual relations with multiple prostitutes is factored in, it puts prostitutes, pimps, and johns in a dangerous place with regard to risk factors in the illicit sex trade.

Pimps and Violence

The literature has suggested a strong correlation between pimping and violence directed at the prostitutes in a pimp's stable, with some comparing violent pimps to batterers and victimized prostitutes to victims of domestic violence. Studies have found a high rate of pimp perpetrated violence with prostitute victims being sexually assaulted, gang raped, punched, beaten, stabbed, burned, tortured, and even murdered.[47] In a survey of streetwalkers, more than two-thirds reported frequently being physically assaulted by their pimps.[48] Another study found that more than half the associations between pimps and prostitutes included violence.[49] The U.S. Department of Justice reported that the mortality rate for prostitution-engaged females is 40 times that of the national average.[50] Much of the pimp violence has to do with respect, or lack of, not bringing in enough money to satisfy him, breaking the rules, setting an example for other girls in his stable, and as a means to keep a prostitute from leaving him.

The following is one such example of the often violent-coercive methods used by a pimp to control a prostituted teenager:

> In New York City, a girl's pimp kept her on the street six nights a week. She hated being a prostitute, but the pimp was the only person who had shown her any kindness. When she could stand it no longer and told him she had to quit, he broke her jaw. At the hospital where her jaw was wired shut, she was given pain pills and told to rest. But her pimp put her on the street the next night.
>
> Later she tried to commit suicide using the pills, but she vomited, breaking the wires in her jaw. Her pimp would not allow her to return to the hospital and sent her back on the street. . . . She turned herself in to the police.
>
> When asked her age, she replied, "I'll be 15 tomorrow."[51]

According to the chilling words of a pimp regarding violence toward a prostitute, "I have to confess that I have broken fingers and done some damage. Quite a few times I've had to do that to protect myself and that's with whores and straight women."[52] Research on pimp behavior toward prostitutes has found that the pimps tended to minimize the degree of violence used as "pimp slapping," instead of the serious violence often perpetrated on prostitutes.[53] Some pimps have admitted using other prostitutes or female acquaintances to physically assault prostitutes who "had it coming" for such reasons as insolence or failure to meet a quota.

One study found that violence "appeared to be an accepted aspect of prostitution" for the women and girls who are turned out by pimps.[54] This notwithstanding, there is some debate among experts on the sex trade industry of the extent of pimp violence used to procure prostitutes and keep them in his stable. In a study of juvenile prostitution, the Enablers reported that only 5 percent of all girl prostitutes were actually forced into offering their bodies for pay as a result of violence or threats thereof by a pimp.[55] In the book *Baby-Pros*, author Dorothy Bracey reached a similar conclusion.[56]

Prostitution researcher Jennifer James asserted with respect to pimp-generated violence and teenage sexual slavery: "It is not true that pimps force [them] to work against their will, seduce young girls, turn [them] into drug addicts for the purpose of control, give no sexual satisfaction . . . keep them from ever leaving their stable, and are never married to prostitutes who work for them."[57]

However, the consensus among many criminologists and other professionals familiar with the dynamics of lower-level prostitution believe that violence is endemic in pimp-controlled prostitution, including customer violent behavior.

Keeping Prostituted Females from Leaving the Stable

Once a pimp has a female in his stable, it is often in his best interests to keep her there for as long as she can be profitable to him. Pimps generally use a combination of smooth talking, emotional coercion, violence, drug dependency, belittling, isolation, and branding to maintain their stables. Some experts believe that love may be the pimp's most powerful weapon in keeping a prostitute tied to him, for if he can "successfully convince her of *his love*, the pimp can convince her of almost anything—including that she should stay with him *and* that he needs other girls for sex, prostitution, and profit."[58] This may be particularly effective in manipulating the runaway or thrownaway prostituted girl, already emotionally scarred and vulnerable, often with a history of child sexual abuse and lack of support within a dysfunctional family, into believing he loves her and will do anything for her.

In spite of the pimp's investment in the pretense of love, studies show that few prostitutes believe their relationship with a pimp is based on mutual love. In one survey, only 4 percent of prostituted girls reported being in love with their pimp.[59] For a high percentage of girl prostitutes, any early love felt toward a pimp often turns into hatred and deep resentment once the façade diminishes, and he becomes more abusive and intolerable.[60]

Violence is seen by many authorities on the sex trade industry as the primary means for pimps to maintain respect and try to hold onto their stable, if not to recruit. According to Wikipedia, some:

pimps have been known to employ a "pimp stick," which is two coat hangers wrapped together, in order to subdue unruly prostitutes. A variation is a "pimp cane," a cane used for similar purposes. Another punishment for unruly prostitutes is to "trunk" them, where the pimp locks the prostitute in the trunk of a car. Although prostitutes are supposedly free to move between pimps, this movement sometimes leads to violence. For example, a prostitute could be punished for merely looking at another pimp; this is considered "reckless eyeballing."[61]

Another example of violence, degradation, and sexual slavery perpetrated by pimps in controlling and breaking prostituted teenage girls can be seen in the following description from a national report on the commercial exploitation of children:

> BG is an African American male in his fifties. He has been a pimp all his working life. He traffics girls between Los Angeles, Seattle, Honolulu, and Vancouver. He mostly recruits girls in Vancouver, brings them to Hawaii and keeps all their papers so they can't leave. He drugs them, handcuffs them, and makes them have sex with his dog. He photographs these sex acts and then uses the photos as blackmail, threatening to send them to magazines or family members. Other methods of controlling the girls include locking them in a bathroom and making them drink water from the toilet and eat out of dog food bowls; and walking them up and down the track/strip while his girls are working—with the dog he makes them have sex with.[62]

Many pimps' violence and debasing include branding their stable of prostitutes as a symbol of "ownership." Tattoos often tend to bear the pimp's likeness, a street he operates on, or another reflection of his domain. The "mark might be as discreet as [an] ankle tattoo, or blatant as a neck tattoo, or large scale font across the prostitute's lower back, thigh, chest, or buttocks."[63] Should a prostitute become another pimp's "property," she could be rebranded by her new pimp and/or attempt to alter or remove the previous pimp's tattoo.

Pimps also rely on social isolation to keep prostituted females tied to them. This includes preventing them from having female friends or talking on the phone, restricting their freedom of movement, putting them on a curfew, and sometimes even forbidding them from contacting family.[64] In many instances, because family friction was a key factor in runaway girls taking to the streets in the first place, pimps often do not have to worry as much about prostituted girls in their stable seeking to leave them to return home.

Some pimps will allow prostitutes to walk away without harm, so long as they leave without any of their personal belongings. According to one pimp: "They [had] to go broke. . . . That's the only rule for them leaving.

They [couldn't] take anything with them. They [couldn't] take anything from me. If they [left] me they [had to] pay [for walking] out the door."[65]

Irrespective of pimps' efforts to the contrary, the majority of prostituted girls do not stay very long with the pimp that initiated them to the sex trade. More than two-thirds of girls involved in prostitution switch from one pimp to another, often within a few months.[66] Nine out of ten prostitutes will leave a pimp within a year's time.[67] In some cases, when a girl changes pimps, her new pimp will require that she pays him a fee to guarantee her safety from her former pimp, who "may acquire the services of a bounty hunter or 'tracker' to retrieve his 'property.'"[68] In their early years in the sex trade, many prostitutes may have up to four pimps before settling on one, becoming independent sex workers, quitting the business, or returning to prostitution in what becomes an often tumultuous "revolving cycle of prostitute and pimp interrelations."[69]

Protection of Prostitutes by Pimps

Although pimps seek to present to their stable toughness and the ability to protect them from harm that could be inflicted by customers, most pimps are more concerned with intervening when there is a conflict regarding payment for services rendered than assaults aimed at the prostitutes. According to prostitution researchers Michael Scott and Kelly Dedel, pimps offer little protection to prostituted women from violent clients.[70] On the contrary, in many instances the pimp may have "offered" the prostitute's services to friends, associates, fellow gang members or drug dealers, pornographers or pedophiles and, as such, may have an even more vested interest with the victimizer than victim. Moreover, as much customer violence takes place away from the street corners where pimps may lurk, they are often not in a position to come to the rescue of victimized prostitutes or go after perpetrators who may be long gone before the pimp becomes aware of the situation.

Pimps tend to be more protective of their prostitutes when it comes to aggression by other pimps as a measure of maintaining territory and image, as well as keeping a prostitute in his stable and the money she brings in. However, there is a certain brotherhood among pimps and so some violence against prostitutes may be tolerated to keep the peace or facilitate a business relationship between pimps and/or other sexual exploiters such as gangs or pornographers.

When it comes to protecting prostitutes from law enforcement, pimps have only limited capabilities. In her study of sex workers, sociologist

Elizabeth Bernstein found that pimps offered prostituted women virtually no protection from police stings and arrests.[71] However, many pimps attempt to circumvent the authorities by moving their stable of prostitutes from state to state, city to city, or off the streets and into massage parlors, escort services, topless bars, and strip joints to keep law enforcement from zeroing in on them.[72] As a reflection of the transient population in the sex trade industry, one retired New York City police officer estimated that only about 15 percent of pimps operating in the city were local.[73]

Pimps and Arrests

Even though few would argue that pimps are a driving force in the street-level prostitution subculture and, aside from turning many young females into prostitutes, are often directly responsible for violence they endure, pimps are far less likely to be arrested on prostitution or commercialized vice-related charges or otherwise put into the criminal justice system than the prostitutes in their stable.[74] With police departments focusing much of their prostitution efforts on the face of prostitution, that being the prostituted women and girls plying the trade, fewer stings target pimps directly, or customers for that matter. This is generally due to having less visibility than streetwalkers, many of whom work for pimps; moving their prostitutes from place to place to reduce the risk for association with them as their pimp; and often maintaining a low profile to make it tougher for authorities to make an arrest.

However, recent years have seen a greater focus by law enforcement on the men who prostitute females and pay for their services, such as the following high profile cases:[75]

- In October 2009, more than 60 alleged pimps were arrested by the FBI in a nationwide sweep dubbed "Operation Cross Country" involving teenage prostitution.
- In December 2005, in one of the largest concentrated efforts against juvenile prostitution dubbed "Innocence Lost," the Justice Department charged more than 30 people covering a number of states on child prostitution-related charges.
- In August 1999, in St. Paul, Minnesota, members of the King Mafia Crips gang were charged with forcing 14- and 15-year-old girls to have paid sex with men in motels and hotels throughout the city.
- In November 1998, a Fresno, California, sex slave ring involving Southeast Asian girls being raped and sold into prostitution resulted in raids in three states with charges filed against 18 gang members.

- In November 1996, a San Diego teenage prostitution ring was broken up by authorities after going on for two years. The five arrestees were charged with pandering, pimping, and child abduction.
- In 1995, San Francisco's vice squad began concentrating on pimps rather than prostitutes, resulting in a number of arrests and convictions.

In spite of these strides in going after pimps, as well as new laws resulting in lengthier sentences for convicted pimps, prosecutors have often found it difficult to get convictions with prostitutes unwilling to testify against their pimps due to fear, intimidation, and even misplaced love, complicating prosecution efforts.[76] The challenges of getting reluctant prostituted females to break the hold pimps have on them and their psyche was described by Washington State prosecutor Sean O'Donnell:

I've seen moms of pimps threaten girls. I had one young witness flee to Louisiana. I had the FBI track her down, but once I brought her back here I didn't have anywhere to house her and she disappeared again. When we finally got her on the stand, she said, "I'm not telling you a thing." All that pressure on a 14- or 16-year-old? It's extraordinary.[77]

Given that most pimps also are active in other criminal activity not always directly related to prostitution or trafficking charges, many such offenders are more likely to be arrested and incarcerated for offenses including drug-related, violent crimes, domestic violence, child pornography, property crimes, and gang offenses.

Chapter 11

Customers of Sex Workers

When one thinks of the customers or johns that prostitutes service, an image of Richard Gere might come to mind when he played the part of a wealthy businessman who picked up a streetwalker on Hollywood Boulevard in the movie *Pretty Woman*. Or perhaps Hugh Grant, an actor who solicited the services of a streetwalker prostitute in Los Angeles for oral sex and was caught by the police. More recently, a more prominent john was exposed—the former governor of New York, Eliot Spitzer—who paid $4,300 for the company of a high-class escort prostitute. Referred to as "Client Number 9," Spitzer spent $80,000 on prostitutes over a number of years and was forced to resign from office.[1] As with these examples, prostitutes' clients are predominantly male (though some females solicit the services of male gigolos, including now in a legal brothel in Nevada). Customers of sex workers come from all walks of life, every racial and ethnic group, nationality, and educational and income level. They also purchase sexual favors while serving in the United States armed forces and through sex tourism. John violence against prostitutes is a common occurrence and the risk for sexually transmitted diseases (STDs) is high.

The Internet has become a key component in the sex trade industry and proliferation of prostitute-customer relations, and has also given law enforcement authorities a new weapon in pursuing johns for prosecution. John schools have developed in recent years across the country, aimed at giving the arrested clients of prostitutes an opportunity to avoid jail time. Prostituted individuals continue to be much more likely to face arrest and involvement with the criminal justice system than the men they sell their bodies to, or the pimps who control a segment of the sex trade industry at the lower level.

The Number of Johns Seeking Sexual Favors

Given the various levels of john-prostitute sexual transactions, involvement, and meeting places in which customers of different income brackets pay for the services of streetwalkers to brothel prostitutes to elite sex workers and prostituted individuals in between, it is all but impossible to know the number of persons who go to prostitutes. There are studies and surveys that illustrate the magnitude of this side of the commercial sex-for-sale industry and the sexual exploitation of prostitution-involved women, teenagers, and males. According to *The Prostitution of Women and Girls*, 20 percent of all males in the United States are estimated to have solicited a sex worker.[2] Similarly, in Victor Malarek's book *The Johns: Sex for Sale and the Men Who Buy It*, the author estimated that 16 percent of men in this country had paid a prostitute to have sex at one time or another.[3]

Prostitution researchers Michael Scott and Kelly Dedel indicated that between 10 and 20 percent of men admit to paying to have sex, with only around 1 percent regularly paying prostitutes for sexual favors.[4] Other research suggest that as many as one in three men have used a prostitute for sex.[5] Some experts believe the percentage of American males who pay for sex may be far greater at anywhere from 69 to 84 percent.[6]

Surveys also provide some context on the men doling out money for sexual relations. According to a 2004 ABC News *Primetime Live* American sex survey, 15 percent of adult males have paid a prostitute to have sex, whereas about 30 percent of unmarried men over the age of 30 have offered payment for sexual services.[7] A *Playboy* magazine survey found that one in five men admitted they sought out the services of a prostitute within the past five years,[8] while a recent survey of some of the country's richest men revealed that more than one in three had paid to have sex inside the last five years.[9]

In terms of raw numbers, it has been conservatively estimated that some 1.5 million adult males go to prostitutes in this country every week.[10] According to the Southside Prostitution Task Force, in Minneapolis alone between 15,000 and 30,000 johns are estimated to spend money daily to have prostituted sex with the city's estimated 1,500 female sex workers.[11] Many experts in the sex trade industry believe that the majority of customers of prostitutes are repeat offenders, paying to receive sexual services "multiple times with multiple prostitutes."[12] As a result of the demand for paid sex, an estimated $14 billion in revenue is generated from the sex-for-sale industry in the United States every year.[13]

Customers' Use of the Internet to Pay for Sex

In modern times, the males who solicit the services of prostitutes have turned to the Internet in their search and can usually find countless references to the trading of sex for cash. A search in Google for "prostitutes" brings up around 8.4 million results. That nearly doubles when you change the search term to "prostitution." Other terms such as "escort services" and "massage parlors" also show millions of results, which may seem like a virtual gold mine to those who seek sexual favors online under the cloak of anonymity. Such searches can be narrowed to specific locations, giving johns the opportunity to arrange meetings and the particular services with prostitutes in any city they travel to within the United States or abroad.

The Internet has changed the landscape for participating in the sex trade by providing a platform that makes it relatively easy to solicit sexual favors for those seeking them. According to Malarek, with respect to buying and selling sex, for many men:

> the marketplace of choice in many corners . . . is the nebulous not-quite-anonymous web of sex online. Men in the hunt for purchased sex stalk Web sites and discussion boards that offer photographs, ads, and tips. . . . The Internet has become a non-stop shop for johns—a Yellow Pages directory, support group, and travel advisory all rolled into one. . . . In the relative comfort of their homes, and under the guise of a screen name, the johns share their reasons for wanting or needing paid sex. . . . Without these high-speed connections, and the validation they bring, men would still be cowering in the closet.[14]

Some escort agency Web sites advertise hundreds of prostitutes, as reported by Wikipedia, organizing them by race, ethnicity, and physical features, among other things. The men looking for sex workers "have the ability to search by type of service they want. The Web sites generally include photographs where the girls are rarely in provocative poses, but are usually scantily clad[, along with] pricing, usually by the hour or by sex act."[15]

Internet prostitution is flourishing in the 21st century with more and more males moving away from the riskier street prostitution, in terms of arrest and exposure, to the much wider and harder to detect landscape of the worldwide Web where prostitution-involved women, men, and even children are available for a range of prices, services, specialties, and situations.

Types of Johns

Although all johns enter the sex trade to purchase the time and bodies of prostitutes, they are not homogenous as a group. The male (as well as female) customers of sex workers run the gamut insofar as age, race, ethnic background, nationality, physical characteristics, marital status, education, occupation, income level, and other individual traits and circumstances. Prostitutes are just as likely, for example, to encounter a married doctor or politician as a single college student or unemployed john. A wealthy customer may choose the services of a streetwalker just as easily as a high-class call girl, depending on his individual preference, money he wishes to spend, and the circumstances in which he decides to purchase sex.

In general, most male clients of sex workers tend to be in their twenties through fifties, but some are younger and older. Many johns are married. According to one upper-class prostitute, 90 percent of her clients were married.[16] Some studies suggest that single men make up the majority of johns.[17] Many of these, however, may have girlfriends or other romantic attachments. Although most johns who solicit female prostitutes are heterosexual, some are bisexual. Others are gay and seek male prostitutes. Johns can also be pedophiles who go after young boys for sex; as well as rapists, wife batterers, gang members, drug dealers, and substance abusers, among other types.

In the book *The Comfort of Sin*, author Richard Goodall described eight types of male customers of prostitutes:[18]

1. Men who are deprived of sexual pleasure or regular sexual relations.
2. Young men who are shy and/or with limited sexual experience.
3. Lonely men.
4. Unlucky men (those who are blind, deformed, or unattractive).
5. Occupational johns (such as those in the military).
6. Deviant males (such as sexual perverts, sadomasochists, or exhibitionists).
7. Menopausal men (husbands of menopausal women whose interest in sex has diminished).
8. Castrated males (men under psychological pressure due to contemporary women's availability and ascendancy).

Another type of male customer identified is the therapeutically motivated john—or one who seeks out the sex worker for therapeutic purposes or "to provide an outlet for venting problems or frustrations . . . and to receive in return a sympathetic and somewhat impersonal listening ear."[19] For these johns, this motivation may be as strong, if not stronger than paid sex.

The men who pay for sex can also be broken down by the prostitutes they predominantly solicit or who solicit them. Some wealthy johns, for example, seek out exclusively upper-class call girls, while some men only go to streetwalkers. Others may choose to avoid the risk of arrest and exposure by going exclusively to legal brothel prostitutes. Gay johns tend to solicit only male prostitutes, whereas pedophile johns go after mostly young prostituted boys. (See Chapter 9.)

The sexual services these men seek from prostitutes vary and include straight sex, oral and anal sex, as well as bestial and ritual sex, pair sex, and triolism, or combinations thereof. As one researcher pointed out, "Some men crave the excitement, thrill, and risk of what they perceive to be down and dirty sex."[20]

Apart from the male clients of female and male prostitutes, some women are also clients of male sex workers or gigolos. Recently a legal brothel in Nevada began hiring the first male prostitutes to serve primarily female johns.[21] But women have purchased sex with illegal prostitutes for much longer (as fictionalized in the 1980 motion picture *American Gigolo*).[22] The types of females who go to men for paid sex include unhappily married women; businesswomen or those in relationships who seek a discreet, no-strings-attached sexual involvement; unattractive women or those with disabilities who may be unable to have a normal relationship or have a low self-esteem; and women who simply choose to enjoy a risqué sexual encounter in the same manner that men do in paying for sex whenever they wish.[23]

There are some heterosexual or homosexual couples who solicit female and/or male prostitutes for group sex, according to experts.[24] Many of them may also proposition sex workers as individuals, while other customers of prostitutes may combine the use of pornography or erotica with paying for sexual favors.

Reasons Why Johns Go to Prostitutes

Why do men choose to pay for sex with a prostitute when they are at risk of contracting a STD or being arrested for breaking the law in the vast majority of the United States? Even for those men who go to Nevada's regulated licensed brothels, it is an alternative to not paying for sex that carries a stigma and, as such, is often done surreptitiously. Yet, the men who solicit prostitutes are many and show no sign of abating in their desire to do business in the sex trade industry.

According to Susan Bakos—whose article, "The Hugh Grant Syndrome: Why Nice Guys Go to Hookers," appeared in *McCall's* magazine—in contrast to popular opinion that such men must be unappealing or desperate to pay for what they are unable to have for free: "Based on interviews I conducted with call girls and prostitutes, I concluded that the men most likely to use prostitutes are not losers who can't get a woman any other way, but married men, often attractive and successful, traveling on business."[25] Similar conclusions were made by researcher Esther Davidowitz in a *Women's Day* article on men who pay for sex: "These men are not unique. . . . It's not just the old, the weird, and perverted who visit prostitutes. And it's not only the cheap, drug-addicted and dim-witted women who go into the business."[26]

Males go to prostitutes for various or multiple reasons, which rarely include their own physical appearance. However, for some men who are physically unappealing, having paid sex with an attractive sex worker may give them a greater sense of self-esteem if such a person is believed to be unattainable otherwise. In a survey of more than 200 johns who responded to sex-trade industry classified ads in Chicago for interviews, 83 percent described their solicitation of prostitutes as a type of addiction.[27] Forty percent of the men claimed to be inebriated when paying for sexual favors, while 57 percent believed that the prostitutes they propositioned had been victims of child abuse.

Prostitution experts on the surge in Internet-era prostitution point toward a number of other reasons why men typically pay for sex, including:[28]

- *Oral sex:* which most johns prefer over sexual intercourse with prostitutes and may be seen as less risky and more acceptable in crossing boundaries.
- *Sexual intercourse:* for variety, experimentation, adventure, and daring.
- *Power and control:* allows men to have this with a prostitute that may not be possible in their real world.
- *Intimacy issues:* fear of intimacy, or an emotional attachment.
- *Madonna-whore notion:* separating the acceptable or good woman, such as a wife, from the unacceptable or bad woman (the prostitute).
- *Preservation of marriage:* by paying for sex rather than having an affair or getting a divorce.
- *Danger and thrills:* the adventure of prostitution while calculating the risk of being exposed.
- *Kinky or unnatural sex acts:* such as sadomasochistic sex, anal sex, mammary sex, and coprolagnia that may be unacceptable to partners or other women.

- *Developing self-esteem:* as a result of being pampered, pleased, and listened to by the prostitute, who is seen as nonjudgmental and positive-oriented.

Building self-esteem, in particular, appears to be a key motivating factor for paid sex. In a four-year study of sex workers and their customers, it was found that the most important reason men gave for going to a prostitute was regarding her being, in effect, a "paraprofessional therapist." The johns often believed that the occasion "raised their self-esteem and self-awareness, eased burdens [at] home or on the job, and restored confidence in their own sexuality."[29]

However, not all clients of prostitutes regard their get-together as a "therapy session," or for anything other than paid sex. According to one john:

> I don't hire prostitutes for the conversation. That's not what I'm paying for. . . . I pay a prostitute for a good time and that means using her mouth for my pleasure. . . . In my book when you pay the money, you're the boss. I give the orders and she follows them.[30]

The Girlfriend and Boyfriend Experience

For many johns, the most popular feature of being with a prostitute is the so-called Girlfriend Experience, or GFE, where a client pays a prostitute to pretend to be his girlfriend during the session, making it seem more real than simply a business arrangement. According to one client of high-end sex workers:

> GFE [girlfriend experience] is popular for (a) the service that it most likely implies and (b) the illusion it presents. The reality is that with very, very rare exceptions, the lady is with the guy because she is being compensated for it. Sure, if the guy and gal see each other 20–30 days in a year then the relationship will generally evolve to more than what a one-time encounter is; even so the gal is unlikely to be there if she is not getting compensated. But, during those hours, night or days together, the illusion of a girlfriend has to be there or the extended engagement doesn't work that well.[31]

Some johns have taken this GFE a step further and created a Boyfriend Experience, or BFE. Malarek quotes an example of the BFE from a john:

> When you come along and they feel that "BFE" from you . . . your attentiveness and willingness to listen and treat them . . . like a regular woman, they

pour into you more and that to me is when you will have your best experience because she is comfortable and there is a level of trust.[32]

Another customer of female prostitutes offered a similar perspective on the BFE:

My feeling is that a lady who feels that she is getting the BFE will be just a little different than with a gent who approaches things in a very businesslike fashion. There is disagreement on this among the guys, but that is how I have found things.[33]

The GFE and BFE may make it seem as though the prostitute-john are approximating a real couple, but once the session has ended, so too does the paid fantasy. (See more on GFE in Chapters 4 and 5.)

Johns and Sex Tourism in the Military

The international sex tourism industry has long been fueled in large part by members of the U.S. armed forces, as military johns have paid for prostituted sex around the world, particularly in Third World countries such as Thailand and the Philippines. Historically, female prostitutes have been regarded by U.S. soldiers as "part of the spoils of war—and foreign women of color are viewed by many in the military as theirs for the taking—even in the absence of armed conflict."[34]

Sex tourism, defined as "travel to engage in sexual activity with prostitutes," is a multibillion-dollar industry that includes international and domestic sex tourism where women and girls, in particular, are subject to sexual exploitation mainly by the men who journey to various destinations "with the intention of exploiting permissive or poorly enforced local laws concerning sex."[35]

During the mid-1960s, an agreement between the United States and Thailand made Thai ports the "way-station for soldiers on leave from the Vietnam War," with the Thai government providing American troops with "rest and relaxation" services, including "government-sponsored" selling of sex by Thai prostitutes, setting a standard for generations of soldiers to follow.[36] According to an international prostitution expert: "Where the [U.S.] military has established bases, prostitution economics have grown up around them—that is, economics based on the prostitution of a nation's women to the American occupying forces."[37]

In his research on johns, Malarek revealed that

> soldiers on R & R . . . and sailors on shore leave are notorious in paying for sex. For them, it is also a rite of passage, usually the last course after a wild night of chugging copious jugs of beer. . . . [The] tacit approval by military brass worldwide has created a sense of entitlement among young men in uniform.[38]

The magnitude of military johns and the sexual exploitation of prostituted females around the world is reflected on the "scores of sex Web sites, [where] military men and Veterans . . . boast about their sexual conquests while serving their country."[39] Traditionally, most friendly countries have been pretty reluctant to prosecute U.S. servicemen on charges related to prostitution and the sex trade. Moreover, the U.S. armed forces has routinely stood behind soldiers accused of sex crimes, especially prostitution. For instance, the U.S. Navy "has been known to give accused servicemen certificates to 'prove' they were on duty when a crime occurred. Another method is to ship an accused serviceman out of the country before a case can be filed in court."[40]

Under current U.S. law, with the PROTECT Act of 2003, Americans can now be prosecuted for engaging in commercial sex or other illicit sexual conduct with minors while traveling abroad.[41] This notwithstanding, sexual commerce between U.S. soldiers and foreign underage and adult prostitutes continues to flourish.

Sexually Transmitted Diseases

Although most prostitutes at all levels use condoms while plying their trade to try and protect themselves from STDs such as HIV that may be carried by johns, the risk for contracting an STD remains high. This is also true in reverse, as customers of prostitutes run the risk of becoming infected with an STD from a sex worker, including genital warts, herpes, gonorrhea, syphilis, hepatitis B, and HIV. Aside from the inconsistent use of condoms by many prostitutes while on duty and off, some johns prefer to engage in sexual relations without protection, thereby increasing the prospects for exposure to an STD. One prostitute noted the pressure often put on cash-strapped or drug-dependent prostitutes from johns: "Many men today offer hookers more money to have sex without a condom."[42] With streetwalkers, prostituted teenagers, and drug-addicted prostitutes often desperate to earn as much as they can from johns, it is not difficult to understand why they might give in to their demands, even at risk to their health and their client's health.

In one of the few studies of johns and AIDS, only around 2 percent of the sample tested positive for its precursor, HIV.[43] Half of this group had other risk factors, such as participating in gay sexual relations or being intravenous (IV) drug users. The other half had no apparent additional risk factors besides involvement with a prostitute. Even with this low percentage of HIV-positive johns, it still leaves potentially thousands of men infected with the virus, many of whom may be unaware of their exposure while continuing to have unprotected sex or paid sex with multiple unsuspecting partners. Some studies have shown that customers of prostitutes are very susceptible to STDs because of the high-risk nature of the sex-for-sale business of multiple sex acts, multiple partners, IV drug use, and irregular use of condoms while having sex with potentially STD-infected prostitutes.[44]

Oral sex is thought by many to be a safe alternative to intercourse in the sex trade, and is the most preferred sex act by johns. One study of prostitute-client contacts found that three-quarters of these were limited to oral copulation.[45] However, experts advise that unprotected oral sex carries a risk of contracting an STD from a sex worker or john through open sores or lacerations in the mouth or genitals, bleeding gums, or other methods of transmission.[46] Even when condoms are used during oral sex, an infected prostitute could still pass on an STD through an exposed area of a john's genitalia that may already be compromised or otherwise susceptible to infection. (See Chapter 6 for further discussion on oral sex and STDs.)

Violence and Johns

Violence is a common occurrence in the sex trade industry, as many prostitutes are prone to victimization by violent johns. Studies indicate that most female prostitutes, particularly street level and teenage, have been sexually or physically assaulted at one time or another by the men they service for pay.[47] In one study of sex worker-related violence, 70 percent of the prostituted females were reportedly raped repeatedly by customers for an average of 31 sexual assaults a year.[48] The research also found that 65 percent of the prostitutes were victims of frequent abuse and assaults. A high incidence of rape and violence during the course of prostituting was reported by Jody Miller and Martin Schwartz, based on their interviews with streetwalking sex workers.[49] In a government publication with case histories of prostitutes, one streetwalker described being raped as many as 20 times and physically assaulted by johns on approximately 30 different "occasions . . . [often] within the context of a robbery or sexual assault."[50] Other studies have indicated a high rate of customer violence directed at male prostitutes as well.[51]

Prostitutes are 40 times as likely to be victims of homicide as other women.[52] Johns are the perpetrators for the majority of prostitute murders. Serial killers such as Robert Pickton, Gary Ridgway, Peter Sutcliffe, Robert Hanson, and Kendall Francois, among others, targeted teenage runaways and prostitutes to sexually exploit and kill.[53] According to University of Houston criminologist Steven Egger, prostitutes are "the most at-risk people for serial killers," primarily because

> they are vulnerable and they are vulnerable because they are available. This provides relative anonymity for the killer because when you pick up a prostitute in an area where they ply their trade, everyone expects to see cars picking them up. No one pays much attention to the so-called Johns.[54]

A further perspective on serial killers and prostitutes was given by Neil Boyd, a criminology professor at Simon Fraser University, who contended that streetwalkers were the most vulnerable class of sex workers: He held that their murders were

> both a crime of opportunity as well as a symbolic crime. There are obviously opportunities for men who want to act with sexual violence against women. But . . . these acts are also something of a symbolic statement about the perpetrator's attitudes toward women. It is really in some sense an expression of male power, male rage taken out against the most vulnerable members of society because these are people who through a variety of reasons don't have the protections that most prostitutes do have.[55]

Aside from perpetrating prostitute killings, johns can also be the victims of sex trade-related homicides, with the prostitute often being the likely killer. Perhaps the most well-known example is that of Aileen Wuornos, a prostitute serial killer who murdered seven of her customers who she claimed raped or tried to rape her.[56] However, in most cases of john murder and other violent victimization, robbery is the motive, often in relation to the prostitute's drug addiction or under the command of her pimp.[57]

A recent example of a john who was robbed and murdered by a female prostitute occurred in East Harlem. According to WPIX.com, the 52-year-old victim:

> was found in his parked 2007 Dodge Magnum [on] Thursday morning, hours after he was reportedly seen buying condoms. . . . His hands [were] tied behind his back and a cord wrapped around his neck, tied to the headrest. He had been stabbed in the chest and robbed, police sources said. According to written reports, a prostitute whom he regularly visited and two of her friends tortured [the john] for his bank card PIN code. Police say his wallet—which contained a debit card and credit cards—was stolen.[58]

John victimizations notwithstanding, they are far more likely to be the perpetrators of violence directed toward prostitutes.

Arrests and Forfeiture Laws

Customers of sex workers are far less likely to be arrested than the prostitutes they solicit. The U.S. Justice Department's Uniform Crime Reports, which collects arrest data from law enforcement agencies nationwide, does not differentiate male arrests for prostitution and commercialized vice by customers and prostitutes. However, even when combining male john and prostitute arrestees for prostitution and commercialized vice in the United States in 2008, arrests totaled 18,012.[59] By comparison, there were 40,772 female arrests that year, or more than twice as many for prostitution-related charges, the vast majority undoubtedly for solicitation.[60] Though the latter figure likely also included multiple arrests of the same prostitute, it is clear that johns have not been held accountable for their role in violating prostitution laws to the same degree. Since female prostitutes are arrested much more often than male prostitutes, a gender bias appears to be a factor, in addition to the greater visibility of street-based female sex workers for police stings, and a concentrated effort by some law enforcement agencies to take teenage prostitutes off the streets and away from pimps and potentially harmful johns.

Recently law enforcement departments across the country have stepped up efforts to go after the men who pay prostitutes for sex. A number of semi-regular police stings have led to numerous arrests of prostitutes' customers for solicitation and related prostitution and commercialized vice charges.[61]

Many cities have also used vehicle forfeiture laws against johns—which gives police the right to impound cars of persons arrested on prostitution charges—as a means to punish, embarrass, make money, clean the streets of prostitution, and deter such men from soliciting prostitutes. These laws recognize, in effect, that "johns degrade not only women who are prostitutes, but also others by assuming that any females in a given area are for sale."[62]

For example, in Wayne County, Michigan, "the Forfeiture Unit is a specialized unit within the Special Operations Division of the Prosecutor's Office."[63] With regard to vehicles "used or intended to be used to engage in prostitution," the Forfeiture Unit

> also operates a sub-unit: the *Vehicle Seizure Unit*. The *Vehicle Seizure Unit* operates a program designed to discourage the use of vehicles . . . to solicit prostitutes, known as the OTE program. Police agencies located within Wayne County seize vehicles used or attempted to be used for [such] illegal purposes and cooperate with the Wayne County Prosecutor's Office in processing the cases in a combined effort to successfully clean the streets from those who participate in these vices in Wayne County. The Forfeiture Unit processed over 3,900 vehicle seizure cases in 2005.[64]

According to a *Detroit News* article on police profits from the vehicle forfeiture program:

> Vehicles seized under authority of Wayne County prosecutors for alleged civil [prostitution] infractions become county property if the owner does not pay the fine, plus towing and storage fees, within [30] days. . . . Each subsequent time someone's vehicle is seized, another $900 is added to the charge to get it back.[65]

The Wayne County Prosecutor Kym Worthy defended the practice, stating: "If people are soliciting prostitutes, selling drugs or otherwise profiting from criminal activity, as prosecutors we have the right under the law to forfeit property."[66]

By and large, these forfeiture laws have been successful in terms of making clients of prostitutes pay a price for illegally soliciting, and reducing street prostitution. For example, recently in Memphis, Tennessee, a few dozen suspects were arrested during a three-day police sting. They had their cars seized and were arrested for soliciting prostitutes. In response to the sting operation and its consequences for the johns, the Memphis Police

Director Larry Godwin spoke of the "domino effect" he hoped this would have on the city's sex trade:

> You think about the johns that are robbed. You think about the pimps that are behind the prostitutes. Do I think it's excessive? I say seize every dad-gummed vehicle and keep them, do whatever we've got to do. We need to send a message of what they are doing to the little girls, what they are doing to somebody's daughter and what is happening out there.[67]

John School

Apart from arrest, vehicle forfeiture, and in some places public exposure, another weapon used to combat prostitution and the sexual exploitation of women and teenage girls and boys is something called "john school." Offered to or imposed on arrested johns or sex workers' customers, it is described as:

> a type of educational intervention aimed at johns, or male clients of prostitutes; john schools are usually a diversion program, but can also be a condition of a criminal sentence. In most jurisdictions in which john schools exist, a man arrested for soliciting the services of a prostitute, or another related offense, may be offered john school as an alternative to criminal prosecution. He will pay a fine, which covers the cost of the program and sometimes contributes to programs to aid prostitutes, and attend a single class or series of classes. In some jurisdictions, courts may sentence men to attend a john school program as a condition of probation.[68]

The first john school, First Offender Prostitution Program, opened in San Francisco in 1995. Since then, other such programs have been established in more than 40 cities, including New York City; Los Angeles; Pittsburgh; Washington, D.C.; Brooklyn, New York; and West Palm Beach, Florida. The classes are for first-time offenders and "purport to teach [them] about the reality of prostitution, such as the abuse histories of many prostitutes, the sexually transmitted disease risks of prostitution, and the effects of prostitution on families and communities."[69]

In an ABC News article, "Inside a Brooklyn John School," a typical class session is described:

> Almost like traffic school, attendees are served bagels and coffee as they sit through a four-hour lecture. Classes can be as long as seven hours depending

on the city. Each class member pays a $250 fee and hears from prosecutors, police, community advocates, and an ex-prostitute. Also included in the lecture is a graphic slideshow about sexually transmitted diseases presented by a Health and Human Services representative. After attending, the arrest is dropped from each john's record as long as he isn't caught soliciting a prostitute again within six months. If the men opt against john school, they face trial on a Class B misdemeanor and a possible sentence of 90 days in jail. Defendants with violent criminal records cannot participate.[70]

Experts and speakers at john schools seek to create a mindset among attendees that prostitutes are, for the most part, victims rather than merely paid sex workers, emphasizing the young age of many prostitutes, their troubled backgrounds, and the daily violence and victimization they endure while working in the sex trade. According to one participant in a john school who seemed to have gotten the message: "It's opened up my eyes, gave me a lot of information about the girls, the community problems, and really graphic pictures which make people really not want to have sex."[71]

There is a low recidivism rate for attendees at john schools across the United States. In Brooklyn, for example, "only nine out of more than 2,000 attendees have been arrested a second time for soliciting prostitution."[72] In spite of the apparent success of john schools, participating johns represent only a fraction of the men who pay for sex in this country and sustain the sex trade industry and its sexual exploitation of voluntary and involuntary prostitutes.

Notes

Chapter 1

1. Cited in Wikipedia, the Free Encyclopedia, "Prostitution," http://en.wikipedia.org/wiki/Prostitution.

2. Cited in Wikipedia, the Free Encyclopedia, "Prostitution in the United States," http://en.wikipedia.org/wiki/Prostitution_in_the_United_States.

3. Quoted in "Sex Work Emerges from Shadows," *CBS News* (March 12, 2008), http://www.cbsnews.com/video/watch/?id=3928272n. See also Norma J. Almodovar, *Cop to Call Girl: Why I Left the LAPD to Make an Honest Living as a Beverly Hills Prostitute* (New York: Simon and Schuster, 1993).

4. "Dirty Money: The Business of High End Prostitution," *CNBC* (October 30, 2008), http://www.cnbc.com/id/26869953?__source=vty|dirtymoney|&par=vty.

5. Alice Gomstyn, "The Perks of High End Prostitution," *ABC News* (May 11, 2008), http://abcnews.go.com/Business/IndustryInfo/story?id=4428608&page=1.

6. Jacquelyn A. Ingles, "Caught in the Web of Internet Prostitution," *Medill Reports Chicago* (July 25, 2007), http://news.medill.northwestern.edu/chicago/news.aspx?id=41347.

7. R. Barri Flowers, *Street Kids: The Lives of Runaway and Thrownaway Teens* (Jefferson, NC: McFarland, 2010); R. Barri Flowers, *Runaway Kids and Teenage Prostitution: America's Lost, Abandoned, and Sexually Exploited Children* (New York: Praeger, 2001).

8. Cited in Mia Spangenberg, "Prostituted Youth in New York City: An Overview," *ECPAT-US* (2001), http://www.libertadlatina.org/US_ECPAT_Child_Prostitution_NYC.htm.

9. Ibid.

10. Flowers, *Runaway Kids and Teenage Prostitution.*

11. See, for example, "52 Kids Rescued in U.S. Prostitution Sweep," *CBS News* (October 26, 2009), http://www.cbsnews.com/stories/2009/10/26/national/main5422063.shtml?tag=cbsnewsTwoColLowerPromoArea;morenews; Russell Goldman, "Parents Who Pimp Their Children: The FBI Steps Up Efforts to Catch Parents and the Predators Who Want Their Kids for Sex," *ABC News* (October 8, 2007), http://abcnews.go.com/US/story?id=3691604&page=1.

12. Cited in Wikipedia, the Free Encyclopedia, "Pornography in the United States," http://en.wikipedia.org/wiki/Pornography_in_the_United_States.

13. Ibid.

14. Cited in Rebecca Leung, "Porn in the U.S.A.," *CBS News* (November 21, 2003), http://www.cbsnews.com/stories/2004/08/31/60minutes/main639674.shtml?tag=mncol;lst;10.

15. Ibid.

16. Ibid.

17. Ibid.

18. "Pornography in the United States."

19. See, for example, Desperate Amateurs, www.desperateamateurs.com; *Amateurs Online*, www.amateursonline.com.

20. National Center for Missing and Exploited Children, "What Is Child Pornography?" http://www.missingkids.com/missingkids/servlet/PageServlet?Language Country=en_US&PageId=1504. See also Possession of Child Pornography, 18 U.S.C. §2252 (2008).

21. Cited in Wikipedia, the Free Encyclopedia, "Child Pornography," http://en.wikipedia.org/wiki/Child_porn.

22. Cited in "What Is Child Pornography?" See also Janis Wolak, David Finkelhor, and Kimberly Mitchell, *Child-Pornography Possessors Arrested in Internet-Related Crimes: Findings from the National Juvenile Online Victimization Study* (Alexandria, VA: National Center for Missing and Exploited Children, 2005).

23. "Child Pornography;" Richard J. Estes and Neil A. Weiner, *The Commercial Sexual Exploitation of Children in the U.S., Canada, and Mexico* (Philadelphia: University of Pennsylvania, 2002).

24. U.S. Department of Justice, Child Exploitation and Obscenity Section (CEOS), "Child Pornography" (November 6, 2007), http://www.justice.gov/criminal/ceos/childporn.html; Richard Wortley and Stephen Smallbone, "Child Pornography on the Internet," *Problem Oriented Guides for the Police* (May 2006), http://www.cops.usdoj.gov/files/RIC/Publications/e04062000.txt.

25. Cited in Wikipedia, the Free Encyclopedia, "Child Pornography."

26. Ibid. See also "27 Charged in Child Porn Sting," *CNN* (March 16, 2006), http://www.cnn.com/2006/LAW/03/15/childporn.arrests/index.html.

27. U.S. Department of Health and Human Services, The Campaign to Rescue and Restore Victims of Human Trafficking, "Fact Sheet: Sex Trafficking" (May 27, 2010), http://www.acf.hhs.gov/trafficking/about/fact_sex.html.

28. Ibid.; Trafficking Victims Protection Act of 2000, P.L. 106–386.

29. Cited on *The Oprah Winfrey Show*, "Child Sex Trafficking: The Facts" (November 15, 2005), http://www.oprah.com/oprahshow/Child-Sex-Trafficking—The-Facts; Ashtar A. Marcus, "Lucy Liu, USAID Highlight Human Trafficking," *Frontlines* (November 2009), http://www.usaid.gov/press/frontlines/fl_nov09/p01 liu091103.html.

30. "Fact Sheet: Sex Trafficking."

31. Marcus, "Lucy Liu, USAID Highlight Human Trafficking;" U.S. Department of Justice, Child Exploitation and Obscenity Section, "Trafficking and Sex Tourism," http://www.justice.gov/criminal/ceos/trafficking.html.

32. Cited in "Child Sex Trafficking: The Facts."

33. Cited in Wikipedia, the Free Encyclopedia, "Sexual Slavery," http://en .wikipedia.org/wiki/Sexual_slavery. See also Kathryn Farr, *Sex Trafficking: The Global Market in Women and Children* (New York: Worth Publishers, 2004); National Crime Victims' Rights Week, "Human Trafficking" (April 10–16, 2005), http://www.ojp .usdoj.gov/ovc/ncvrw/2005/pg5l.html.

34. Cited in Bridgette Carr, "Sex Trafficking: An American Problem Too," *CNN* (November 25, 2009), http://www.cnn.com/2009/OPINION/11/25/carr .human.trafficking. See also Eric M. Strauss, "Domestic Sex Trafficking in the U.S.," *ABC News/Primetime* (July 14, 2008), http://abcnews.go.com/Primetime/ story?id=5326721&page=1.

35. See, for example, *Cosmopolitan*, http://www.cosmopolitan.com; *Maxim*, http://www.maxim.com.

36. The Internet Movie Database, Box Office/Business for *Pretty Woman* (1990), http://www.imdb.com/title/tt0100405/business.

37. Almodovar, *Cop to Call Girl*; Xaviera Hollander, *The Happy Hooker* (New York: Dell, 1984); Sydney Biddle Barrows, *Mayflower Madam: The Secret Life of Sydney Biddle Barrows* (New York: Arbor House, 1989); Jody B. Gibson, *Secrets of a Hollywood Super Madam* (Los Angeles, CA: Corona Books, 2007); Jeannette Angell, *Callgirl: Confessions of an Ivy League Lady of Pleasure* (New York: HarperCollins, 2005). See also Natalie McLennan, *The Price: My Rise and Fall as Natalia, New York's #1 Escort* (Beverly Hills, CA: Phoenix Books, 2008).

Chapter 2

1. Merriam-Webster Online, "Prostitution," http://www.merriam-webster.com/ dictionary/prostitution.

2. Charles Winick and Paul M. Kinsie, *The Lively Commerce: Prostitution in the United States* (Chicago: Triangle Books, 1971), 3.

3. Richard Goodall, *The Comfort of Sin: Prostitutes and Prostitution in the 1990s* (Kent, UK: Renaissance Books, 1995), 1.

4. Abraham Flexner, *Prostitution in Europe* (New York: Century, 1914), 11.

5. Quoted in U.S. Legal Definitions, "Prostitution Law and Legal Definition," http://definitions.uslegal.com/p/prostitution.

6. Quoted in R. Barri Flowers, *The Prostitution of Women and Girls* (Jefferson, NC: McFarland, 2009), 6.

7. Cited in Wikipedia, the Free Encyclopedia, "Prostitution," http://en. wikipedia .org/wiki/Prostitution.

8. Howard B. Woolston, *Prostitution in the United States* (New York: Century, 1921), 35.

9. Cited in Wikipedia, "Prostitution."

10. R. Barri Flowers and H. Loraine Flowers, *Murders in the United States: Crimes, Killers and Victims of the Twentieth Century* (Jefferson, NC: McFarland, 2009), 96–97, 105; Ann Rule, *Green River, Running Red: The Real Story of the Green River Killer—America's Deadliest Serial Murderer* (New York: Free Press, 2004).

11. YourDictionary.com, "Panderer Legal Definition," http://www.yourdictionary .com/law/panderer.

12. R. Barri Flowers, *Runaway Kids and Teenage Prostitution: America's Lost, Abandoned, and Sexually Exploited Children* (New York: Praeger, 2001), p. 119.

13. Wikipedia, the Free Encyclopedia, "American Pimp," http://en.wikipedia .org/wiki/American_Pimp.

14. Merriam-Webster Online, "Madam," http://www.merriam-webster.com/ dictionary/madam.

15. Sydney Biddle Barrows and William Novak, *Mayflower Madam: The Secret Life of Sydney Biddle Barrows* (New York: HarperCollins, 1986); Xaviera Hollander, Robin Moore, and Yvonne Dunleavy, *Happy Hooker: My Own Story* (New York: HarperCollins, 2002).

16. Cited in Wikipedia, the Free Encyclopedia, "Prostitution in the United States," http://en.wikipedia.org/wiki/Prostitution_in_the_United_States.

17. Flowers, *The Prostitution of Women and Girls*, 11, 15.

18. Cited in Wikia Education, The Psychology Wiki, "Prostitution," http:// psychology.wikia.com/wiki/Prostitution.

19. Mandi L. Burnette, Emma Lucas, Mark Ilgen, Susan M. Frayne, Julia Mayo, Julie C. Weitlauf, "Prevalence and Health Correlates of Prostitution among Patients Entering Treatment for Substance Use Disorders," *Archives of General Psychiatry* 65, 3 (2008): 337–44.

20. Cited in Wikia Education, The Psychology Wiki, "Prostitution of Children," http://psychology.wikia.com/wiki/Child_prostitution. See also Richard J. Estes and Neil A. Weiner, *The Commercial Sexual Exploitation of Children in the U.S., Canada, and Mexico* (Philadelphia: University of Pennsylvania, 2002), 140–45.

21. Flowers, *Runaway Kids and Teenage Prostitution*, 87.

22. Cited in Wikipedia, the Free Encyclopedia, "Sexual Slavery," http://en .wikipedia.org/wiki/Sexual_slavery.

23. Cited in Wikipedia, the Free Encyclopedia, "Human Trafficking in the United States," http://en.wikipedia.org/wiki/Human_trafficking_in_the_United_States.

24. Cited in Wikipedia, "Prostitution in the United States."

25. Ibid.

26. Wikipedia, the Free Encyclopedia, "Prostitution in Rhode Island," http:// en.wikipedia.org/wiki/Prostitution_in_Rhode_Island.

27. Flowers, *The Prostitution of Women and Girls*, 8.

28. Ibid.

29. Cited in "Sex Work Emerges from Shadows," *CBS News* (March 12, 2008), http://www.cbsnews.com/video/watch/?id=3928272n.

30. U.S. Department of Justice, Federal Bureau of Investigation, *Crime in the United States 2008*, Table 29 (September 2009), http://www.fbi.gov/ucr/cius2008/data/table_29.html.

31. Flowers, *The Prostitution of Women and Girls*, 8.

32. Harry Benjamin and R. E. L. Masters, *Prostitution and Morality* (New York: Julian Press, 1964), 36.

33. Paul J. Goldstein, *Prostitution and Drugs* (Lexington, MA: Lexington Books, 1979), 34.

34. Jennifer James, "Prostitutes and Prostitution," in *Deviants: Voluntary Actors in a Hostile World*, ed. Edward Sagarin and Fred Montanino, 390–91 (Morrison, NJ: General Learning Press, 1977), Jennifer James, "Two Domains of Streetwalker Argot," *Anthropological Linguistics* 14 (1972): 174–75.

35. Cited in Flowers, *The Prostitution of Women and Girls*, 55.

36. Ibid., 48.

37. Ibid., 49.

38. Flowers, *Runaway Kids and Teenage Prostitution*, 130–34; R. Barri Flowers, *Street Kids: The Lives of Runaway and Thrownaway Teens* (Jefferson, NC: McFarland, 2010), 147–49.

39. Nicholas Ray, *Lesbian, Gay, Bisexual, and Transgender Youth: An Epidemic of Homelessness* (New York: National Gay and Lesbian Task Force Policy Institute and National Coalition for the Homeless, 2006), 1; Michael C. Clatts, W. Rees Davis, Jo L. Sotheran, and Aylin Atillasoy, "Correlates and Distribution of HIV Risk Behaviors among Homeless Youths in New York City: Implications for Prevention and Policy," *Child Welfare* 77, 2 (1998): 195–207.

40. See, for example, David M. Fergusson, L. John Horwood, and Annette L. Beautrais, "Is Sexual Orientation Related to Mental Health Problems and Suicidality in Young People?" *Archives of General Psychiatry* 56, 10 (1999): 876–80; Stephen Gaetz, "Safe Streets for Whom? Homeless Youth, Social Exclusion, and Criminal Victimization," *Canadian Journal of Criminology and Criminal Justice* 46, 6 (2004): 423–55.

41. Flowers, *Street Kids*, pp. 117–18; R. Barri Flowers, *The Victimization and Exploitation of Women and Children: A Study of Physical, Mental and Sexual Maltreatment in the United States* (Jefferson, NC: McFarland, 1994), 72.

42. Flowers, *Runaway Kids and Teenage Prostitution*, 108–109; R. Barri Flowers, *Children and Criminality: The Child as Victim and Offender* (Westport, CT: Greenwood, 1986), 134–37.

43. U.S. Department of Health and Human Services, The Campaign to Rescue and Restore Victims of Human Trafficking, "Fact Sheet: Sex Trafficking" (May 27, 2010), http://www.acf.hhs.gov/trafficking/about/fact_sex.html; Bridgette Carr,

"Sex Trafficking: An American Problem Too," *CNN* (November 25, 2009), http://www.acf.hhs.gov/trafficking/about/fact_sex.html; *The Oprah Winfrey Show*, "Child Sex Trafficking: The Facts" (November 15, 2005).

44. "Human Trafficking in the United States;" U.S. Department of Justice, Child Exploitation and Obscenity Section (CEOS), "Trafficking and Sex Tourism," http://www.justice.gov/criminal/ceos/trafficking.html; Eric M. Strauss, "Domestic Sex Trafficking in the U.S.," ABC News/Primetime (July 14, 2008), http://abcnews.go.com/Primetime/story?id=5326721&page=1.

45. Mimi H. Silbert and Ayala M. Pines, "Entrance into Prostitution," *Youth and Society* 13 (1982): 471–500; Estes and Weiner, *The Commercial Sexual Exploitation of Children*, 92.

46. Flowers, *Street Kids*, 144; Neil R. Coombs, "Male Prostitution: A Psychosocial View of Behavior," *American Journal of Orthopsychiatry* 44 (1974): 782–89.

47. Flowers, *The Prostitution of Women and Girls*, 51; Jennifer James, "Prostitute-Pimp Relationships," *Medical Aspects of Human Sexuality* 7 (1973): 147–63; Kit R. Roane, "Gangs Turn to New Trade: Young Prostitutes," *New York Times* (July 11, 1999), 23.

48. Nancy E. Walker, "Executive Summary: How Many Teens Are Prostituted?" fce.msu.edu/Family_Impact_Seminars/pdf/2002-2.pdf. See also Claire E. Sterk, *Tricking and Tripping: Prostitution in the Era of AIDS* (Putnam Valley, NY: Social Change Press, 2000).

49. National Center for Missing and Exploited Children, *Female Juvenile Prostitution: Problem and Response*, 2nd ed. (Alexandria, VA: National Center for Missing and Exploited Children, 2002), x, 15.

50. Martin A. Plant, "Sex Work, Alcohol, Drugs, and AIDS," in *AIDS, Drugs, and Prostitution,* ed. Martin A. Plant, 4 (London: Routledge, 1990).

51. Cited in Flowers, *The Prostitution of Women and Girls*, 32.

52. Ibid.

53. Flowers, *Street Kids*, 99–101; R. L. Sticof, L. F. Novick, and J. T. Kennedy, "HIV Seroprevalence in Facilities for Runaway and Homeless Adolescents in Four States: Florida, Texas, Louisiana and New York" (paper presented at the Sixth International Conference on AIDS, San Francisco, June 20–24, 1990).

54. Cited in Patricia Hersch, "Coming of Age on City Streets," *Psychology Today* (July 20, 1986), 37.

55. Mary Ann Chiasson, Alan R. Lifson, Rand L. Stoneburner, William Ewing, Deborah Hilderbrandt, and Harold W. Jaffe, "HIV-1 Seroprevalence in Male and Female Prostitutes in New York City" (abstracts from the Sixth International Conference on AIDS, Stockholm, Sweden, June 1988).

56. Timothy P. Johnson, Jennie R. Aschkenasy, Mary R. Herbers, and Stephen A. Gillenwater, "Self-Reported Risk Factors for AIDS among Homeless Youth," *AIDS Education and Prevention* 8 (1996): 308–22.

57. Cited in Flowers, *The Prostitution of Women and Girls*, 49.

58. Cited in "Prostitution Facts;" RapeIs.org, http://www.rapeis.org/activism/prostitution/prostitutionfacts.html.

59. Anastasia Volkonsky, "Legalizing the 'Profession' Would Sanction the Abuse," *Insight on the News* 11 (1995): 20.

60. Ibid.; Flowers, *The Prostitution of Women and Girls*, 49.

61. Anne Rasmusson, "Commercial Sexual Exploitation of Children: A Literature Review," Alliance for Speaking the Truths on Prostitution and Center for Urban and Regional Affairs (June 1, 1999), http://members.shaw.ca/pdg/exploitation_of_children.html#_Toc452540114. See also Stephen W. Baron, "Street Youth Violence and Victimization," *Trauma, Violence, and Abuse* 4 (2003): 22–44.

62. Cited in Ray, *Lesbian, Gay, Bisexual, and Transgender Youth*, 3.

Chapter 3

1. Cesare Lombroso and William Ferrero, *The Female Offender* (New York: Appleton, 1900).

2. Earnest A. Hooton, *The American Criminal* (Cambridge, MA: Harvard University Press, 1939); Earnest A. Hooton, *Crime and the Man* (Cambridge, MA: Harvard University Press, 1939).

3. Charles B. Goring, *The English Convict: A Statistical Study* (London: H.M.S., 1913).

4. Enrico Ferri, *Criminal Sociology* (London: T. Fisher Unwin, 1895).

5. R. Barri Flowers, *The Prostitution of Women and Girls* (Jefferson, NC: McFarland, 2009), 24.

6. Sigmund Freud, *New Introductory Lectures in Psychoanalysis* (New York: W.W. Norton, 1933).

7. R. Barri Flowers, *Women and Criminality: The Woman as Victim, Offender, and Practitioner* (Westport, CT: Greenwood Press, 1987), 121.

8. Ibid.

9. Jennifer James, "Motivations for Entrance into Prostitution," in *The Female Offender*, ed. Laura Crites, 190 (Lexington, MA: Lexington Books, 1976).

10. R. Barri Flowers, *Street Kids: The Lives of Runaway and Thrownaway Teens* (Jefferson, NC: McFarland, 2010), 97–98; R. Barri Flowers, *Runaway Kids and Teenage Prostitution: America's Lost, Abandoned, and Sexually Exploited Children* (New York: Praeger, 2001), 90–91; Jennifer B. Unger, Michele D. Kipke, Thomas R. Simon, Susanne B. Montgomery, and Christine J. Johnson, "Homeless Youths and Young Adults in Los Angeles: Prevalence of Mental Health Problems and the Relationship between Mental Health and Substance Abuse Disorders," *American Journal of Community Psychology* 25, no. 3 (1997): 371–94.

11. Cited in Flowers, *The Prostitution of Women and Girls*, 28–29.

12. Cited in Joan J. Johnson, *Teen Prostitution* (Danbury, CT: Franklin Watts, 1992), 131.

13. William I. Thomas, *Sex and Society: Studies in the Social Psychology of Sex* (Boston, MA: Little, Brown, 1907); William I. Thomas, *The Unadjusted Girl: With Cases and Standpoint for Behavioral Analysis* (New York: Harper and Row, 1923).

14. Joy Pollock, "Early Theories of Female Criminality," in *Women, Crime, and the Criminal Justice System,* ed. Lee H. Bowker (Lexington, MA: Lexington Books, 1978), 45.

15. Sheldon Glueck and Eleanor Glueck, *Five Hundred Delinquent Women* (New York: Alfred A. Knopf, 1934).

16. Otto Pollak, *The Criminality of Women* (Philadelphia: University of Philadelphia Press, 1950).

17. Quoted in Flowers, *The Prostitution of Women and Girls*, 25. See also Charles Winick and Paul M. Kinsie, *The Lively Commerce: Prostitution in the United States* (Chicago: Quadrangle Books, 1971).

18. Kingsley Davis, "The Sociology of Prostitution," *American Sociological Review* 2 (1937): 744–55.

19. Flowers, *Women and Criminality*, 121–22.

20. Edwin M. Lemert, *Social Pathology* (New York: McGraw-Hill, 1951), 237.

21. Roger E. Faris, *Social Disorganization* (New York: Ronald Press, 1955), 271.

22. Flowers, *The Prostitution of Women and Girls*, 122.

23. Ibid.; James, "Motivations for Entrance into Prostitution," 186.

24. Winick and Kinsie, *The Lively Commerce*, 271.

25. Lemert, *Social Pathology.*

26. James, "Motivations for Entrance into Prostitution," 194.

27. Johnson, *Teen Prostitution*, 102–103.

28. Flowers, *Street Kids*, 121.

29. Mimi H. Silbert, "Delancey Street Study: Prostitution and Sexual Assault, Summary of Results," Delancey Street Foundation, San Francisco, 1982, 3.

30. National Center for Missing and Exploited Children, *Prostitution of Children and Child-Sex Tourism* (Alexandria, VA: National Center for Missing and Exploited Children, 1999), 2. See also Ronald L. Simons and Les B. Whitbeck, "Sexual Abuse as a Precursor to Prostitution and Victimization among Adolescent and Adult Homeless Women," *Journal of Family Issues* 12, no. 3 (1991): 375.

31. Stephen Gaetz, "Safe Streets for Whom? Homeless Youth, Social Exclusion, and Criminal Victimization," *Canadian Journal of Criminology and Criminal Justice* 46, no. 6 (2004): 426.

32. Heather Worth, "Up on K Road on a Saturday Night: Sex, Gender and Sex Work in Auckland," *Venereology* 13, no. 1 (2000): 15–24. See also Gabe Kruks, "Gay and Lesbian Homeless/Street Youth: Special Issues and Concerns," *Journal of Adolescent Health* 12 (1991): 515–18.

33. Christina Hoag, "New Laws Treat Teen Prostitutes as Abuse Victims," *ABC News* (April 19, 2009), http://www.abcnews.go.com/US/Wire Story? id=7370496& page=2.

34. Cited in R. Barri Flowers, *The Victimization and Exploitation of Women and Children: A Study of Physical, Mental and Sexual Maltreatment in the United States* (Jefferson, NC: McFarland, 1994), 44.

35. Johnson, *Teen Prostitution*, 97.

36. National Survey on Drug Use and Health, *The NSDUH Report*, "Substance Abuse among Youths Who Had Run Away from Home" (July 2, 2004), http://www.oas.samhsa.gov/2k4/runAways/runAways.htm.

37. Shelley Mallett, Doreen Rosenthal, and Deborah Keys, "Young People, Drug Use and Family Conflict: Pathways into Homelessness," *Journal of Adolescence* 28, no. 2 (2005): 185–99.

38. Cited in June Wyman, "Drug Abuse among Runaway and Homeless Youths Calls for Focused Outreach Solutions," *NIDA Notes* 12, no. 3 (1997), http://www.nida.nih.gov/NIDA_Notes/NNVol12N3/Runaway.html.

39. R. Barri Flowers, *Drugs, Alcohol and Criminality in American Society* (Jefferson, NC: McFarland, 2008), 99–111; Michele D. Kipke, Susanne B. Montgomery, Thomas R. Simon, and Ellen F. Iverson, "Substance Abuse Disorders among Runaway and Homeless Youth," *Substance Use and Misuse* 32 (1997): 969–86.

40. National Center for Missing and Exploited Children, *The Prostitution of Children and Child-Sex Tourism*, 9.

41. Safe Schools Coalition, "Homeless LGBT Youth and LGBT Youth in Foster Care" (July 6, 2009), http://www.safeschoolscoalition.org/RG-homeless.html.

42. Michael C. Clatts, W. Rees Davis, Jo L. Sotheran, and Aylin Atillasoy, "Correlates and Distribution of HIV Risk Behaviors among Homeless Youths in New York City: Implications for Prevention and Policy," *Child Welfare* 77, no. 2 (1998): 195–207.

43. Cited in "Homeless LGBT Youth and LGBT Youth in Foster Care."

44. Cited in Frank York and Robert H. Knight, "Reality Check on Homeless Gay Teens," *Family Policy* (1998), http://www.frc.org/fampol/fp98fcv.htm.

45. Gaetz, "Safe Streets for Whom?" 423–55.

46. Nicholas Ray, *Lesbian, Gay, Bisexual, and Transgender Youth: An Epidemic of Homelessness* (New York: National Gay and Lesbian Task Force Policy Institute and National Coalition for the Homeless, 2006), 3.

47. Pam Oliver, "A Review of Literature on Child Prostitution," *Social Policy Journal of New Zealand* 19 (2002), http://www.thefreelibrary.com/_/print/PrintArticle.aspx?id=99849275.

48. Jody M. Greene, Susan T. Ennett, and Christopher L. Ringwalt, "Prevalence and Correlates of Survival Sex among Runaway and Homeless Youth," *American Journal of Public Health* 89, 9 (1999): 1406. See also David Barrett and William Beckett, "Child Prostitution: Reaching Out to Children Who Sell Sex to Survive," *British Journal of Nursing* 5 (1996): 1120–25.

49. Richard J. Estes and Neil A. Weiner, *The Commercial Sexual Exploitation of Children in the U.S., Canada, and Mexico* (Philadelphia: University of Pennsylvania, 2002), 11.

50. Ray, *Lesbian, Gay, Bisexual, and Transgender Youth*, 57.

51. Wikipedia, the Free Encyclopedia, "Sexual Slavery," http://en.wikipedia .org/wiki/Sexual_slavery; Wikipedia, the free Encyclopedia, "Forced prostitution," http://en.wikipedia.org/wiki/Forced_prostitution.

52. Susan Moran, "New World Havens of Oldest Profession," *Insight on the News* 9 (1993): 14.

53. Evelina Giobbe, "An Analysis of Individual, Institutional and Cultural Pimping," *Michigan Journal of Gender and Law* 1 (1983): 43.

54. Flowers, *The Prostitution of Women and Girls*, 97.

55. Ibid.

56. Dorothy H. Bracey, *"Baby-Pros": Preliminary Profiles of Juvenile Prostitutes* (New York: John Jay Press, 1979), 23.

57. Cited in York and Knight, "Reality Check on Homeless Gay Teens."

58. Pamela Miller, Peter Donahue, Dave Este, and Marvin Hofer, "Experiences of Being Homeless or at Risk of Being Homeless among Canadian Youths," *Adolescence* 39, 156 (2004): 741.

59. Quoted in R. Barri Flowers, *The Adolescent Criminal: An Examination of Today's Juvenile Offender* (Jefferson, NC: McFarland, 2009), 59.

60. Flowers, *The Prostitution of Women and Girls*, 58–59.

Chapter 4

1. Cited in Wikipedia, the Free Encyclopedia, "Prostitution in Nevada," http:// en.wikipedia.org/wiki/Prostitution_in_Nevada.

2. Ibid., "Prostitution and the Law," http://en.wikipedia.org/wiki/Prostitution_ and_the_Law. See also Melissa H. Ditmore, *Encyclopedia of Prostitution and Sex Work*, Vol. 2 (Westport, CT: Greenwood, 2006); Marina Della Giusta, Maria Di Tommaso, and Steinar Strom, *Sex Markets: The Denied Industry* (New York: Routledge, 2008).

3. See, for example, Katherine Gregory, *The Everyday Lives of Sex Workers in the Netherlands* (New York: Routledge, 2005); Wikipedia, the Free Encyclopedia, "Prostitution in the United Kingdom," http://en.wikipedia.org/wiki/Prostitution_ in_the_United_Kingdom.

4. See, for example, Wikipedia, the Free Encyclopedia, "Prostitution in Canada," http://en.wikipedia.org/wiki/Prostitution_in_Canada; Wikipedia, the Free Encyclopedia, "Prostitution in Australia," http://en.wikipedia.org/wiki/Prostitution_ in_Australia.

5. Wikipedia, "Prostitution and the Law."

6. Ibid. See also Wikipedia, the Free Encyclopedia, "Prostitution," http://en .wikipedia.org/wiki/Prostitution; New World Encyclopedia, "Prostitution," http:// www.newworldencyclopedia.org/entry/Prostitution.

7. Wikipedia, "Prostitution and the Law."

8. Cited in R. Barri Flowers, *The Prostitution of Women and Girls* (Jefferson, NC: McFarland, 2009), 171. See also Petrien Venema and Jan Visser, "Safer Prostitution: New Approach in Holland," in *AIDS, Drugs, and Prostitution,* ed. Martin A. Plant, 42 (London: Routledge, 1990).

9. Wikipedia, the Free Encyclopedia, "De Wallen," http://en.wikipedia.org/wiki/De_Wallen.

10. Wikipedia, the Free Encyclopedia, "Prostitution in the Netherlands," http://en.wikipedia.org/wiki/Prostitution_in_the_Netherlands.

11. Cited in Marlise Simons, "Amsterdam Tries Upscale Fix for Red-Light District Crime," *New York Times,* February 24, 2008, http://www.nytimes.com/2008/02/24/world/europe/24amsterdam.html?_r=1&scp=1&sq=amersterdam%20tries%20upscale%20fix%20for%20red%20light%20district%20crime&st=cse.

12. Venema and Visser, "Safer Prostitution," 42.

13. Wikipedia, "Prostitution in the Netherlands."

14. Quoted in Simons, "Amsterdam Tries Upscale Fix for Red-Light District Crime."

15. Wikia Education, the Psychology Wiki, "Prostitution," http://psychology.wikia.com/wiki/Prostitution.

16. Wikipedia, the Free Encyclopedia, "Prostitution in the United Kingdom," http://en.wikipedia.org/wiki/Prostitution_in_the_United_Kingdom.

17. Ibid.

18. Cited in Flowers, *The Prostitution of Women and Girls*, 173.

19. Sheron Boyle, *Working Girls and Their Men* (London: Smith Grypon, 1994), 68.

20. Flowers, *The Prostitution of Women and Girls*, p. 173; Boyle, *Working Girls and Their Men*, 161; Ruth Thomas, "AIDS Risks: Alcohol, Drugs, and the Sex Industry," in *AIDS, Drugs, and Prostitution,* ed. Martin A. Plant, 88 (London: Routledge, 1990).

21. Flowers, *The Prostitution of Women and Girls*, 165–75; Richard Goodall, *The Comfort of Sin: Prostitutes and Prostitution in the 1990s* (Kent, UK: Renaissance Books, 1995), 12–13, 210, 218; Lynn Darling, "Havana at Midnight," *Esquire* 123 (May 1995), 98.

22. Barbara G. Brents, Crystal A. Jackson, and Kathryn Hausbeck, *The State of Sex: Tourism, Sex and Sin in the New American Heartland* (New York: Routledge, 2009); Alexa Albert, *Brothel: Mustang Ranch and Its Women* (New York: Random House, 2002).

23. "Prostitution in Nevada;" Wikia Education, "Prostitution."

24. Cited in Sarah Netter, "Prostitution Not Just for Women: Nevada Brothel Cleared to Hire Men," *ABC News/Money* (January 7, 2010), http://abcnews.go.com/Business/shady-lady-ranch-cleared-legal-male-prostitutes/story?id=9493257&page=1.

25. Ibid. Melissa Farley, *Prostitution and Trafficking in Nevada: Making the Connections* (San Francisco: Prostitution Research and Education, 2007).

26. Cited in Netter, "Prostitution Not Just for Women."

27. Cited in "Prostitution in America: Diane Sawyer Special Examines World's Oldest Profession," *ABC News/20/20* (March 19, 2008), http://abcnews.go.com/2020/story?id=4480892&page=1.

28. Wikipedia, "Prostitution in Nevada."

29. World Famous Mustang Ranch, http://www.worldfamousbrothel.com/wfhome.php; Albert, *Brothel: Mustang Ranch and Its Women.*

30. Wikipedia, the Free Encyclopedia, "Mustang Ranch," http://en.wikipedia.org/wiki/Mustang_Ranch.

31. Neal Karlinsky and Alyssa Litoff, "Economic Tough Times Hit Nevada Brothel," *ABC News* (November 22, 2008), http://abcnews.go.com/Business/Economy/story?id=6308834&page=1.

32. Ibid.; World Famous Mustang Ranch.

33. Wikipedia, the Free Encyclopedia, "Love Ranch," http://en.wikipedia.org/wiki/Love_Ranch; The Internet Movie Database, *Love Ranch*, http://www.imdb.com/title/tt1125929/.

34. Wikipedia, the Free Encyclopedia, "Moonlite BunnyRanch," http://en.wikipedia.org/wiki/Moonlite_BunnyRanch; *The Oprah Winfrey Show*, "Inside the Moonlite BunnyRanch" (April 29, 2009), http://www.oprah.com/oprahshow/Moonlite-Bunny-Ranch.

35. Ibid.; The Internet Movie Database, *Cathouse* (2002), http://www.imdb.com/title/tt0359056/.

36. Wikipedia, "Prostitution in Nevada."

37. Ibid.

38. Ibid.

39. Ibid.; Netter, "Prostitution Not Just for Women."

40. Wikipedia, "Prostitution in Nevada."

41. Elizabeth Joseph, "Sex for Hire: Real Stories of Prostitution in America," ABC News (March 24, 2008), http://abcnews.go.com/2020/story?id=4495721&page=1.

42. Wikipedia, "Prostitution in Nevada."

43. Ibid.

44. Quoted in Joseph, "Sex for Hire."

45. "Prostitution in America."

46. Alice Gomstyn, "The Perks of High End Prostitution," *ABC News* (May 11, 2008), http://abcnews.go.com/Business/IndustryInfo/story?id=4428608&page=1.

47. "Prostitution in Nevada."

48. Quoted in Alice Gomstyn, "The Perks of High End Prostitution."

49. Karlinsky and Litoff, "Economic Tough Times Hit Nevada Brothel."

50. Ibid.

51. Joseph, "Sex for Hire."

52. Ibid.

53. Ibid.

54. Wikipedia, "Prostitution in America."

55. Joseph, "Sex for Hire."

56. Netter, "Prostitution Not Just for Women."

57. Wikipedia, the Free Encyclopedia, "Shady Lady Ranch," http://en.wikipedia .org/wiki/Shady_Lady_Ranch; Kasey Jones, "Los Angeles Porn Actor Now the First Legal Gigolo in the US," *LA Examiner,* January 22, 2010, http://www.examiner .com/x-28270-LA-Headlines-Examiner~y2010m1d22-Los-Angeles-porn-actor- now-the-first-legal-gigolo-in-the-US.

58. Netter, "Prostitution Not Just for Women."

59. Ibid.

60. Ibid.

61. Tracy Quan, "Male Prostitution Comes to Nevada," *Guardian,* January 20, 2010, http://www.guardian.co.uk/commentisfree/cifamerica/2010/jan/20/male- prostitution-nevada-brothel.

62. "Shady Lady Ranch."

63. Netter, "Prostitution Not Just for Women."

64. Quoted in Ibid.

65. "Shady Lady Ranch."

66. Flowers, *The Prostitution of Women and Girls*, 161.

67. Julie Bindel, "It's Like You Sign a Contract to Be Raped," *Guardian,* September 2, 2007, http://www.guardian.co.uk/world/2007/sep/07/usa.gender; Farley, *Prostitution and Trafficking In Nevada*; Barbara G. Brents and Kathryn Hausbeck, "Violence and Legalized Brothel Prostitution in Nevada: Examining Safety, Risk and Prostitution Policy," *Journal of Interpersonal Violence* 20, 3 (2005): 270–95; Ronald Weitzer, ed., *Sex for Sale: Prostitution, Pornography and the Sex Industry* (New York: Taylor and Francis, 1999).

68. Rosemary Black, "Pregnant 'Cathouse' Star Brooke Phillips Was Shot, Stabbed, and Slashed, the Autopsy Reveals," *New York Daily News,* November 24, 2009, http:// www.nydailynews.com/news/national/2009/11/24/2009-11-24_pregnant_cathouse_ star_brooke_phillips_was_shot_stabbed_and_slashed_the_autopsy_.htm.

69. Anastasia Volkonsky, "Legalizing the 'Profession' Would Sanction the Abuse," *Insight on the News* 11 (1995): 21.

70. Ibid.

71. Quoted in "Prostitution in Nevada."

72. Volkonsky, "Legalizing the 'Profession,'" 21; Laura Miller, "Prostitution," *Harper's Bazaar* 3400 (March 1995), 210.

73. Flowers, *The Prostitution of Women and Girls*, 161.

74. Bob Herbert, "Op-Ed Columnist; Fantasies, Well Meant," *New York Times,* September 11, 2007, http://query.nytimes.com/gst/fullpage.html?res=9E03E0DF 1430F932A2575AC0A9619C8B63&sec=&spon=&&scp=8&sq=bob%20herbert+ nevada%20brothel%20prostitution&st=cse.

75. Quoted in "Prostitution in Nevada."

76. Cited in Ibid.

77. Flowers, *The Prostitution of Women and Girls*, 154–55.

78. Elizabeth Bernstein, *Temporarily Yours: Intimacy, Authenticity, and the Commerce of Sex* (Chicago: University of Chicago Press, 2007), 78.

79. Quoted in Miller, "Prostitution," 210.

80. Cited in Flowers, *The Prostitution of Women and Girls*, 155.

81. Quoted in Miller, "Prostitution," 210.

82. Ibid.

83. Ibid.

84. Bernstein, *Temporarily Yours*, 77.

85. Flowers, *The Prostitution of Women and Girls*, 160.

Chapter 5

1. Merriam-Webster Online, "Call Girl," http://www.merriam-webster.com/dictionary/call+girl.

2. Quoted in R. Barri Flowers, *The Prostitution of Women and Girls* (Jefferson, NC: McFarland, 2009), 54.

3. Ibid., 55.

4. Karen E. Rosenblum, "Female Deviance and the Female Sex Role: A Preliminary Investigation," *British Journal of Sociology* 26 (1975): 173–78.

5. Flowers, *The Prostitution of Women and Girls*, 55.

6. R. Barri Flowers, *Female Crime, Criminals and Cellmates: An Exploration of Female Criminality and Delinquency* (Jefferson, NC: McFarland, 2009), 110.

7. "Ex 'Hollywood Madam' Heidi Fleiss Hit with Felony Drug Charge," Fox News (July 11, 2008), http://www.foxnews.com/story/0,2933,381131,00.html; Sydney Biddle Barrows and William Novak, *Mayflower Madam: The Secret Life of Sydney Biddle Barrows* (New York: HarperCollins, 1986); Jody B. Gibson, *Secrets of a Hollywood Super Madam* (Los Angeles: Corona Books, 2007); Wikipedia, the Free Encyclopedia, "Deborah Jeane Palfrey," en.wikipedia.org/wiki/Deborah_Jeane_Palfrey.

8. Alice Gomstyn, "The Perks of High End Prostitution," *ABC News* (March 11, 2008), http://abcnews.go.com/Business/IndustryInfo/story?id=4428608&page=1.

9. Wikipedia, the Free Encyclopedia, "Emperors Club VIP," http://en.wikipedia.org/wiki/Emperors_Club_VIP; Kimberly Launter and Katie Escherich, "Ashley Dupré Exclusive: 'My Side of the Story,'" *ABC News/20/20* (November 19, 2008), http://abcnews.go.com/2020/story?id=6280407&page=1.

10. Joseph D. Wilcox, "Madam Offers Few Regrets about Demise of Brothel," *TribLive.com* (October 11, 2002), http://www.pittsburghlive.com/x/dailycourier/sports/s_96266.html.

11. Ibid.

12. Quoted in Linda Lee, "The World (and Underworld) of the Professional Call Girl," *New Woman* (January 1988), 61.

13. Wikipedia, the Free Encyclopedia, "Brothel," http://en.wikipedia.org/wiki/Brothel.

14. Oskar Garcia, "Country's First Legal Gigolo Starts Work in Nevada," *Seattle Times,* January 22, 2010, http://seattletimes.nwsource.com/html/nationworld/2010859290_apusnevadagigolo.html.

15. Gomstyn, "The Perks of High End Prostitution;" Wilcox, "Madam Offers Few Regrets about Demise of Brothel;" "A Crackdown on Call Girls," *Newsweek* (September 2, 2002), http://www.newsweek.com/2002/09/01/a-crackdown-on-call-girls.html.

16. Brian Kates, "Elaborate Hooker Ring Busted," *New York Daily News,* September 29, 2002, http://www.nydailynews.com/archives/news/2002/09/29/2002-09-29_elaborate_hooker_ring_busted.html.

17. Glynn Wilson, "New Orleans Abuzz with Canal Street Brothel," *The Southerner* (June 16, 2002), http://www.southerner.net/v3n1_2002/brothel.html

18. Wilcox, "Madam Offers Few Regrets about Demise of Brothel."

19. Kates, "Elaborate Hooker Ring Busted."

20. Quoted in Robert Karen, "The World of the Middle Class Prostitute," *Cosmopolitan* 202 (January 1987), 205.

21. Quoted in "Wolseley Home Used as Brothel, ex-Prostitute Confirms," *CBC News* (September 10, 2009), http://www.cbc.ca/canada/manitoba/story/2009/09/10/mb-brothel-leblanc-winnipeg.html. See also Jeff Wilkins and Alison Gendar, "Vice Cops Raid Grimy Midtown Teen Sex Brothel," *New York Daily News,* August 14, 2009, http://www.nydailynews.com/news/ny_crime/2009/08/15/index.html.

22. Wikipedia, the Free Encyclopedia, "Escort Agency," http://en.wikipedia.org/wiki/Escort_agency.

23. Ibid.; Wikia Education, the Psychology Wiki, "Prostitution," http://psychology.wikia.com/wiki/Prostitution.

24. Quoted in Mike Celizic, "Former Call Girl Opens Up about the Industry," TodayShow.com (March 12, 2008), http://www.msnbc.msn.com/id/23589422.

25. Marcus Baram, "What Makes a Woman Become an Escort?" *ABC News* (March 14, 2008), http://abcnews.go.com/US/story?id=4451781&page=1.

26. Quoted in Ibid.

27. Quoted in Launier and Escherich, "Ashley Dupré Exclusive."

28. Ibid.

29. Elizabeth Bernstein, *Temporarily Yours: Intimacy, Authenticity, and the Commerce of Sex* (Chicago: University of Chicago Press, 2007), 126.

30. Wikipedia, the Free Encyclopedia, "Girlfriend Experience," http://en.wikipedia.org/wiki/Girlfriend_experience.

31. Elizabeth Joseph, "Sex for Hire: Real Stories of Prostitution in America," *ABC News* (March 24, 2008), http://abcnews.go.com/2020/story?id=4495721&page=1.

32. Olivia Perkins, "I Am a High-Class Call Girl," *Cosmopolitan* 215 (October 1993), 96. See also Barbara Ignoto, *Confessions of a Part-Time Call Girl* (New York: Dell, 1986).

33. Quoted in Baram, "What Makes a Woman Become an Escort?"

34. Quoted in Gomstyn, "The Perks of High End Prostitution."

35. Cited in "Dirty Money: The Business of High End Prostitution," *CNBC*, http://www.cnbc.com/id/26869953?__source=vty|dirtymoney|&par=vty.

36. "The Economics of High End Prostitution," MoreIntelligentLife.com (April 10, 2008), http://moreintelligentlife.com/node/964. See also Viviana A. Zelizer, *The Purchase of Intimacy* (Princeton, NJ: Princeton University Press, 2007).

37. William Sherman, "Inside the World of High-Priced Hookers," *New York Daily News,* March 16, 2008, http://www.nydailynews.com/news/2008/03/16/2008-03-16_inside_the_world_of_highpriced_hookers.html.

38. Quoted in Ibid.

39. Ibid.

40. Ibid.

41. "Dirty Money: The Business of High End Prostitution."

42. Ibid. See also John Dececco, Kerwin Brook, Jill Nagle, and Baruch Gould, *Male Lust: Pleasure, Power, and Transformation* (New York: Routledge, 2000).

43. "The Economics of High End Prostitution."

44. Quoted in Bernstein, *Temporarily Yours,* 123. See also Katherine Frank, *G-Strings and Sympathy: Strip Club Regulars and Male Desire* (Durham, NC: Duke University Press, 2002), 25.

45. Bernstein, *Temporarily Yours,* 123. See also Kerr Fuffle and Roscoe Spanks, *Paying for Sex: The Gentlemen's Guide to Web Porn, Strip Clubs, Prostitutes & Escorts—Without Humiliation, Job Loss, Bankruptcy, Infection, Bloodshed or Incarceration* (Bloomington, IN: Trafford Publishing, 2006).

46. Quoted in Jane Ridley, "Secrets of the High-End Hookers," *New York Daily News,* August 10, 2006, http://www.nydailynews.com/archives/entertainment/2006/08/10/2006-08-10_secrets_ofthe_high-end_hooke.html.

47. Vicky Ward, "The Business Side of Prostitution," *CNBC* (November 9, 2008), http://www.cnbc.com/id/15840232?video=924626302&play=1.

48. Sherman, "Inside the World of High-Priced Hookers."

49. Tracy Quan, "The Work Ethic," *CNBC* (October 26, 2008), http://www.cnbc.com/id/15840232?video=907167785&play=1.

50. Cited in "Dirty Money: The Business of High End Prostitution;" Flowers, *Female Crime, Criminals and Cellmates.*

51. "Emperors Club: All about Eliot Spitzer's Alleged Prostitution Ring," *Huffington Post* (March 10, 2008), http://www.huffingtonpost.com/2008/03/10/emperors-club-all-about-e_n_90768.html.

52. Quoted in Ibid.

53. Scott Michels, "Craigslist Threatened with Criminal Investigation," *ABC News* (May 5, 2009), http://abcnews.go.com/TheLaw/story?id=7507090&page=1; "Lawsuit Accuses Craigslist of Promoting Prostitution," *CNN* (May 5, 2009), http://www.cnn.com/2009/CRIME/03/05/craigs.list.prostitution/index.html;

"The Craigslist Killer: Seven Days of Rage," *48 Hours Mystery* (September 16, 2009), http://www.cbsnews.com/stories/2009/09/16/48hours/main5315790.shtml.

54. Bernstein, *Temporarily Yours*, 93.

55. Quoted in Ibid.

56. Quoted in "Dirty Money: The Business of High End Prostitution."

57. John Stossel, Catherine Brosseau, and Andrew Kirell, "New Dating Web Sites Bring Sugar Daddies, Babies Together at Last," ABC News (August 20, 2009), http://abcnews.go.com/2020/Stossel/story?id=8364856.

58. Ibid.

59. Cited in Flowers, *The Prostitution of Women and Girls*, 59.

60. John E. Exner, Jr., Joyce Wylie, Antonnia Laura, Tracey Parrill, "Some Psychological Characteristics of Prostitutes," *Journal of Personality Assessment* 41 (1977): 483.

61. Freda Adler, *Sisters in Crime: The Rise of the New Female Criminal* (New York: McGraw-Hill, 1975), 73.

62. Martha L. Stein, *Lovers, Friends, Slaves: The Nine Male Sexual Types, Their Psycho-Sexual Transactions with Call Girls* (New York: Berkley, 1974), 22.

63. Harold Greenwald, *The Elegant Prostitute: A Social and Psychoanalytic Study* (New York: Walker and Company, 1970). See also Harold Greenwald, *Call Girls* (San Diego, CA: Libra Publishers, 1988).

64. Ibid., 242.

65. Quoted in Lee H. Bowker, *Women, Crime, and the Criminal Justice System* (Lexington, MA: Lexington Books, 1978), 151–52.

66. James H. Bryan, "Occupational Ideologies and Individual Attitudes of Call Girls," *Social Problems* 13 (1966): 441–50; James H. Bryan, "Apprenticeship in Prostitution," *Social Problems* 12 (1965): 287–97.

67. Stein, *Lovers, Friends, Slaves*, 1–2, 317, 320.

68. Ibid., 317; Flowers, *The Prostitution of Women and Girls*, 60.

69. Quoted in Lee, "The World (and Underworld) of the Professional Call Girl," 63. See also Delores French, *Working: My Life as a Prostitute* (Chicago: Trafalgar Square Publishing, 1977).

70. See, for example, "A Crackdown on Call Girls;" "D.C. Madam Found Hanged," CNN (May 1, 2008), http://www.cnn.com/2008/POLITICS/05/01/dc.madam/index.html; Natalie McLennan, *The Price: My Rise and Fall as Natalia, New York's #1 Escort* (Beverly Hills, CA: Phoenix Books, 2008); William Rashbaum, "Spitzer Antagonist Advises Ex-Madam's Campaign," *New York Times,* April 16, 2010, http://www.nytimes.com/2010/04/17/nyregion/17stone.html.

71. Anthony Cormier, "Police Raid Sarasota Escort Service," *HeraldTribune .com* (February 4, 2010), http://www.heraldtribune.com/article/20100204/article/2041095?p=all&tc=pgall; "Suspect Arrested in Call Girl Ring," *Houston News,* March 18, 2009, http://www.click2houston.com/news/18961545/detail.html; "Brooklyn Woman Pleads Guilty to Laundering Money Earned from Prostitution Businesses,"

FBI Press Release (June 21, 2007), http://newhaven.fbi.gov/dojpressrel/2007/nh062107a.htm.

Chapter 6

1. YourDictionary.com, "Streetwalker Definition," http://www.yourdictionary.com/streetwalker.

2. Paul J. Goldstein, *Prostitution and Drugs* (Lexington, MA: Lexington Books, 1979), 35.

3. Wikipedia, the Free Encyclopedia, "Street Prostitution," http://en.wikipedia.org/wiki/Street_prostitution.

4. Barbara Goldsmith, "Women on the Edge: A Reporter at Large," *New Yorker* 69 (April 26, 1993), 66.

5. "Oakland Battles Wave of Teenage Prostitution," *KTVU.com* (May 7, 2009), http://www.ktvu.com/news/19388341/detail.html.

6. Adrian N. LeBlanc, "I'm a Shadow," *Seventeen* 52 (March 1993), 214.

7. R. Barri Flowers, *The Prostitution of Women and Girls* (Jefferson, NC: McFarland, 2009), 48.

8. Quoted in Wikipedia, the Free Encyclopedia, "Estella Marie Thompson," http://en.wikipedia.org/wiki/Estella_Marie_Thompson.

9. Flowers, *The Prostitution of Women and Girls*, 48.

10. Ibid., 48–49.

11. R. Barri Flowers, *Street Kids: The Lives of Runaway and Thrownaway Teens* (Jefferson, NC: McFarland, 2010), 134–36; R. Barri Flowers, *Runaway Kids and Teenage Prostitution: America's Lost, Abandoned, and Sexually Exploited Children* (New York: Praeger, 2001), 107–10.

12. Flowers, *The Prostitution of Women and Girls*, 49; Mia Spangenberg, "Prostituted Youth in New York City: An Overview," *ECPAT-US* (2001), http://www.libertadlatina.org/US_ECPAT_Child_Prostitution_NYC.htm.

13. Flowers, *The Prostitution of Women and Girls*, 21. See also Eleanor M. Miller, *Street Woman* (Philadelphia: Temple University Press, 1987).

14. Ibid., p. 49; Goldsmith, "Women on the Edge," 66.

15. Cited in Spangenberg, "Prostituted Youth in New York City."

16. Ibid.

17. The Enablers, *Juvenile Prostitution in Minnesota: The Report of a Research Project* (St. Paul, MN: The Enablers, 1978), 18; Sparky Harlan, Luanne L. Rodgers, and Brian Slattery, *Male and Female Adolescent Prostitution: Huckleberry House Sexual Minority Youth Services Project* (Washington, DC: U.S. Department of Health and Human Services, 1981), 7.

18. Cited in Flowers, *The Prostitution of Women and Girls*, 21.

19. R. Barri Flowers, *Female Crime, Criminals and Cellmates: An Exploration of Female Criminality and Delinquency* (Jefferson, NC: McFarland, 2009), 151; Mimi

H. Silbert, *Sexual Assault of Prostitutes: Phase One* (Washington, DC: National Institute of Health, 1980), 10.

20. LeBlanc, "I'm a Shadow," 214.

21. Ibid.

22. See, for example, George Gardner, "Hookers Go Hi-Tech, Advertise on Craigslist," *Tech.Blorge* (July 26, 2007), http://tech.blorge.com/Structure:%20/ 2007/07/26/hookers-go-hi-tech-advertise-on-craigslist; Ben Winslow, "Ogden Police Make Prostitution Bust," *Deseret News*, February 29, 2008, http://www.deseretnews .com/article/1,5143,695257579,00.html.

23. Celia Williamson and Lynda M. Baker, "Women in Street-Based Prostitution," *Qualitative Social Work* 8, no. 1 (2009): 27–44.

24. Jennifer James, "Two Domains of Streetwalker Argot," *Anthropological Linguistics* 14 (1972): 174–75.

25. Flowers, *The Prostitution of Women and Girls*, 50.

26. Ibid.

27. Elizabeth Bernstein, *Temporarily Yours: Intimacy, Authenticity, and the Commerce of Sex* (Chicago: University of Chicago Press, 2007), 44.

28. Ibid., 42–43.

29. Ibid., 44.

30. Ibid., 48–49.

31. National Center for Missing and Exploited Children, *Female Juvenile Prostitution: Problem and Response*, 2nd ed. (Alexandria, VA: National Center for Missing and Exploited Children, 2002), 20.

32. Flowers, *The Prostitution of Women and Girls*, 18.

33. Flowers, *Street Kids*, 134–7; Kathleen Barry, *The Prostitution of Sexuality* (New York: New York University Press, 1995), 198.

34. Flowers, *Runaway Kids and Teenage Prostitution*, 119–23. See also Clare Tattersall, *Drugs, Runaways, and Teen Prostitution* (New York: Rosen, 1999); U.S. Department of Health and Human Services, Family Youth and Services Bureau, *Youth with Runaway, Throwaway, and Homeless Experiences: Prevalence, Drug Use, and Other At-Risk Behaviors* (Silver Springs, MD: National Clearinghouse on Families and Youth, 1995).

35. Richard J. Estes and Neil A. Weiner, *The Commercial Sexual Exploitation of Children in the U.S., Canada, and Mexico* (Philadelphia: University of Pennsylvania, 2002), 64.

36. Flowers, *The Prostitution of Women and Girls*, 50; Joan J. Johnson, *Teen Prostitution* (Danbury, CT: Franklin Watts, 1992), 78.

37. Bernstein, *Temporarily Yours*, 54.

38. Ibid.

39. Michael S. Scott and Kelly Dedel, *Street Prostitution*, 2nd ed. (Washington, DC: Office of Community Oriented Policing Services, 2006), http://www.cops .usdoj.gov/files/RIC/Publications/e10062633.txt; Anne Rasmusson, "Commercial

Sexual Exploitation of Children: A Literature Review," Alliance for Speaking the Truths on Prostitution and Center for Urban and Regional Affairs (June 1, 1999), http://members.shaw.ca/pdg/exploitation_of_children.html#_Toc452540153.

40. Ibid.

41. Spangenberg, "Prostituted Youth in New York City."

42. Bernstein, *Temporarily Yours*, 42–43.

43. Ibid.

44. Ibid., 44.

45. Ibid.

46. Gardner, "Hookers Go Hi-Tech."

47. Cited in Wikipedia, "Street Prostitution."

48. Scott and Dedel, *Street Prostitution*.

49. Harlan, Rodgers, and Slattery, *Male and Female Adolescent Prostitution*, 21.

50. Mimi H. Silbert, "Delancey Street Study: Prostitution and Sexual Assault," summary of Results, Delancey Street Foundation, San Francisco, 1982, 3.

51. Ronald L. Simons and Les B. Whitbeck, "Sexual Abuse as a Precursor to Prostitution and Victimization among Adolescent and Adult Homeless Women," *Journal of Family Issues* 12, 3 (1991): 361–79.

52. Flowers, *Runaway Kids and Teenage Prostitution*; Flowers, *Street Kids*.

53. Cited in Flowers, *The Prostitution of Women and Girls*, 52.

54. Jennifer James, "Prostitutes and Prostitution," in Edward Sagarin and Fred Montanino, eds., *Deviants: Voluntary Actors in a Hostile World* (Morrison, NJ: General Learning Press, 1977), 390–91.

55. Scott and Dedel, *Street Prostitution*.

56. Ibid.

57. Ibid.

58. Ibid.

59. Ibid.; Flowers, *Street Kids*.

60. Amanda Roxburgh, Louisa Degenhardt, Jan Copeland, and Briony Larance, "Drug Dependence and Associated Risks among Female Street-Based Sex Workers in the Greater Sydney Area, Australia," *Substance Use and Misuse* 43, 8/9 (2008): 1202–17.

61. Qing Li, Xiaoming Li, and Bonita Stanton, "Alcohol Use among Female Sex Workers and Male Clients: An Integrative Review of Global Literature," *Alcohol and Alcoholism* 45, 2 (2010): 188–99.

62. National Center for Missing and Exploited Children, *Prostitution of Children and Child-Sex Tourism* (Alexandria, VA: National Center for Missing and Exploited Children, 1999), 2.

63. Ibid., 6.

64. Jessica M. Edwards, Carolyn T. Halpern, and Wendee M. Wechsberg, "Correlates of Exchanging Sex for Drugs or Money among Women Who Use Crack Cocaine," *AIDS Education and Prevention* 18, no. 5 (2006): 420–29.

65. Scott and Dedel, *Street Prostitution.*

66. Kara M. Brawn and Dominique Roe-Sepowitz, "Female Juvenile Prostitutes: Exploring the Relationship to Substance Use," *Children and Youth Services Review* 30, no. 12 (2008): 1395–1402.

67. LeBlanc, "I'm a Shadow," 214.

68. Brenda Mosedale, Christos Kouimtsidis, and Martina Reynolds, "Sex Work, Substance Misuse and Service Provision: The Experiences of Female Sex Workers in South London," *Drugs: Education, Prevention and Policy* 16, no. 4 (2009): 355–63.

69. Spangenberg, "Prostituted Youth in New York City."

70. Ibid.

71. Nancy E. Walker, "Executive Summary: How Many Teens Are Prostituted?" fce.msu.edu/Family_Impact_Seminars/pdf/2002-2.pdf.

72. Tattersall, *Drugs, Runaways, and Teen Prostitution*, 28.

73. Flowers, *Street Kids*, pp. 98–101; John Noell, Paul Rohde, John Seeley, and Linda Ochs, "Childhood Sexual Abuse, Adolescent Sexual Coercion and Sexually Transmitted Infection Acquisition among Homeless Female Adolescents," *Child Abuse and Neglect* 25 (2001): 137–48; Doreen Rosenthal and Susan Moore, "Homeless Youths: Sexual and Drug-Related Behavior, Sexual Beliefs and HIV/AIDS Risk," *AIDS Care* 6, no. 1 (1994): 83–94.

74. Scott and Dedel, *Street Prostitution.*

75. Ronald Weitzer, ed., *Sex for Sale: Prostitution, Pornography and the Sex Industry* (New York: Taylor and Francis, 1999).

76. Goldsmith, "Women on the Edge," 65–66.

77. Cited in Ibid., 65.

78. Cited in Flowers, *The Prostitution of Women and Girls*, 60.

79. Cited in Jo Moreland, "Area Study Says Female Teen Prostitution 'Common,'" *North County Times*, November 2, 2005, http://nctimes.com/news/local/sdcounty/article_f7d2d30c-f678-5a86-855e-89843f668fd2.html.

80. Cited in *Prostitution of Children and Child–Sex Tourism*, 8.

81. Cited in Flowers, *Street Kids*, 101. See also Mary J. Rotheram-Borus, Heino Meyer-Bahlburg, Cheryl Koopman, Margaret Rosario, Theresa M. Exner, Ronald Henderson, Marjory Matthieu, and Rhoda Gruen, "Lifetime Sexual Behavior among Runaway Males and Females," *Journal of Sex Research* 29, no. 1 (1992): 15–29.

82. Cited in the National Network for Youth, "NN4Y Issue Brief: Unaccompanied Youth Overview," p. 5, http://www.nn4youth.org/system/files/IssueBrief_Unaccompanyed_youth.pdf.

83. Wikipedia, the Free Encyclopedia, "Mammary Intercourse," http://en.wikipedia.org/wiki/Mammary_intercourse.

84. Ibid., Wikipedia, the Free Encyclopedia, "Oral Sex," http://en.wikipedia.org/wiki/Oral_sex.

85. Goldsmith, "Women on the Edge," 65.

86. Ibid., 74.

87. Linda Lee, "The World (and Underworld) of the Professional Call Girl," *New Woman* (January 1988), 62.

88. W. Robert Lange, Frederick R. Snyder, David Lozovsky, Vivek Kaistha, Mary A. Kaczaniuk, and Jerome H. Jaffe, "HIV Infection in Baltimore: Antibody Seroprevalence Rates among Parenteral Drug Abusers and Prostitutes," *Maryland Medical Journal* 36, no. 9 (1987): 757–61.

89. Flowers, *Street Kids*, 107–109; *Prostitution of Children and Child-Sex Tourism*, 7–8; Janice G. Raymond, "Health Effects of Prostitution," in Donna M. Hughes and Claire M. Roche, eds., *Making the Harm Visible: Global Sexual Exploitation of Women and Girls* (New York: Coalition Against Trafficking in Women, 1999); Rasmusson, "Commercial Sexual Exploitation of Children."

90. Cited in Flowers, *The Prostitution of Women and Girls*, 49.

91. Cited in Spangenberg, "Prostituted Youth in New York City."

92. Raymond, "Health Effects of Prostitution."

93. *Youth with Runaway, Throwaway, and Homeless Experiences*, 7.

94. Nicholas Ray, *Lesbian, Gay, Bisexual, and Transgender Youth: An Epidemic of Homelessness* (New York: National Gay and Lesbian Task Force Policy Institute and National Coalition for the Homeless, 2006), 58; Linda L. Halcon and Alan R. Lifson, "Prevalence and Predictors of Sexual Risks among Homeless Youth," *Journal of Youth and Adolescence* 33, no. 1 (2004): 75–76.

95. Flowers, *The Prostitution of Women and Girls*, 50.

96. Goldsmith, "Women on the Edge," 66.

97. Raymond, "Health Effects of Prostitution;" Flowers, *Street Kids*, 108–109; *Prostitution of Children and Child-Sex Tourism*, 8; James A. Farrow, Robert W. Deisher, Richard Brown, John W. Kulig, and Michele Kipke, "Health and Health Needs of Homeless and Runaway Youth," *Journal of Adolescent Health* 13 (1992): 717–26.

98. Cited in "Street Prostitution."

99. Flowers, *The Prostitution of Women and Girls*, 49.

100. Cited in Goldsmith, "Women on the Edge," 65–66.

101. Quoted in Spangenberg, "Prostituted Youth in New York City."

102. Ibid.

103. See, for example, R. Barri Flowers and H. Loraine Flowers, *Murders in the United States: Crimes, Killers and Victims of the Twentieth Century* (Jefferson, NC: McFarland, 2009); C. Gabrielle Salfati, Alison R. James, and Lynn Ferguson, "Prostitute Homicides: A Descriptive Study," *Journal of Interpersonal Violence* 23, no. 4 (2008): 505–43.

104. See, for example, Flowers and Flowers, *Murders in the United States*; Trevor Marriot, *Jack the Ripper: The 21st Century Investigation* (London: John Blake, 2005); Ann Rule, *Green River, Running Red: The Real Story of the Green River Killer—America's Deadliest Serial Murderer* (New York: Free Press, 2004); Linda Rosencrance, *Ripper* (New York: Pinnacle, 2008).

105. U.S. Department of Justice, Federal Bureau of Investigation, *Crime in the United States 2008*, Table 40 (September 2009), http://www.fbi.gov/ucr/cius2008/data/table_40.html.

106. Cited in "Street Prostitution."

107. R. Barri Flowers, *Women and Criminality: The Woman as Victim, Offender, and Practitioner* (Westport, CT: Greenwood Press, 1987), 129.

108. Flowers, *Runaway Kids and Teenage Prostitution*, 97–99; *Crime in the United States 2008*, Table 39; Nicholas Kristof, "The Pimp's Slaves," *New York Times*, March 16, 2008, http://www.nytimes.com/2008/03/16/opinion/16kristof.html?_r=2&oref=slogin&oref=slogin; Laura Trujillo, "Escort Services Thriving Industry in Portland Area," *Oregonian* (June 7, 1996), B1.

109. See, for example, Geraldine Sealey, "Exposing America's Ugly Child Sex Secret," *ABC News* (December 13, 2009), http://abcnews.go.com/US/story?id=90557&page=1; Aisha Ali, "Washington, DC, A Sexual Playground for Pimps and Johns: Exposing Child Prostitution Rings in DC," *Examiner*, March 17, 2009, http://www.examiner.com/x-1207-DC-Youth-Issues-Examiner~y2009m3d17-Washington-DC-a-sexual-playground-for-child-sex-exploiters-Exposing-child-prostitution.

110. John L. Mitchell, "Prostitute with HIV Faces Felony," *Los Angeles Times*, July 22, 2002, http://articles.latimes.com/2002/jul/22/local/me-hooker22.

Chapter 7

1. Geraldine Sealey, "Exposing America's Ugly Child Sex Secret," ABC News (December 13, 2009), http://abcnews.go.com/US/story?id=90557&page=1.

2. Mia Spangenberg, "Prostituted Youth in New York City: An Overview," *ECPAT-US* (2001), http://www.libertadlatina.org/US_ECPAT_Child_Prostitution_NYC.htm.

3. Ibid.

4. Cited in R. Barri Flowers, *The Prostitution of Women and Girls* (Jefferson, NC: McFarland, 2009), 71; R. Barri Flowers, *Street Kids: The Lives of Runaway and Thrownaway Teens* (Jefferson, NC: McFarland, 2010), 131. See also Michelle Stransky and David Finkelhor, *How Many Juveniles Are Involved in Prostitution in the United States?* (Durham, NC: Crimes against Children Research Center, 2008).

5. National Runaway Switchboard, "Keeping America's Runaway and At-Risk Youth Safe and Off the Streets," http://www.1800runaway.org/.

6. U.S. Department of Health and Human Services, Family Youth and Services Bureau, *Youth with Runaway, Throwaway, and Homeless Experiences: Prevalence, Drug Use, and Other At-Risk Behaviors* (Silver Spring, MD: National Clearinghouse on Families and Youth, 1995), E6.

7. R. Barri Flowers, *The Adolescent Criminal: An Examination of Today's Juvenile Offender* (Jefferson, NC: McFarland, 2009), 49–55; Clare Tattersall, *Drugs, Runaways, and Teen Prostitution* (New York: Rosen, 1999), 8.

8. Flowers, *The Adolescent Criminal*, 58. See also D. Kelly Weisberg, *Children of the Night: A Study of Adolescent Prostitution* (Lexington, MA: Lexington Books, 1985), 107.

9. Cited in Flowers, *The Prostitution of Women and Girls*, 82. See also The Enablers, *Juvenile Prostitution in Minnesota: The Report of a Research Project* (St. Paul, MN: The Enablers, 1978), 18.

10. Flowers, *The Adolescent Criminal*, p. 56; Jennifer James, *Entrance into Juvenile Prostitution* (Washington, DC: National Institute of Mental Health, 1980), 19.

11. Flowers, *The Prostitution of Women and Girls*, 82; James, *Entrance into Juvenile Prostitution*, 10.

12. Cited in Flowers, *The Prostitution of Women and Girls*, 82. See also R. Barri Flowers, *Sex Crimes: Perpetrators, Predators, Prostitutes and Victims*, 2nd ed. (Springfield, IL: Charles C. Thomas, 2006), 134–35; Susan Moran, "New World Haven of Oldest Profession," *Insight on the News* 9 (1993): 12–16.

13. Mimi H. Silbert, *Sexual Assault of Prostitutes: Phase One* (Washington, DC: National Institute of Health, 1980), 15.

14. James, *Entrance into Juvenile Prostitution*, 10; Jennifer James, *Entrance into Juvenile Prostitution: Progress Report* (Washington, DC: National Institute of Mental Health, 1978), 53.

15. Sealey, "Exposing America's Ugly Child Sex Secret."

16. Maura G. Crowley, "Female Runaway Behavior and Its Relationship to Prostitution," Master's thesis, Sam Houston State University, Institute of Contemporary Corrections and Behavioral Sciences, 1977.

17. Sparky Harlan, Luanne L. Rodgers, and Brian Slattery, *Male and Female Adolescent Prostitution: Huckleberry House Sexual Minority Youth Services Project* (Washington, DC: U.S. Department of Health and Human Services, 1981), 14.

18. Diana Gray, "Turning Out: A Study of Teenage Prostitution," Master's thesis, University of Washington, 1971, 25.

19. Harlan, Rodgers, and Slattery, *Male and Female Adolescent Prostitution*, 21; Evelina Giobbe, "Confronting the Liberal Lies about Prostitution," in Dorchen Leidholdt and Janice G. Raymond, eds., *The Sexual Liberals and the Attack on Feminism* (New York: Pergamon Press, 1990).

20. Weisberg, *Children of the Night*.

21. See, for example, Susan M. Nadon, Catherine Koverola, and Eduard H. Schudermann, "Antecedents to Prostitution: Childhood Victimization," *Journal of Interpersonal Violence* 13 (1998): 206–21; Daniel S. Campagna and Donald Poffenberger, *The Sexual Trafficking in Children: An Investigation of the Child Sex Trade* (Dover, MA: Auburn House, 1988), 65.

22. R. Barri Flowers, *Runaway Kids and Teenage Prostitution: America's Lost, Abandoned, and Sexually Exploited Children* (New York: Praeger, 2001), 107–11.

23. Susan F. McClanahan, Gary M. McClelland, Karen M. Abram, and Linda A. Teplin, "Pathways into Prostitution among Female Jail Detainees and Their Implications for Mental Health Services," *Psychiatric Services* 50 (1999): 1606–13.

24. National Center for Missing and Exploited Children, *Female Juvenile Prostitution: Problem and Response*, 2nd ed. (Alexandria, VA: National Center for Missing and Exploited Children, 2002), 8.

25. Howard N. Snyder and Melissa Sickmund, *Juvenile Offenders and Victims: 1999 National Report* (Washington, DC: Office of Juvenile Justice and Delinquency Prevention, 1999), 38.

26. Alma C. Molino, "Characteristics of Help-Seeking Street Youth and Non-Street Youth," 2007 National Symposium on Homelessness Research, March 1–2, 2007, http://aspe.hhs.gov/hsp/homelessness/symposium07/molino/index.htm;. National Runaway Switchboard, "NRS Call Statistics," http://www.nrscrisisline.org/news_events/call_stats.html. See also Rebecca P. Sanchez, Martha W. Waller, and Jody M. Greene, "Who Runs? A Demographic Profile of Runaway Youth in the United States," *Journal of Adolescent Health* 39, no. 5 (2006): 778–81.

27. Cited in Patricia Hersch, "Coming of Age on City Streets," *Psychology Today* (July 20, 1986), 31.

28. Quoted in Stephanie Arbarbanel, "Women Who Make a Difference," *Family Circle* 107 (January 11, 1994), 11.

29. Cited in John Blankenship, "Runaways: Juvenile Prostitution Increases with More Teens Fleeing Their Homes," *Register Herald,* August 16, 2008, http://register-herald.com/features/local_story_228110706.html?

30. Arbarbanel, "Women Who Make a Difference," 11.

31. Laurie Schaffner, "Searching for Connection: A New Look at Teenaged Runaways," *Adolescence* 33, no. 31 (1998): 619–28.

32. P. David Kurtz, Gail L. Kurtz, and Sara Jarvis, "Problems of Maltreated Runaway Youth," *Adolescence* 26 (1991): 543–55.

33. See, for example, Kimberly A. Tyler, Les B. Whitbeck, Danny R. Hoyt, and Ana Mari Cauce, "Risk Factors for Sexual Victimization among Male and Female Homeless and Runaway Youth," *Journal of Interpersonal Violence* 19 (2004): 503–20.

34. Myrna Kostash, "Surviving the Streets," *Chatelaine* 67 (October 1994), 103–4. See also Flowers, *The Prostitution of Women and Girls*, 84–85; Weisberg, *Children of the Night*, 117–19.

35. Deidre Pike, "On the Run," *Las Vegas City Life* (August 11, 2004), http://www.lasvegascitylife.com/articles/2004/08/11/cover_story/cover.txt.

36. Dotson Rader, "I Want to Die So I Won't Hurt No More," *Parade Magazine* (August 18, 1985), 5–6.

37. Molino, "Characteristics of Help-Seeking Street Youth and Non-Street Youth."

38. Flowers, *Street Kids*, 82; Marjorie J. Robertson and Paul A. Toro, "Homeless Youth: Research, Intervention, and Policy," in Linda B. Fosburg and Deborah

L. Dennis, eds., *Practical Lessons, the 1998 National Symposium on Homelessness Research* (Washington, DC: U.S. Department of Housing and Urban Development, 1999. http://aspe.hhs.gov/ProgSys/homeless/symposium/3-Youth.htm.

39. *Youth with Runaway, Throwaway, and Homeless Experiences*, 5–6.

40. Pam Oliver, "A Review of Literature on Child Prostitution," *Social Policy Journal of New Zealand* 19 (2002), http://www.thefreelibrary.com/_/print/ PrintArticle.aspx?id=99849275. See also Farquan Haq, "U.S. Children: Street Kids Turn to Sex to Survive," *Inter-Press Service* (March 27, 1996).

41. Richard J. Estes and Neil A. Weiner, *The Commercial Sexual Exploitation of Children in the U.S., Canada, and Mexico* (Philadelphia: University of Pennsylvania, 2002), 11.

42. Oliver, "A Review of Literature on Child Prostitution."

43. David Kihara, "Giuliani's Suppressed Report on Homeless Youth," *The Village Voice* 44, 33 (August 24, 1999), http://village voice.com.

44. Cited in Nicholas Ray, *Lesbian, Gay, Bisexual, and Transgender Youth: An Epidemic of Homelessness* (New York: National Gay and Lesbian Task Force Policy Institute and National Coalition for the Homeless, 2006), 56.

45. Ibid., 57.

46. Flowers, *Street Kids*, 120–21.

47. Nadon, Koverola, and Schudermann, "Antecedents to Prostitution," 206–21.

48. Martin L. Forst and Martha E. Blomquist, *Missing Children: Rhetoric and Reality* (New York: Lexington Books, 1991).

49. Mimi H. Silbert and Ayala M. Pines, "Occupational Hazards of Street Prostitutes," *Criminal Justice and Behavior* 8 (1981): 397; Susan K. Hunter, "Prostitution Is Cruelty and Abuse to Women and Children," *Michigan Journal of Gender and Law* 1, no. 91 (1993): 91–104.

50. Spangenberg, "Prostituted Youth in New York City."

51. Marcia I. Cohen, *Identifying and Combating Juvenile Prostitution: A Manual for Action* (Washington, DC: National Association of Counties Research, 1987); Miriam Saphira, *The Commercial Exploitation of Children* (Auckland, New Zealand: ECPAT, 2001).

52. Spangenberg, "Prostituted Youth in New York City."

53. Quoted in Ibid.

54. "Oakland Battles Wave of Teenage Prostitution," *KTVU.com* (May 7, 2009), http://www.ktvu.com/news/19388341/detail.html.

55. Anne Rasmusson, "Commercial Sexual Exploitation of Children: A Literature Review," Alliance for Speaking the Truths on Prostitution and Center for Urban and Regional Affairs (June 1, 1999), http://members.shaw.ca/pdg/exploitation_of_ children.html#_Toc452540153.

56. Flowers, *Runaway Kids and Teenage Prostitution*, 108–109; Joan J. Johnson, *Teen Prostitution* (Danbury, CT: Franklin Watts, 1992), 108.

57. Flowers, *The Prostitution of Women and Girls*, 80. See also Johnson, *Teen Prostitution*.

58. Flowers, *Street Kids*, 134–37.

59. Cited in Johnson, *Teen Prostitution*, 78. See also Celia Williamson and Terry Cluse-Tolar, "Pimp-Controlled Prostitution: Still an Integral Part of Street Life," *Violence against Women* 8 (2002): 1074–92.

60. Flowers, *Street Kids*, 134–37.

61. Spangenberg, "Prostituted Youth in New York City;" Nicholas Kristof, "The Pimp's Slaves," *New York Times*, March 16, 2008, http://www.nytimes.com/2008/03/16/opinion/16kristof.html?_r=2&oref=slogin&oref=slogin.

62. Flowers, *The Prostitution of Women and Girls*, 80.

63. Spangenberg, "Prostituted Youth in New York City." See also Amy Schalet, Geoffrey Hunt, and Karen Joe-Laidler, "Respectability and Autonomy: The Articulation and Meaning of Sexuality among the Girls in the Gang," *Journal of Contemporary Ethnography* 32 (2003): 108–43; Kit R. Roane, "Gangs Turn to New Trade: Young Prostitutes," *New York Times,* July 11, 1999, 23.

64. Cited in Russell Goldman, "Parents Who Pimp Their Children: The FBI Steps Up Efforts to Catch Parents and the Predators Who Want Their Kids for Sex," *ABC News* (October 8, 2007), http://abcnews.go.com/US/story?id=3691604&page=1.

65. Margot Hornblower, "The Skin Trade," *Time* 141 (June 21, 1993), 44.

66. Flowers, *Runaway Kids and Teenage Prostitution*, 119–24.

67. Flowers, *Street Kids*, 134–36.

68. Hersch, "Coming of Age on City Streets," 32.

69. Deborah Jones, "Pimped," *Chatelaine* 67 (November 1994), 111.

70. Kamika Dunlap and Barbara Grady, "City Comes to Grips with Teen Prostitution," *Oakland Tribune,* April 21, 2008, http://www.insidebayarea.com/teenprostitution/ci_9000424.

71. Flowers, *The Prostitution of Women and Girls*, 79.

72. Quoted in Ibid., 51.

73. Anastasia Volkonsky, "Legalizing the 'Profession' Would Sanction the Abuse," *Insight on the News* 11 (1995): 20.

74. Quoted in Kristof, "The Pimps' Slaves."

75. Quoted in "Oakland Battles Wave of Teenage Prostitution."

76. Quoted in Jones, "Pimped," 112.

77. Michael S. Scott and Kelly Dedel, *Street Prostitution*, 2nd ed. (Washington, DC: Office of Community Oriented Policing Services, 2006), http://www.cops.usdoj.gov/files/RIC/Publications/e10062633.txt; Rasmusson, "Commercial Sexual Exploitation of Children."

78. Barbara Goldsmith, "Women on the Edge: A Reporter at Large," *New Yorker* 69 (April 26, 1993), 65.

79. Adrian N. LeBlanc, "I'm a Shadow," *Seventeen* 52 (March 1993), 216.

80. Quoted in Dunlap and Grady, "City Comes to Grips with Teen Prostitution."

81. Spangenberg, "Prostituted Youth in New York City."

82. Scott and Dedel, *Street Prostitution*, 6.

83. "Crack: A Cheap and Deadly Cocaine Is a Spreading Menace," *Time* 127 (June 12, 1986), p. 18.

84. Kathleen Barry, *The Prostitution of Sexuality* (New York: New York University Press, 1995), 41.

85. Flowers, *The Adolescent Criminal*, 58.

86. Rasmusson, "Commercial Sexual Exploitation of Children." See also Mimi H. Silbert and Ayala M. Pines, "Victimization of Street Prostitutes," *Victimology* 7 (1982): 122–33.

87. Flowers, *Street Kids*, 138–39.

88. Nancy E. Walker, "Executive Summary: How Many Teens Are Prostituted?" fce.msu.edu/Family_Impact_Seminars/pdf/2002-2.pdf. See also Claire E. Sterk, *Tricking and Tripping: Prostitution in the Era of AIDS* (Putnam Valley, NY: Social Change Press, 2000).

89. National Center for Missing and Exploited Children, *Prostitution of Children and Child-Sex Tourism* (Alexandria, VA: National Center for Missing and Exploited Children, 1999), 8. See also Timothy P. Johnson, Jennie R. Aschkenasy, Mary R. Herbers, and Stephen A. Gillenwater, "Self-Reported Risk Factors for AIDS among Homeless Youth," *AIDS Education and Prevention* 8 (1996): 308–22.

90. Tattersall, *Drugs, Runaways, and Teen Prostitution*, 28.

91. Flowers, *Runaway Kids and Teenage Prostitution*, 113–14.

92. Hersch, "Coming of Age on City Streets," 37.

93. Oliver, "A Review of Literature on Child Prostitution."

94. U.S. Department of Justice, Federal Bureau of Investigation, *Crime in the United States 2008*, Tables 39 and 40 (September 2009), http://www.fbi.gov/ucr/cius2008/data/table_40.html.

95. R. Barri Flowers, *Female Crime, Criminals and Cellmates: An Exploration of Female Criminality and Delinquency* (Jefferson, NC: McFarland, 2009); David Finkelhor and Richard Ormrod, *Prostitution of Juveniles: Patterns from NIBRS* (Washington, DC: Office of Justice Programs, 2004), 1–2.

96. Weisberg, *Children of the Night*, 124–28.

97. Bill Callahan, "Prisoners without Chains: For Teen-agers Like Peaches, Coming Back Is an Uphill Battle," *San Diego Union-Tribune*, June 21, 1998, A19.

98. Flowers, *Street Kids*, pp. 139–41; Flowers, *Runaway Kids and Teenage Prostitution*, 95–96.

Chapter 8

1. R. Barri Flowers, *Sex Crimes: Perpetrators, Predators, Prostitutes and Victims*, 2nd ed. (Springfield, IL: Charles C Thomas, 2006), 131. See also Kevin Bales and

Ron Soodalter, *The Slave Next Door: Human Trafficking and Slavery in America Today* (Berkeley, CA: University of California Press, 2009).

2. Wikipedia, the Free Encyclopedia, "Human Trafficking," http://en.wikipedia .org/wiki/Human_trafficking.

3. Ibid. See also Kathryn Cullen-Dupont, Jessica Neuwirth, and Taina Bien-Aime, *Human Trafficking (Global Issues)* (New York: Facts on File, 2009).

4. UN Protocol to Prevent, Suppress, and Punish Trafficking in Persons, Article 3 (February 14, 2006), http://www.unodc.org/unodc/en/trafficking_human_beings .html.

5. Victims of Trafficking and Violence Protection Act of 2000, P.L. 100–386, Sec. 103 (8); U.S. Department of State, *Trafficking in Persons Report, Office to Monitor and Combat Trafficking in Persons* (June 3, 2005), http://www.state.gov/g/tip/ris/ tiprpt/2005/46606.htm.

6. Flowers, *Sex Crimes*, 132.

7. Cited from the United Nations in Frontline, "Sex Slaves" (February 7, 2006), http://www.pbs.org/wgbh/pages/frontline/slaves/etc/stats.html; *Oprah Winfrey Show*, "Child Sex Trafficking: The Facts" (November 15, 2005), http://www.oprah.com/ oprahshow/Child–Sex-Trafficking-The-Facts.

8. Elizabeth P. Salett, "Human Trafficking and Modern-Day Slavery," *National Multicultural Institute*, http://www.nmci.org/news/news_items/trafficking.html; Wikipedia, the Free Encyclopedia, "Human Trafficking."

9. Cited in "Sex Slaves."

10. Marisa B. Ugarte, Laura Zarate, and Melissa Farley, "Prostitution and Trafficking of Women and Children from Mexico to the United States," *Journal of Trauma Practice* 2, no. 3/4 (2003): 147–65.

11. U.S. Department of Justice, Child Exploitation and Obscenity Section (CEOS), "Trafficking and Sex Tourism," http://www.justice.gov/criminal/ceos/ trafficking.html.

12. Cited in High Road for Human Rights, "Sexual Slavery/Human Trafficking," http://www.highroadforhumanrights.org/education/slavery.html; U.S. Department of State, "Trafficking in Persons: Ten Years of Partnering to Combat Modern Slavery," Bureau of Public Affairs Fact Sheet (June 14, 2010), http://www.state.gov/r/pa/ scp/fs/2010/143115.htm.

13. Cited in Salett, "Human Trafficking and Modern-Day Slavery." See also Heather J. Clawson, Nicole Dutch, Amy Solomon, and Lisa G. Grace, *Human Trafficking into and within the United States: A Review of the Literature* (Washington, DC: U.S. Department of Health and Human Services, 2009).

14. Cited in "Study: Ohio at Center of Child Sex Trade," *CBS News* (February 11, 2010), http://www.cbsnews.com/stories/2010/02/11/national/main6196454 .shtml?tag=mncol;lst;4.

15. "U.S. Estimates Thousands of Victims, Efforts to Find Them Fall Short," HumanTrafficking.org (September 24, 2007), http://www.humantrafficking

.org/updates/711; Samantha M. Berg, "Sex Trafficking Strikes Closer to Home Than Thought," *The Portland Alliance* (November 18, 2004), http://www .theportlandalliance.org/2004/nov/pdxtrafficking.htm.

16. Clawson, Dutch, Solomon, and Grace, *Human Trafficking into and within the United States*; Bridgette Carr, "Sex Trafficking: An American Problem Too," *CNN* (November 25, 2009), http://www.cnn.com/2009/OPINION/11/25/carr .human.trafficking/; Richard J. Estes and Neil A. Weiner, *The Commercial Sexual Exploitation of Children in the U.S., Canada, and Mexico* (Philadelphia: University of Pennsylvania, 2002), 139–51.

17. Cited in Flowers, *Sex Crimes*, 33

18. Wikipedia, the Free Encyclopedia, "Human Trafficking in the United States," http://en.wikipedia.org/wiki/Human_trafficking_in_the_United_States.

19. Amy O'Neill-Richard, *International Trafficking in Women in the United States: A Contemporary Manifestation of Slavery and Organized Crime* (Washington, DC: Center for the Study of Intelligence, 1999), 13.

20. *Trafficking in Persons Report.*

21. Quoted in Wikipedia, "Human Trafficking."

22. O'Neill-Richard, *International Trafficking in Women in the United States.* See also Kevin Bales and Steven Lize, *Trafficking in Persons in the United States* (unpublished report to the National Institute of Justice, Washington, DC, U.S. Department of Justice, November 2005), 14–15.

23. R. Barri Flowers, *Street Kids: The Lives of Runaway and Thrownaway Teens* (Jefferson, NC: McFarland, 2010); R. Barri Flowers, *The Prostitution of Women and Girls* (Jefferson, NC: McFarland, 2009).

24. *Trafficking in Persons Report.*

25. Bales and Lize, *Trafficking in Persons in the United States*, p. 15. See also Frank Laczko and Elzbieta M. Gozdziak, *Data and Research on Human Trafficking: A Global Survey* (Geneva, Switzerland: International Organization for Migration, 2005).

26. Flowers, *Sex Crimes*, 134.

27. Bales and Lize, *Trafficking in Persons in the United States*, 15.

28. Donna M. Hughes, Janice G. Raymond, and Carol J. Gomez, *Sex Trafficking of Women in the United States: International and Domestic Trends* (North Amherst, MA: Coalition Against Trafficking in Women, 2001), 55.

29. Ibid.

30. Ibid.

31. Flowers, *Sex Crimes*, 134–35.

32. Hughes, Raymond, and Gomez, *Sex Trafficking of Women in the United States*, 56.

33. Rebecca Leung, "Rescued from Sex Slavery: *48 Hours* Goes Undercover into the International Sex Slave Trade," *CBS News* (February 23, 2005), http://www .cbsnews.com/stories/2005/02/23/48hours/main675913.shtml?tag=currentVideo Info;segmentTitle.

34. Ibid.

35. *Trafficking in Persons Report.* See also Kathryn Farr, *Sex Trafficking: The Global Market in Women and Children* (New York: Worth Publishers, 2004).

36. "Trafficking and Sex Tourism."

37. Daniel S. Campagna and Donald Poffenberger, *The Sexual Trafficking in Children: An Investigation of the Child Sex Trade* (Dover, MA: Auburn House, 1988), 4.

38. Robert Moossy, "Sex Trafficking: Identifying Cases and Victims," *National Institute of Justice Journal* 262 (March 2009), http://www.ojp.usdoj.gov/nij/journals/262/sex-trafficking.htm. See also Siddharth Kara, *Sex Trafficking: Inside the Business of Modern Slavery* (New York: Columbia University Press, 2008).

39. U.S. Department of Health and Human Services, The Campaign to Rescue and Restore Victims of Human Trafficking, "Fact Sheet: Sex Trafficking" (May 27, 2010), http://www.acf.hhs.gov/trafficking/about/fact_sex.html.

40. Ibid.

41. Anne Rasmusson, "Commercial Sexual Exploitation of Children: A Literature Review," Alliance for Speaking the Truths on Prostitution and Center for Urban and Regional Affairs (June 1, 1999), http://members.shaw.ca/pdg/exploitation_of_children.html#_Toc452540130.

42. Ibid.

43. Ibid.

44. Ibid.

45. Cited in Flowers, *Sex Crimes*, 135.

46. Ibid. See also Flowers, *The Prostitution of Women and Girls*, 8–9, 165–95; Penny Venetis, "International Sexual Slavery," *Women's Rights Law Reporter* 18, no. 3 (1997): 263–70; Siriporn Skrobanek, Nattaya Boonpakdi, and Chutima Janthakeero, *The Traffic in Women: Human Realities of the International Sex Trade* (New York: Zed Books Ltd., 1997).

47. "Human Trafficking." See also Leonard Territo and George Kirkham, *International Sex Trafficking of Women & Children* (Flushing, NY: Looseleaf Law Publications, 2009).

48. "Fact Sheet: Sex Trafficking."

49. Ibid.

50. Moossy, "Sex Trafficking."

51. Hughes, Raymond, and Gomez, *Sex Trafficking of Women in the United States*, 25.

52. Ugarte, Zarate, and Farley, "Prostitution and Trafficking of Women and Children from Mexico to the United States."

53. Dorchen A. Leidholdt, "Prostitution and Trafficking in Women: An Intimate Relationship," *Journal of Trauma Practice* 2, no. 3/4 (2003): 167–83.

54. Cited in *Trafficking in Persons Report.*

55. Cited in "Human Trafficking."

56. "Sex Trafficking Strikes Closer to Home Than Thought."

57. Salett, "Human Trafficking and Modern-Day Slavery."

58. Quoted in "Human Trafficking in the United States."

59. Cited in Ibid.

60. Ibid.

61. Ibid.

62. Hughes, Raymond, and Gomez, *Sex Trafficking of Women in the United States*, 48.

63. Ibid.

64. Ibid.

65. "Trafficking and Sex Tourism;" U.S. Department of Justice, Child Exploitation and Obscenity Section (CEOS), "Child Prostitution," http://www.justice.gov/criminal/ceos/prostitution.html.

66. Estes and Weiner, *The Commercial Sexual Exploitation of Children*, 140–50; Eliott C. McLaughlin, "Child Traffickers Target Runaways," *CNN* (November 18, 2009), http://www.cnn.com/2009/CRIME/11/18/domestic.child.trafficking/index.html?iref=allsearch.

67. Clawson, Dutch, Solomon, and Grace, *Human Trafficking into and within the United States*.

68. Carr, "Sex Trafficking."

69. "Study: Ohio at Center of Child Sex Trade."

70. Greg Kaufman, "Human Trafficking: Not Someone Else's Problem," *CBS News* (June 15, 2010), http://www.cbsnews.com/stories/2010/06/15/opinion/main6586310.shtml?tag=mncol;lst;1; U.S. Department of State, "Trafficking in Persons Report 2010" (June 14, 2010), http://www.state.gov/g/tip/rls/tiprpt/2010/index.htm.

71. "Sex Trafficking Charges against Reputed Mobsters," *CBS News* (April 20, 2010), http://www.cbsnews.com/stories/2010/04/20/national/main6415114.shtml?tag=mncol;lst;3.

72. "The Realities of Human Trafficking," *CBS News* (September 12, 2007), http://www.cbsnews.com/stories/2007/09/11/earlyshow/main3250963.shtml?tag=mncol;lst;1.

73. Huma Khan, "Child Sex Trafficking Growing in the U.S.: 'I Got My Child Taken from Me," *ABC News* (May 5, 2010), http://abcnews.go.com/US/domestic-sex-trafficking-increasing-united-states/story?id=10557194&page=1.

74. Ibid.

75. Victims of Trafficking and Violence Protection Act; "President signs H.R. 972, Trafficking Victims Protection Reauthorization Act" (January 10, 2006), http://www.whitehouse.gov/news/releases/2006/01/20060110-3.html. See also Joan Fitzpatrick, "Trafficking as a Human Rights Violation: The Complex Intersection of Legal Frameworks for Conceptualizing and Combating Trafficking," *Michigan Journal of International Law* 24 (2003): 1143.

76. Flowers, *Sex Crimes*, p. 138; Christina Hoag, "New Laws Treat Teen Prostitutes as Abuse Victims," *ABC News* (April 19, 2009), http://www.abcnews.go.com/US/WireStory?id=7370496&page=2.

77. U.S. Immigration and Customs Enforcement, News Release, "Human Trafficking: 21st Century Slavery" (January 7, 2010), http://www.ice.gov/pi/nr/1001/100107washingtondc.htm.

78. Ibid.

Chapter 9

1. R. Barri Flowers, *The Prostitution of Women and Girls* (Jefferson, NC: McFarland, 2009), 134.

2. *Encyclopedia of Sex and Sexuality*, "Prostitution" (September 2007), http://www.sexuality-encyclopedia.com/dr-ruth/Prostitution.

3. Connie Sponsler, "Juvenile Prostitution Prevention Project," *WHISPER* 13, 2 (1993): 3–4. See also Robin Erb and Roberta de Boer, "Males Who Work as Prostitutes: A Little-Known Part of Sex Industry," *ToledoBlade.com* (December 29, 2006), http://toledoblade.com/apps/pbcs.dll/article?AID=/20061229/NEWS03/612290302.

4. Robin Lloyd, *For Money or Love: Boy Prostitution in America* (New York: Ballantine, 1976), 58–72.

5. U.S. Department of Justice, Office of Juvenile Justice and Delinquency Prevention, *Prostitution of Children and Child–Sex Tourism* (Alexandria, VA: National Center for Missing and Exploited Children, 1999), 2; Mia Spangenberg, "Prostituted Youth in New York City: An Overview" (2001), http://www.libertadlatina.org/US_ECPAT_Child_Prostitution_NYC.htm.

6. *Prostitution of Children and Child–Sex Tourism*, 2.

7. Spangenberg, "Prostituted Youth in New York City."

8. Linda L. Halcon and Alan R. Lifson, "Prevalence and Predictors of Sexual Risks among Homeless Youth," *Journal of Youth and Adolescence* 33, no. 1 (2004): 75–76.

9. Donald M. Allen, "Young Male Prostitutes: A Psychosocial Study," *Archives of Sexual Behavior* 9 (1980): 418.

10. Flowers, *The Prostitution of Women and Girls*, 136–37.

11. Matt Dougherty, "A Day in the Life of a Male Prostitute," *Everyday Life and Health* (December 2, 2005), http://soc.hfac.uh.edu/artman/publish/article_311.shtml.

12. Flowers, *The Prostitution of Women and Girls*, 138.

13. Ibid.; Sivan E. Caukins and Neil Coombs, "The Psychodynamics of Male Prostitution," *American Journal of Psychotherapy* 30 (1976): 450.

14. Flowers, *The Prostitution of Women and Girls*, pp. 138–39.

15. Allen, "Young Male Prostitutes."

16. Neil Coombs, "Male Prostitution: A Psychosocial View of Behavior," *American Journal of Orthopsychiatry* 44 (1974): 782–89.

17. Ibid.

18. Christopher M. Earls and Helene David, "A Psychosocial Study of Male Prostitution," *Archives of Sexual Behavior* 18 (1989): 401–19.

19. "Prostitution."

20. Flowers, *The Prostitution of Women and Girls*, p. 138. See also Caukins and Coombs, "The Psychodynamics of Male Prostitution;" Joan J. Johnson, *Teen Prostitution* (Danbury, CT: Franklin Watts, 1992), 118.

21. Cited in Wikipedia, the free Encyclopedia, "Male Prostitution," http://en.wikipedia.org/wiki/Rent_boy.

22. Ibid.

23. Nicholas Ray, *Lesbian, Gay, Bisexual, and Transgender Youth: An Epidemic of Homelessness* (New York: National Gay and Lesbian Task Force Policy Institute and National Coalition for the Homeless, 2006), 55.

24. Caukins and Coombs, "The Psychodynamics of Male Prostitution," 441.

25. Ibid., 441–51.

26. Dan Waldorf and Sheigla Murphy, "Intravenous Drug Use and Syringe-Sharing Practices of Call Men and Hustlers," in *AIDS, Drugs, and Prostitution,* ed. Martin A. Plant (London: Routledge, 1990), 109–31.

27. Klass Kids Foundation, "The HT Report" (February 2009), http://www.klaaskids.org/pg-ht-report.htm; Richard J. Estes and Neil A. Weiner, *The Commercial Sexual Exploitation of Children in the U.S., Canada, and Mexico* (Philadelphia: University of Pennsylvania, 2002), 92.

28. Earls and David, "A Psychosocial Study of Male Prostitution," 401–19.

29. Coombs, "Male Prostitution."

30. Allen, "Young Male Prostitutes."

31. Les B. Whitbeck, Danny R. Hoyt, Kevin A. Yoder, Ana Mari Cauce, and Matt Paradise, "Deviant Behavior and Victimization among Homeless and Runaway Adolescents," *Journal of Interpersonal Violence* 16 (2001): 1175–1204.

32. Gil Griffin, "Running on Empty: Kids Take to the Streets When They Don't Feel Loved at Home," *San Diego Union-Tribune* (July 26, 1997), E1.

33. Ray, *Lesbian, Gay, Bisexual, and Transgender Youth*, 2; Tamar Stieber, "The Boys Who Sell Sex to Men in San Francisco," *Sacramento Bee* (March 4, 1984), A22.

34. Griffin, "Running on Empty."

35. Z. M. Lukman, "The Prevalence of Running Away from Home among Prostituted Children in Malaysia," *Journal of Social Sciences* 5, no. 3 (2009): 158.

36. Martin L. Forst and Martha E. Blomquist, *Missing Children: Rhetoric and Reality* (New York: Lexington Books, 1991), 37.

37. Ray, *Lesbian, Gay, Bisexual, and Transgender Youth*, 52.

38. John Lowman, "Taking Young Prostitutes Seriously," *Canadian Review of Sociology and Anthropology* 21, no. 1 (1987): 99–116.

39. Quoted online in Dan Allman, "Demographic Information and Sex Work in Canada," in *M Is for Mutual, A Is for Acts: Male Sex Work and AIDS in Canada*, Chapter 6 (Toronto: Health Canada, 1999), http://www.walnet.org/members/dan_allman/mutualacts/chapter06.html.

40. Cited in Hilary Abramson, "Sociologists Try to Reach Young Hustlers," *Sacramento Bee*, September 3, 1984, A8.

41. D. Kelly Weisberg, *Children of the Night: A Study of Adolescent Prostitution* (Lexington, MA: Lexington Books, 1985), 61.

42. Johnson, *Teen Prostitution*, 100.

43. Caukins and Coombs, "The Psychodynamics of Male Prostitution," 450; R. Barri Flowers, *Street Kids: The Lives of Runaway and Thrownaway Teens* (Jefferson, NC: McFarland, 2010), 142, 150–51.

44. Johnson, *Teen Prostitution*, 110.

45. Weisberg, *Children of the Night*, 19.

46. Ibid.

47. R. Barri Flowers, *Runaway Kids and Teenage Prostitution: America's Lost, Abandoned, and Sexually Exploited Children* (New York: Praeger, 2001), 130–31.

48. Flowers, *The Prostitution of Women and Girls*, 140.

49. Ibid.; Flowers, *Street Kids*, 146–47.

50. Quoted in Alfred Danna, "Juvenile Male Prostitution: How Can We Reduce the Problem?" *USA Today* 113 (May 1988), 87.

51. Ibid., 88.

52. Garrett Prestage, "Male and Transsexual Prostitution," in Roberta Perkins, Garrett Prestage, Rachel Sharp, and Frances Lovejoy, eds., *Sex Work and Sex Workers in Australia* (Sydney: University of New South Wales Press, 1994), 177.

53. Cited in Flowers, *The Prostitution of Women and Girls*, 143.

54. Edward V. Morse, Patricia M. Simon, and Paul M. Balson, "Sexual Behavior Patterns of Customers of Male Street Prostitutes," *Archives of Sexual Behavior* 21, no. 4 (1992): 347–57.

55. Richard R. Pleak and Heino Meyer-Bahlburg, "Sexual Behavior and AIDS Knowledge of Young Male Prostitutes in Manhattan," *Journal of Sex Research* 27 (1990): 557–88.

56. Timothy P. Johnson, Jennie R. Aschkenasy, Mary R. Herbers, and Stephen A. Gillenwater, "Self-Reported Risk Factors for AIDS among Homeless Youth," *AIDS Education and Prevention* 8 (1996): 308–22.

57. A. R. Markos, A. A. Wade, and M. Walzman, "The Adolescent Male Prostitute and Sexually Transmitted Diseases, HIV and AIDS," *Journal of Adolescence* 17 (1994): 123–30.

58. U.S. Department of Justice, Federal Bureau of Investigation, *Crime in the United States 2008*, Table 37 (September 2009), http://www.fbi.gov/ucr/cius2008/data/table_37.html.

59. David Finkelhor and Richard Ormrod, *Prostitution of Juveniles: Patterns from NIBRS* (Washington, DC: Office of Justice Programs, 2004), 1–2.

60. Weisberg, *Children of the Night*, 75.

61. See, for example, Aisha Ali, "Washington DC a Sexual Playground For Pimps and Johns: Exposing Child Prostitution Rings in DC," *Examiner* (March 17, 2009), http://www.examiner.com/x-1207-DC-Youth-Issues-Examiner~y2009m3d17-Washington-DC-a-sexual-playground-for-child-sex-exploiters-Exposing-child-prostitution; Christine Lagorio, "Crackdown on Child Prostitution: Justice Department Charges More Than 30 across Several States," *CBS News* (December 16, 2005), http://www.cbsnews.com/stories/2005/12/16/national/main1133570.shtml.

Chapter 10

1. Iceberg Slim, *Pimp: The Story of My Life* (Los Angeles, CA: Holloway House, 1969). See also Christina Milner and Richard Milner, *Black Players: The Secret World of Black Pimps* (New York: Little, Brown, 1973); Bob Adelman and Susan Hall, *Gentleman of Leisure: A Year in the Life of a Pimp* (Brooklyn, NY: Power-House Books, 2006).

2. The Free Dictionary, "Pimp," http://www.thefreedictionary.com/pimp; R. Barri Flowers, *Runaway Kids and Teenage Prostitution: America's Lost, Abandoned, and Sexually Exploited Children* (New York: Praeger, 2001).

3. Michael S. Scott and Kelly Dedel, *Street Prostitution*, 2nd ed. (Washington, DC: Office of Community Oriented Policing Services, 2006), http://www.cops.usdoj.gov/files/RIC/Publications/e10062633.txt.

4. Ibid.

5. Cited in Mia Spangenberg, "Prostituted Youth in New York City: An Overview," *ECPAT-US* (2001), http://www.libertadlatina.org/US_ECPAT_Child_Prostitution_NYC.htm.

6. R. Barri Flowers, *The Prostitution of Women and Girls* (Jefferson, NC: McFarland, 2009), 100.

7. Ibid.

8. See, for example, "Sex Trafficking Problem Growing Quickly," Austin News (December 1, 2009), http://www.kxan.com/dpp/news/national/sex-trafficking-problem-growing-quickly; Carey Goldberg, "Sex Slavery, Thailand to New York; Thousands of Indentured Asian Prostitutes May Be in U.S.," *New York Times,* September 11, 1995, B1; Susan Moran, "New World Havens of Oldest Profession," *Insight on the News* 9 (1993): 12–16.

9. Spangenberg, "Prostituted Youth in New York City."

10. Cited in Ibid.

11. Ibid.

12. Ibid.; Kevin A. Yoder, Les B. Whitbeck, and Danny R. Hoyt, "Gang Involvement and Membership among Homeless and Runaway Youth," *Youth and Society* 34,

no. 4 (2003): 441–67; Kayleen Hazelhurst and Cameron Hazelhurst, eds., *Gangs and Youth Subcultures: International Explorations* (New Brunswick, NJ: Transaction Publishers, 1989).

13. Wikipedia, the Free Encyclopedia, "Pimp," http://en.wikipedia.org/wiki/Pimp.

14. Anne Rasmusson, "Commercial Sexual Exploitation of Children: A Literature Review," Alliance for Speaking the Truths on Prostitution and Center for Urban and Regional Affairs (June 1, 1999), http://members.shaw.ca/pdg/exploitation_of_children.html#_Toc452540114.

15. Ibid.

16. Ibid. See also R. Barri Flowers, *Street Kids: The Lives of Runaway and Thrownaway Teens* (Jefferson, NC: McFarland, 2010), 135–36.

17. Joan J. Johnson, *Teen Prostitution* (Danbury, CT: Franklin Watts, 1992), 76–77. See also James F. Hodgson, *Games Pimps Play: Players and Wives-in-Law: A Qualitative Analysis of Street Prostitution* (Toronto: Canadian Scholars' Press, 1997).

18. Cited in Johnson, *Teen Prostitution*, 77.

19. National Center for Missing and Exploited Children, *Female Juvenile Prostitution: Problem and Response*, 2nd ed. (Alexandria, VA: National Center for Missing and Exploited Children, 2002), 23.

20. Ibid.

21. Flowers, *The Prostitution of Women and Girls*, 102.

22. Western Michigan University, "The Pimping Game," http://www.wmich.edu/destinys-end/pimping%20game.htm.

23. Wikipedia, "Pimp."

24. Ibid.

25. Flowers, *The Prostitution of Women and Girls*, 101; Johnson, *Teen Prostitution*, 78; Kathleen Barry, *The Prostitution of Sexuality* (New York: New York University Press, 1995), 198.

26. Quoted in Spangenberg, "Prostituted Youth in New York City."

27. Elizabeth Bernstein, *Temporarily Yours: Intimacy, Authenticity, and the Commerce of Sex* (Chicago: University of Chicago Press, 2007), 54.

28. Ibid. See also Hodgson, *Games Pimps Play*.

29. Quoted in Julia Dahl, "Big Pimping," *The Crime Report* (June 14, 2010), http://thecrimereport.org/2010/06/14/big-pimping/.

30. Minnesota Attorney General's Office, *The Hofstede Committee Report: Juvenile Prostitution in Minnesota*, (August 23, 2000), 6, http://www.ag.state.mn.us/home/files/news/hofstede.htm.

31. Deborah Jones, "Pimped," *Chatelaine* 67 (November 1994), 111.

32. See, for example, Wikipedia, "Pimped"; *Female Juvenile Prostitution*, 21.

33. *Female Juvenile Prostitution*, 22–23.

34. Ibid., 27.

35. "The Pimping Game."

36. Ibid.

37. Ibid.

38. Ibid.

39. Ibid. See also Hodgson, *Games Pimps Play.*

40. "The Pimping Game."

41. Flowers, *The Prostitution of Women and Girls*, 45; Marilyn G. Haft, "Hustling for Rights," in *The Female Offender*, ed. Laura Crites, 212 (Lexington, MA: Lexington Books, 1978).

42. Flowers, *Runaway Kids and Teenage Prostitution*, 125–26.

43. Flowers, *The Prostitution of Women and Girls*, 85–86.

44. Ibid., 13; *Female Juvenile Prostitution*, 4; National Center for Missing and Exploited Children, *Prostitution of Children and Child-Sex Tourism* (Alexandria, VA: National Center for Missing and Exploited Children, 1999), 6.

45. Flowers, *The Prostitution of Women and Girls*, p. 104; Johnson, *Teen Prostitution*, 127; Flowers, *Runaway Kids and Teenage Prostitution*, 113–14.

46. Flowers, *Street Kids*, pp. 136–38; Flowers, *The Prostitution of Women and Girls*, 130–31; Barbara Goldsmith, "Women on the Edge: A Reporter at Large," *New Yorker* 69 (April 26, 1993), 65.

47. Flowers, *The Prostitution of Women and Girls*, 49, 51; *Female Juvenile Prostitution*, 3–4, 10, 14–15; *Prostitution of Children and Child-Sex Tourism*, 5–6; Kendra Nixon, Leslie Tutty, Pamela Downe, Kelly Gorkoff, and Jane Ursel, "The Everyday Occurrence: Violence in the Lives of Girls Exploited through Prostitution," *Violence against Women* 8 (2002): 1016–43.

48. Anastasia Volkonsky, "Legalizing the 'Profession' Would Sanction the Abuse," *Insight on the News* 11 (1995): 20.

49. Minouche Kandel, "Whores in Court: Judicial Processing of Prostitutes in the Boston Municipal Court in 1990," *Yale Journal of Law & Feminism* 4 (1992): 329.

50. Cited in Flowers, *The Prostitution of Women and Girls*, 49.

51. John G. Hubbell, "Child Prostitution: How It Can Be Stopped," *Reader's Digest* (June 1984), 202, 205.

52. Quoted in *Female Juvenile Prostitution*, 24.

53. Ibid., 26, 29.

54. Ibid., 14.

55. The Enablers, *Juvenile Prostitution in Minnesota: The Report of a Research Project* (St. Paul, MN: The Enablers, 1978), 57.

56. Dorothy H. Bracey, *"Baby-Pros": Preliminary Profiles of Juvenile Prostitutes* (New York: John Jay Press, 1979), 23.

57. Quoted in Lee H. Bowker, *Women, Crime, and the Criminal Justice System* (Lexington, MA: Lexington Books, 1978), 55. See also Jennifer James, "Prostitute-Pimp Relationships," *Medical Aspects of Human Sexuality* 7 (1973): 147–63.

58. Flowers, *The Prostitution of Women and Girls*, 103.

59. Cited in Johnson, *Teen Prostitution*, 83.

60. Flowers, *The Prostitution of Women and Girls*, 103.

61. Wikipedia, "Pimp."

62. Richard J. Estes and Neil A. Weiner, *The Commercial Sexual Exploitation of Children in the U.S., Canada, and Mexico* (Philadelphia: University of Pennsylvania, 2002), 110.

63. Wikipedia, "Pimp."

64. *Female Juvenile Prostitution*, 24.

65. Ibid.

66. Flowers, *The Prostitution of Women and Girls*, 103.

67. Ibid.

68. Flowers, *Runaway Kids and Teenage Prostitution*, 125; *Prostitution of Children and Child-Sex Tourism*, 5; Evelina Giobbe, "An Analysis of Individual, Institutional, and Cultural Pimping," *Michigan Journal of Gender and Law* 1 (1993): 48.

69. Flowers, *Runaway Kids and Teenage Prostitution*, 125. See also Flowers, *The Prostitution of Women and Girls*, 103; Johnson, *Teen Prostitution*, 83–84.

70. Scott and Dedel, *Street Prostitution*.

71. Bernstein, *Temporarily Yours*, 57.

72. Spangenberg, "Prostituted Youth in New York City."

73. Cited in Ibid.

74. Flowers, *The Prostitution of Women and Girls*, 42; R. Barri Flowers, *Female Crime, Criminals and Cellmates: An Exploration of Female Criminality and Delinquency* (Jefferson, NC: McFarland, 2009), 105; Laura Trujillo, "Escort Services Thriving Industry in Portland Area," *Oregonian* (June 7, 1996), p. B1; D. Kelly Weisberg, *Children of the Night: A Study of Adolescent Prostitution* (Lexington, MA: Lexington Books, 1985), 124–28.

75. See, for example, "52 Kids Rescued in U.S. Prostitution Sweep," *CBS News* (October 26, 2009), http://www.cbsnews.com/stories/2009/10/26/national/main5422063.shtml?tag=cbsnewsTwoColLowerPromoArea;morenews; Christine Lagorio, "Crackdown on Child Prostitution: Justice Department Charges More Than 30 across Several States," *CBS News* (December 16, 2005), http://www.cbsnews.com/stories/2005/12/16/national/main1133570.shtml; Matthew Yi, "Police Say Sex-Slave Ring Is Broken Up," *Associated Press* (November 14, 1998); Carla Marinucci, "S.F. Vice Squad Focuses on Pimps," *San Francisco Chronicle,* July 16, 1995, http://www.sfgate.com/cgi-bin/article.cgi?f=/e/a/1995/07/26/NEWS13830.dtl.

76. Dahl, "Big Pimping."

77. Ibid. See also Geraldine Sealey, "Exposing America's Ugly Child Sex Secret," *ABC News* (December 13, 2009), http://abcnews.go.com/US/story?id=90557&page=1.

Chapter 11

1. Peter Elkind, *Rough Justice: The Rise and Fall of Eliot Spitzer* (New York: Penguin, 2010); Wikipedia, the Free Encyclopedia, "Eliot Spitzer Prostitution Scandal," http://en.wikipedia.org/wiki/Eliot_Spitzer_prostitution_scandal.

2. R. Barri Flowers, *The Prostitution of Women and Girls* (Jefferson, NC: McFarland, 2009), 127; R. Barri Flowers, *The Victimization and Exploitation of Women and Children: A Study of Physical, Mental and Sexual Maltreatment in the United States* (Jefferson, NC: McFarland, 1994), 173.

3. Victor Malarek, *The Johns: Sex for Sale and the Men Who Buy It* (New York: Arcade Publishing, 2009), 12. See also James Elias, Vern L. Bullough, Veronica Elias, and Gwen Brewer, eds., *Prostitution: On Whores, Hustlers, and Johns* (Amherst, NY: Prometheus Books, 1998).

4. Michael S. Scott and Kelly Dedel, *Street Prostitution*, 2nd ed. (Washington, DC: Office of Community Oriented Policing Services, 2006), http://www.cops .usdoj.gov/files/RIC/Publications/e10062633.txt. See also Harold Holzman and Sharon Pines, "Buying Sex: The Phenomenology of Being a John," *Deviant Behavior* 4 (1982): 89–116.

5. Flowers, *The Prostitution of Women and Girls*, 127; Susan Bakos, "The Hugh Grant Syndrome: Why Nice Guys Go to Hookers," *McCall's* 123 (November 1995), 108.

6. Cited in Anne Rasmusson, "Commercial Sexual Exploitation of Children: A Literature Review," Alliance for Speaking the Truths on Prostitution and Center for Urban and Regional Affairs (June 1, 1999), http://members.shaw.ca/pdg/exploitation_ of_children.html#_Toc452540114.

7. ABC News Prime Time, "Poll: American Sex Survey: A Peek Beneath the Sheets" (October 24, 2004), http://abcnews.go.com/Primetime/News/story? id=156921&page=1. See also Teela Sanders, *Paying for Pleasure: Men Who Buy Sex* (London: Wilan Publishing, 2008).

8. Cited in Esther Davidowitz, "Why 'Nice' Men Pay for Sex," *Women's Day* 56 (August 10, 1993), p. 100. See also Kerr Fuffle and Roscoe Spanks, *Paying for Sex: The Gentlemen's Guide to Web Porn, Strip Clubs, Prostitutes & Escorts—Without Humiliation, Job Loss, Bankruptcy, Infection, Bloodshed or Incarceration* (Bloomington, IN: Trafford Publishing, 2006).

9. Cited in "Dirty Money: The Business of High End Prostitution," *CNBC*, http://www.cnbc.com/id/26869953?_source=vty|dirtymoney|&par=vty. See also John Dececco, Kerwin Brook, Jill Nagle, and Baruch Gould, *Male Lust: Pleasure, Power, and Transformation* (New York: Routledge, 2000).

10. Cited in Rasmusson, "Commercial Sexual Exploitation of Children."

11. Cited in Mia Spangenberg, "Prostituted Youth in New York City: An Overview," *ECPAT-US* (2001), http://www.libertadlatina.org/US_ECPAT_Child_Prostitution_ NYC.htm.

12. Flowers, *The Prostitution of Women and Girls*, 127.

13. Cited in "Prostitution in the United States."

14. Malarek, *The Johns*, 3, 9, 190.

15. "Prostitution in the United States."

16. Cited in Bakos, "The Hugh Grant Syndrome," 108.

17. Malarek, *The Johns*, 143–44; John Dececco and Matt Bernstein Sycamore, *Tricks and Treats: Sex Workers Write about Their Clients* (New York: Routledge, 2000).

18. Richard Goodall, *The Comfort of Sin: Prostitutes and Prostitution in the 1990s* (Kent, UK: Renaissance Books, 1995), 69–79.

19. Flowers, *The Prostitution of Women and Girls*, 129.

20. Bakos, "The Hugh Grant Syndrome," 108.

21. Wikipedia, the Free Encyclopedia, "Shady Lady Ranch," http://en.wikipedia .org/wiki/Shady_Lady_Ranch; "Prostitution Not Just for Women: Nevada Brothel Cleared to Hire Men," *ABC News*, http://abcnews.go.com/Business/shady-lady-ranch-cleared-legal-male-prostitutes/story?id=9493257&page=3.

22. The Internet Movie Database, *American Gigolo* (1980), http://www.imdb .com/title/tt0080365/.

23. Hannah Barnes, "Women Who Pay for Sex," *BBC News Magazine* (February 27, 2009), http://news.bbc.co.uk/2/hi/uk_news/magazine/7914639.stm.

24. Cited in Spangenberg, "Prostituted Youth in New York City."

25. Bakos, "The Hugh Grant Syndrome," 108.

26. Davidowitz, "Why 'Nice' Men Pay for Sex," 101.

27. David Heinzmann, "Some Men Say Using Prostitutes Is an Addiction," *Chicago Tribune* (May 6, 2008), 4.

28. Ibid., 101, 107; Flowers, *The Prostitution of Women and Girls*, 129.

29. Martha L. Stein, *Lovers, Friends, Slaves: The Nine Male Sexual Types, Their Psycho-Sexual Transactions with Call Girls* (New York: Berkley, 1974), 1–2.

30. Malarek, *The Johns*, 82.

31. Molly Bedell, "Sex for Sale: Confessions of a Client," *CNBC* (November 10, 2008), http://www.prnewschannel.com/absolutenm/templates/?a=954&z=4. See also Janet Lever and Deanne Dolnick, "Clients and Call Girls: Seeking Sex and Intimacy," in *Sex for Sale: Prostitution, Pornography and the Sex Industry*, ed. Ronald Weitzer, 85–103 (New York: Taylor and Francis, 1999).

32. Malarek, *The Johns*, 72.

33. Bedell, "Sex for Sale."

34. Alice Leuchtag, "Merchants of Flesh: International Prostitution and the War on Women's Rights," *The Humanist* 55, 2 (1995): 14.

35. Wikipedia, the Free Encyclopedia, "Sex Tourism," http://en.wikipedia.org/ wiki/Sex_tourism; The Free Dictionary, "Sex Tourism," http://www.thefreedictionary .com/sex+tourism.

36. Leuchtag, "Merchants of Flesh," 12; Carol Smolenski, "Sex Tourism and the Sexual Exploitation of Children," *Christian Century* 112 (1995): 1080.

37. Leuchtag, "Merchants of Flesh," 15.

38. Malarek, *The Johns*, 24.

39. Ibid., 25.

40. Leuchtag, "Merchants of Flesh," 14.

41. Flowers, *The Prostitution of Women and Girls*, p. 133; PROTECT Act of 2003, P.L. 108–21, 117 Stat. 650, S. 151; Wikipedia, the Free Encyclopedia, "PROTECT Act of 2003," http://en.wikipedia.org/wiki/PROTECT_Act_of_2003.

42. Quoted in Davidowitz, "Why 'Nice' Men Pay for Sex," 100.

43. Cited in Linda Lee, "The World (and Underworld) of the Professional Call Girl," *New Woman* (January 1988), 62. See also Claire E. Sterk, *Tricking and Tripping: Prostitution in the Era of AIDS* (Putnam Valley, NY: Social Change Press, 2000).

44. Flowers, *The Prostitution of Women and Girls*, 131; Martin A. Plant, "Sex Work, Alcohol, Drugs, and AIDS," in *AIDS, Drugs, and Prostitution,* ed. Martin A. Plant, 1–17 (London: Routledge, 1990); Linda L. Halcon and Alan R. Lifson, "Prevalence and Predictors of Sexual Risks among Homeless Youth," *Journal of Youth and Adolescence* 33, no. 1 (2004): 75–76.

45. Cited in Barbara Goldsmith, "Women on the Edge: A Reporter at Large," *New Yorker* 69 (April 26, 1993), 65.

46. Flowers, *The Prostitution of Women and Girls*, 130–31; Wikipedia, the Free Encyclopedia, "Oral Sex," http://en.wikipedia.org/wiki/Oral_sex.

47. See, for example, Flowers, *The Prostitution of Women and Girls*, 130; Joan J. Johnson, *Teen Prostitution* (Danbury, CT: Franklin Watts, 1992), 131; Mimi H. Silbert and Ayala M. Pines, "Victimization of Street Prostitutes," *Victimology* 7 (1982): 122–33.

48. Cited in Anastasia Volkonsky, "Legalizing the 'Profession' Would Sanction the Abuse," *Insight on the News* 11 (1995): 20.

49. Jody Miller and Martin D. Schwartz, "Rape Myths and Violence against Street Prostitutes," *Deviant Behavior* 16, 1 (1995): 1–23.

50. National Center for Missing and Exploited Children, *Female Juvenile Prostitution: Problem and Response,* 2nd ed. (Alexandria, VA: National Center for Missing and Exploited Children, 2002), 5.

51. R. Barri Flowers, *Street Kids: The Lives of Runaway and Thrownaway Teens* (McFarland, 2010), 137–38; Stephen W. Baron, "Street Youth Violence and Victimization," *Trauma, Violence, and Abuse* 4 (2003): 22–44; Nicholas Ray, *Lesbian, Gay, Bisexual, and Transgender Youth: An Epidemic of Homelessness* (New York: National Gay and Lesbian Task Force Policy Institute and National Coalition for the Homeless, 2006), 3, 67.

52. Cited in "Why Serial Killers Target Prostitutes," *CBC News* (December 19, 2006), http://www.cbc.ca/news/background/crime/targeting-prostitutes.html.

53. See, for example, Robert Keppel, *The Riverman: Ted Bundy and I Hunt for the Green River Killer* (New York: Simon and Schuster, 2010); R. Barri Flowers and H. Loraine Flowers, *Murders in the United States: Crimes, Killers and Victims of the Twentieth Century* (Jefferson, NC: McFarland, 2009); Michael Bilton, *Wicked beyond Belief: The Hunt for the Yorkshire Ripper* (New York: HarperCollins, 2003).

54. "Why Serial Killers Target Prostitutes."

55. Ibid.

56. Wikipedia, the Free Encyclopedia, "Aileen Wuornos," http://en.wikipedia
.org/wiki/Aileen_Wuornos; Michael Reynolds, *Dead Ends: The Pursuit, Conviction
and Execution of Female Serial Killer Aileen Wuornos, the Damsel of Death*
(New York: St. Martin's Press, 2003).

57. Flowers, *The Prostitution of Women and Girls*, 130; R. Barri Flowers, *Female
Crime, Criminals and Cellmates: An Exploration of Female Criminality and Delin-
quency* (Jefferson, NC: McFarland, 2009), 153; The Enablers, *Juvenile Prostitution in
Minnesota: The Report of a Research Project* (St. Paul, MN: The Enablers, 1978), 75.

58. Meredith Traina, "LI Motivational Speaker Murdered by Prostitute for
Debit Card PIN," *WPIX* (July 18, 2009), http://www.wpix.com/news/local/
wpix-motivational-speaker-prostitute,0,3703962.story.

59. U.S. Department of Justice, Federal Bureau of Investigation, *Crime in the
United States 2008*, Table 39 (September 2009), http://www.fbi.gov/ucr/cius2008/
data/table_39.html.

60. Ibid., Table 40, http://www.fbi.gov/ucr/cius2008/data/table_40.html.

61. See, for example, Michael Russell, "Springfield-Area School Superintendent
Cited in Prostitution Sting," OregonLive.com (July 13, 2009), http://www.oregonlive
.com/news/index.ssf/2009/07/springfield_school_super_cited.html; "Police Use
Craigslist In Prostitution Sting," *KCTV 5 News* (February 22, 2008), http://www
.kctv5.com/news/15378677/detail.html; Sara J. Green, "Prostitution Sting Leads to
104 Arrests," *Seattle Times,* November 16, 2006, http://seattletimes.nwsource.com/
html/localnews/2003432936_craigslist16m.html.

62. Volkonsky, "Legalizing the 'Profession' Would Sanction the Abuse," 22.

63. Wayne County, Asset Forfeiture Unit, http://www.waynecounty.com/wcpo_
divisions_forfeiture.htm.

64. Ibid.

65. George Hunter and Doug Guthrie, "Wayne Co. Profits from Police Property
Seizures," *Detroit News,* November 13, 2009, http://detnews.com/article/20091113/
METRO/911130372/Wayne-Co.-profits-from-police-property-seizures.

66. Quoted in Ibid.

67. Quoted in Bill Dries, "Law Enforcement Takes Prostitution Fight to New
Level," *The Daily News,* April 28, 2008, http://www.memphisdailynews.com/
editorial/Article.aspx?id=36794.

68. Wikipedia, the Free Encyclopedia, "John School," http://en.wikipedia.org/
wiki/John_school.

69. Ibid.

70. Kristin Pisarcik, "Inside a Brooklyn 'John School'," *ABC News/20/20* (March
20, 2007), http://abcnews.go.com/2020/story?id=4488623&page=1.

71. Quoted in Ibid.

72. Ibid. See also Martin A. Monto and Steve Garcia, "Recidivism among the
Customers of Female Street Prostitutes: Do Intervention Programs Help?" *Western
Criminology Review* 3, 2 (2002): 1–10.

Bibliography

ABC News Prime Time. "Poll: American Sex Survey: A Peek Beneath the Sheets." (October 24, 2004). http://abcnews.go.com/Primetime/News/story?id=156921&page=1.

Abramson, Hilary. "Sociologists Try to Reach Young Hustlers." *Sacramento Bee,* September 3, 1984, A8.

Adelman, Bob, and Susan Hall. *Gentleman of Leisure: A Year in the Life of a Pimp.* Brooklyn, NY: PowerHouse Books, 2006.

Adler, Freda. *Sisters in Crime: The Rise of the New Female Criminal.* New York: McGraw-Hill, 1975.

Albert, Alexa. *Brothel: Mustang Ranch and Its Women.* New York: Random House, 2002.

Ali, Aisha. "Washington DC A Sexual Playground for Pimps and Johns: Exposing Child Prostitution Rings in DC." *Examiner,* March 17, 2009. http://www.examiner.com/x-1207-DC-Youth-Issues-Examiner~y2009m3d17-Washington-DC-a-sexual-playground-for-child-sex-exploiters-Exposing-child-prostitution.

Allen, Donald M. "Young Male Prostitutes: A Psychosocial Study." *Archives of Sexual Behavior* 9 (1980): 418.

Allman, Dan. "Demographic Information and Sex Work in Canada." Chap. 6 in *M Is for Mutual, A Is for Acts: Male Sex Work and AIDS in Canada,* edited by Dan Allman. Toronto: Health Canada, 1999. http://www.walnet.org/members/dan_allman/mutualacts/chapter06.html.

Almodovar, Norma J. *Cop to Call Girl: Why I Left the LAPD to Make an Honest Living as a Beverly Hills Prostitute.* New York: Simon and Schuster, 1993.

Amateurs Online. www.amateursonline.com.

Angell, Jeannette. *Callgirl: Confessions of an Ivy League Lady of Pleasure.* New York: HarperCollins, 2005.

Arbarbanel, Stephanie. "Women Who Make a Difference." *Family Circle* 107 (January 11, 1994): 11.

Bakos, Susan. "The Hugh Grant Syndrome: Why Nice Guys Go to Hookers." *McCall's* 123 (November 1995): 108.

Bales, Kevin, and Ron Soodalter. *The Slave Next Door: Human Trafficking and Slavery in America Today*. Berkeley, CA: University of California Press, 2009.

Bales, Kevin, and Ron Soodalter, and Steven Lize. *Trafficking in Persons in the United States*. Unpublished report to the National Institute of Justice. Washington, DC: U.S. Department of Justice, November 2005, 14–15.

Baram, Marcus. "What Makes a Woman Become an Escort?" *ABC News*. http://abcnews.go.com/US/story?id=4451781&page=1 (March 14, 2008).

Barnes, Hannah. "Women Who Pay for Sex." *BBC News Magazine,* February 27, 2009. http://news.bbc.co.uk/2/hi/uk_news/magazine/7914639.stm.

Baron, Stephen W. "Street Youth Violence and Victimization." *Trauma, Violence, and Abuse* 4 (2003): 22–44.

Barrett, David, and William Beckett. "Child Prostitution: Reaching Out to Children Who Sell Sex to Survive." *British Journal of Nursing* 5 (1996): 1120–25.

Barrows, Sydney Biddle. *Mayflower Madam: The Secret Life of Sydney Biddle Barrows*. New York: Arbor House, 1989.

Barrows, Sydney Biddle, and William Novak. *Mayflower Madam: The Secret Life of Sydney Biddle Barrows*. New York: HarperCollins, 1986.

Barry, Kathleen. *The Prostitution of Sexuality*. New York: New York University Press, 1995.

Bedell, Molly. "Sex for Sale: Confessions of a Client." *CNBC,* November 10, 2008. http://www.prnewschannel.com/absolutenm/templates/?a=954&z=4.

Benjamin, Harry, and R. E. L. Masters. *Prostitution and Morality*. New York: Julian Press, 1964.

Berg, Samantha M. "Sex Trafficking Strikes Closer to Home Than Thought." *The Portland Alliance,* November 18, 2004. http://www.theportlandalliance.org/2004/nov/pdxtrafficking.htm.

Bernstein, Elizabeth. *Temporarily Yours: Intimacy, Authenticity, and the Commerce of Sex*. Chicago: University of Chicago Press, 2007.

Bilton, Michael. *Wicked beyond Belief: The Hunt for the Yorkshire Ripper*. New York: HarperCollins, 2003.

Bindel, Julie. "It's Like You Sign a Contract to Be Raped." *Guardian*, September 2, 2007. http://www.guardian.co.uk/world/2007/sep/07/usa.gender.

Black, Rosemary. "Pregnant 'Cathouse' Star Brooke Phillips Was Shot, Stabbed, and Slashed, the Autopsy Reveals." *New York Daily News,* November 24, 2009. http://www.nydailynews.com/news/national/2009/11/24/2009-11-24_pregnant_cathouse_star_brooke_phillips_was_shot_stabbed_and_slashed_the_autopsy_.htm.

Blankenship, John. "Runaways: Juvenile Prostitution Increases with More Teens Fleeing Their Homes." *Register Herald,* August 16, 2008. http://register-herald.com/features/local_story_228110706.html?

Bowker, Lee H. *Women, Crime, and the Criminal Justice System*. Lexington, MA: Lexington Books, 1978.

Boyle, Sheron. *Working Girls and Their Men*. London: Smith Grypon, 1994.

Bracey, Dorothy H. *"Baby-Pros": Preliminary Profiles of Juvenile Prostitutes*. New York: John Jay Press, 1979.

Brawn, Kara M., and Dominique Roe-Sepowitz. "Female Juvenile Prostitutes: Exploring the Relationship to Substance Use." *Children and Youth Services Review* 30, no. 12 (2008): 1395–1402.

Brents, Barbara G., Crystal A. Jackson, and Kathryn Hausbeck. *The State of Sex: Tourism, Sex, and Sin in the New American Heartland*. New York: Routledge, 2009.

Brents, Barbara G., and Kathryn Hausbeck. "Violence and Legalized Brothel Prostitution in Nevada: Examining Safety, Risk and Prostitution Policy." *Journal of Interpersonal Violence* 20 (2005), 3: 270–95.

"Brooklyn Woman Pleads Guilty to Laundering Money Earned from Prostitution Businesses." FBI Press Release, June 21, 2007. http://newhaven.fbi.gov/dojpressrel/2007/nh062107a.htm.

Bryan, James H. "Apprenticeship in Prostitution." *Social Problems* 12 (1965): 287–97.

Bryan, James H. "Occupational Ideologies and Individual Attitudes of Call Girls." *Social Problems* 13 (1966): 441–50.

Burnette, Mandi L., Emma Lucas, Mark Ilgen, Susan M. Frayne, Julia Mayo, and Julie C. Weitlauf. "Prevalence and Health Correlates of Prostitution among Patients Entering Treatment for Substance Use Disorders." *Archives of General Psychiatry* 65, no. 3 (2008): 337–44.

Callahan, Bill. "Prisoners without Chains: For Teen-agers Like Peaches, Coming Back Is an Uphill Battle." *San Diego Union-Tribune*, June 21, 1998, A19.

Campagna, Daniel S., and Donald Poffenberger. *The Sexual Trafficking in Children: An Investigation of the Child Sex Trade*. Dover, MA: Auburn House, 1988.

Carr, Bridgette. "Sex Trafficking: An American Problem Too." *CNN Opinion*, November 25, 2009. http://www.cnn.com/2009/OPINION/11/25/carr.human.trafficking.

Caukins, Sivan E., and Neil Coombs. "The Psychodynamics of Male Prostitution." *American Journal of Psychotherapy* 30 (1976): 450.

Celizic, Mike. "Former Call Girl Opens Up about the Industry." *TodayShow.com*, March 12, 2008. http://www.msnbc.msn.com/id/23589422.

Chiasson, Mary Ann, Alan R. Lifson, Rand L. Stoneburner, William Ewing, Deborah Hilderbrandt, and Harold W. Jaffe. "HIV-1 Seroprevalence in Male and Female Prostitutes in New York City." Abstracts from the Sixth International Conference on AIDS, Stockholm, Sweden, June 1988.

Clatts, Michael C., W. Rees Davis, Jo L. Sotheran, and Aylin Atillasoy. "Correlates and Distribution of HIV Risk Behaviors among Homeless Youths in New York City: Implications for Prevention and Policy." *Child Welfare* 77, no. 2 (1998): 195–207.

Clawson, Heather J., Nicole Dutch, Amy Solomon, and Lisa G. Grace. *Human Trafficking into and within the United States: A Review of the Literature.* Washington, DC: U.S. Department of Health and Human Services, 2009.

Cohen, Marcia. *Identifying and Combating Juvenile Prostitution: A Manual for Action.* Washington, DC: National Association of Counties Research, Inc., 1987.

Coombs, Neil R. "Male Prostitution: A Psychosocial View of Behavior." *American Journal of Orthopsychiatry* 44 (1974): 782–89.

Cormier, Anthony. "Police Raid Sarasota Escort Service." *HeraldTribune.com,* February 4, 2010. http://www.heraldtribune.com/article/20100204/article /2041095?p=all&tc=pgall.

"Crack: A Cheap and Deadly Cocaine Is a Spreading Menace." *Time* 127 (June 12, 1986): 18.

"The Craigslist Killer: Seven Days of Rage." *48 Hours Mystery: CBS News.* September 16, 2009. http://www.cbsnews.com/stories/2009/09/16/48hours/ main5315790.shtml.

"A Crackdown on Call Girls." *Newsweek* (September 2, 2002). http://www .newsweek.com/2002/09/01/a-crackdown-on-call-girls.html.

Crowley, Maura G. "Female Runaway Behavior and Its Relationship to Prostitution." Master's thesis. Sam Houston State University. Institute of Contemporary Corrections and Behavioral Sciences, 1977.

Cullen-Dupont, Kathryn, Jessica Neuwirth, and Taina Bien-Aime. *Human Trafficking (Global Issues).* New York: Facts on File, 2009.

Dahl, Julia. "Big Pimping." *The Crime Report.* http://thecrimereport.org/2010/06/ 14/big-pimping/ (June 14, 2010).

Danna, Alfred. "Juvenile Male Prostitution: How Can We Reduce the Problem?" *USA Today* 113 (May 1988): 87.

Darling, Lynn. "Havana at Midnight." *Esquire* 123 (May 1995): 98.

Davidowitz, Esther. "Why 'Nice' Men Pay for Sex." *Women's Day* 56 (August 10, 1993): 100.

Davis, Kingsley. "The Sociology of Prostitution." *American Sociological Review* 2 (1937): 744–55.

"D.C. Madam Found Hanged." *CNN,* May 1, 2008. http://www.cnn.com/2008/ POLITICS/05/01/dc.madam/index.html.

Dececco, John, Kerwin Brook, Jill Nagle, and Baruch Gould. *Male Lust: Pleasure, Power, and Transformation.* New York: Routledge, 2000.

Dececco, John, and Matt Bernstein Sycamore. *Tricks and Treats: Sex Workers Write about Their Clients.* New York: Routledge, 2000.

Desperate Amateurs. www.desperateamateurs.com.

"Dirty Money: The Business of High End Prostitution." *CNBC,* October 30, 2008. http://www.cnbc.com/id/26869953?__source=vty|dirtymoney|&par=vty.

Ditmore, Melissa H. *Encyclopedia of Prostitution and Sex Work*. Vol. 2. Westport, CT: Greenwood, 2006.

Dougherty, Matt. "A Day in the Life of a Male Prostitute." *Everyday Life and Health* (December 2, 2005). http://soc.hfac.uh.edu/artman/publish/article_311.shtml.

Dries, Bill. "Law Enforcement Takes Prostitution Fight to New Level." *The Daily News,* April 28, 2008. http://www.memphisdailynews.com/editorial/Article.aspx?id=36794.

Dunlap, Kamika, and Barbara Grady. "City Comes to Grips with Teen Prostitution." *Oakland Tribune,* April 21, 2008. http://www.insidebayarea.com/teenprostitution/ci_9000424.

Earls, Christopher M., and Helene David. "A Psychosocial Study of Male Prostitution." *Archives of Sexual Behavior* 18 (1989): 401–19.

"The Economics of High End Prostitution." *MoreIntelligentLife.com,* April 10, 2008. http://moreintelligentlife.com/node/964.

Edwards, Jessica M., Carolyn T. Halpern, and Wendee M. Wechsberg. "Correlates of Exchanging Sex for Drugs or Money among Women Who Use Crack Cocaine." *AIDS Education and Prevention* 18, 5 (2006): 420–29.

Elias, James, Vern L. Bullough, Veronica Elias, and Gwen Brewer, eds. *Prostitution: On Whores, Hustlers, and Johns.* Amherst, NY: Prometheus Books, 1998.

Elkind, Peter. *Rough Justice: The Rise and Fall of Eliot Spitzer.* New York: Penguin, 2010.

"Emperors Club: All about Eliot Spitzer's Alleged Prostitution Ring." *Huffington Post,* March 10, 2008. http://www.huffingtonpost.com/2008/03/10/emperors-club-all-about-e_n_90768.html.

The Enablers. *Juvenile Prostitution in Minnesota: The Report of a Research Project.* St. Paul, MN: The Enablers, 1978.

Encyclopedia of Sex and Sexuality. "Prostitution." http://www.sexuality-encyclopedia.com/dr-ruth/Prostitution (September 2007).

Erb, Robin, and Roberta de Boer. "Males Who Work as Prostitutes: A Little-Known Part of Sex Industry." *ToledoBlade.com,* December 29, 2006. http://toledoblade.com/apps/pbcs.dll/article?AID=/20061229/NEWS03/612290302.

Estes, Richard J., and Neil A. Weiner. *The Commercial Sexual Exploitation of Children in the U.S., Canada, and Mexico.* Philadelphia: University of Pennsylvania, 2002.

"Ex 'Hollywood Madam' Heidi Fleiss Hit with Felony Drug Charge." *Fox News,* July 11, 2008. http://www.foxnews.com/story/0,2933,381131,00.html.

Exner, John E., Jr., Joyce Wylie, Antonnia Laura, and Tracey Parrill. "Some Psychological Characteristics of Prostitutes." *Journal of Personality Assessment* 41 (1977): 483.

Faris, Roger E. *Social Disorganization.* New York: Ronald Press, 1955.

Farley, Melissa. *Prostitution and Trafficking in Nevada: Making the Connections.* San Francisco: Prostitution Research and Education, 2007.

Farr, Kathryn. *Sex Trafficking: The Global Market in Women and Children*. New York: Worth Publishers, 2004.

Farrow, James A., Robert W. Deisher, Richard Brown, John W. Kulig, and Michele Kipke. "Health and Health Needs of Homeless and Runaway Youth." *Journal of Adolescent Health* 13 (1992): 717–26.

Fergusson, David M., L. John Horwood, and Annette L. Beautrais. "Is Sexual Orientation Related to Mental Health Problems and Suicidality in Young People?" *Archives of General Psychiatry* 56, no. 10 (1999): 876–80.

Ferri, Enrico. *Criminal Sociology*. London: T. Fisher Unwin, 1895.

"52 Kids Rescued in U.S. Prostitution Sweep." *CBS News,* October 26, 2009. http://www.cbsnews.com/stories/2009/10/26/national/main5422063.shtml?tag=cbsnewsTwoColLowerPromoArea;morenews.

Finkelhor, David, and Richard Ormrod. *Prostitution of Juveniles: Patterns from NIBRS*. Washington, DC: Office of Justice Programs, 2004.

Fitzpatrick, Joan. "Trafficking as a Human Rights Violation: the Complex Intersection of Legal Frameworks for Conceptualizing and Combating Trafficking." *Michigan Journal of International Law* 24 (2003): 1143.

Flexner, Abraham *Prostitution in Europe*. New York: Century, 1914.

Flowers, R. Barri. *Children and Criminality: The Child as Victim and Offender*. Westport, CT: Greenwood, 1986.

Flowers, R. Barri. *Women and Criminality: The Woman as Victim, Offender, and Practitioner*. Westport, CT: Greenwood Press, 1987.

Flowers, R. Barri. *The Victimization and Exploitation of Women and Children*. Jefferson, NC: McFarland, 1994.

Flowers, R. Barri. *Runaway Kids and Teenage Prostitution: America's Lost, Abandoned, and Sexually Exploited Children*. New York: Praeger, 2001.

Flowers, R. Barri. *Sex Crimes: Perpetrators, Predators, Prostitutes and Victims*, 2nd ed. Springfield, IL: Charles C Thomas, 2006.

Flowers, R. Barri. *Drugs, Alcohol and Criminality in American Society*. Jefferson, NC: McFarland, 2008.

Flowers, R. Barri. *The Adolescent Criminal: An Examination of Today's Juvenile Offender*. Jefferson, NC: McFarland, 2009.

Flowers, R. Barri. *Female Crime, Criminals and Cellmates: An Exploration of Female Criminality and Delinquency*. Jefferson, NC: McFarland, 2009.

Flowers, R. Barri. *The Prostitution of Women and Girls*. Jefferson, NC: McFarland, 2009.

Flowers, R. Barri. *Street Kids: The Lives of Runaway and Thrownaway Teens*. Jefferson, NC: McFarland, 2010.

Flowers, R. Barri, and H. Loraine Flowers. *Murders in the United States: Crimes, Killers and Victims of the Twentieth Century*. Jefferson, NC: McFarland, 2009.

Forst, Martin L., and Martha E. Blomquist. *Missing Children: Rhetoric and Reality*. New York: Lexington Books, 1991.

Frank, Katherine. *G-Strings and Sympathy: Strip Club Regulars and Male Desire.* Durham, NC: Duke University Press, 2002.

The Free Dictionary. "Pimp." http://www.thefreedictionary.com/pimp.

The Free Dictionary. "Sex Tourism." http://www.thefreedictionary.com/sex+tourism.

French, Delores. *Working: My Life as a Prostitute.* Chicago: Trafalgar Square Publishing, 1977.

Freud, Sigmund. *New Introductory Lectures in Psychoanalysis.* New York: W.W. Norton, 1933.

Fuffle, Kerr, and Roscoe Spanks. *Paying for Sex: The Gentlemen's Guide to Web Porn, Strip Clubs, Prostitutes & Escorts—Without Humiliation, Job Loss, Bankruptcy, Infection, Bloodshed or Incarceration.* Bloomington, IN: Trafford Publishing, 2006.

Gaetz, Stephen. "Safe Streets for Whom? Homeless Youth, Social Exclusion, and Criminal Victimization." *Canadian Journal of Criminology and Criminal Justice* 46, no. 6 (2004): 423–55.

Garcia, Oskar. "Country's First Legal Gigolo Starts Work in Nevada." *Seattle Times,* January 22, 2010. http://seattletimes.nwsource.com/html/nationworld/2010859290_apusnevadagigolo.html.

Gardner, George. "Hookers Go Hi-Tech, Advertise on Craigslist." *Tech.Blorge,* July 26, 2007. http://tech.blorge.com/Structure:%20/2007/07/26/hookers-go-hi-tech-advertise-on-craigslist.

Gibson, Jody B. *Secrets of a Hollywood Super Madam.* Los Angeles: Corona Books, 2007.

Giobbe, Evelina. "An Analysis of Individual, Institutional and Cultural Pimping." *Michigan Journal of Gender and Law* 1 (1983): 43, 48.

Giobbe, Evelina. "Confronting the Liberal Lies about Prostitution." In *The Sexual Liberals and the Attack on Feminism,* edited by Dorchen Leidholdt and Janice G. Raymond. New York: Pergamon Press, 1990.

Giusta, Marina Della, Maria Di Tommaso, and Steinar Strom. *Sex Markets: The Denied Industry.* New York: Routledge, 2008.

Glueck, Sheldon, and Eleanor Glueck. *Five Hundred Delinquent Women.* New York: Alfred A. Knopf, 1934.

Goldberg, Carey. "Sex Slavery, Thailand to New York; Thousands of Indentured Asian Prostitutes May Be in U.S." *New York Times,* September 11, 1995, B1.

Goldman, Russell. "Parents Who Pimp Their Children: The FBI Steps Up Efforts to Catch Parents and the Predators Who Want Their Kids for Sex." *ABC News,* October 8, 2007. http://abcnews.go.com/US/story?id=3691604&page=1.

Goldsmith, Barbara. "Women on the Edge: A Reporter at Large." *New Yorker* 69 (April 26, 1993): 65–66.

Goldstein, Paul J. *Prostitution and Drugs.* Lexington, MA: Lexington Books, 1979.

Gomstyn, Alice. "The Perks of High End Prostitution." *ABC News,* May 11, 2008. http://abcnews.go.com/Business/IndustryInfo/story?id=4428608&page=1.

Goodall, Richard. *The Comfort of Sin: Prostitutes and Prostitution in the 1990s.* Kent, UK: Renaissance Books, 1995.

Goring, Charles B. *The English Convict: A Statistical Study.* London: H.M.S., 1913.

Gray, Diana. "Turning Out: A Study of Teenage Prostitution." Master's thesis, University of Washington, 1971.

Green, Sara J. "Prostitution Sting Leads to 104 Arrests." *Seattle Times,* November 16, 2006.   http://seattletimes.nwsource.com/html/localnews/2003432936_craigslist16m.html.

Greene, Jody M., Susan T. Ennett, and Christopher L. Ringwalt. "Prevalence and Correlates of Survival Sex among Runaway and Homeless Youth." *American Journal of Public Health* 89, no. 9 (1999): 1406.

Greenwald, Harold. *The Elegant Prostitute: A Social and Psychoanalytic Study.* New York: Walker and Company, 1970.

Greenwald, Harold. *Call Girls.* San Diego, CA: Libra Publishers, 1988.

Gregory, Katherine. *The Everyday Lives of Sex Workers in the Netherlands.* New York: Routledge, 2005.

Griffin, Gil. "Running on Empty: Kids Take to the Streets When They Don't Feel Loved at Home." *San Diego Union-Tribune*, July 26, 1997, E1.

Haft, Marilyn G. "Hustling for Rights." In *The Female Offender*, edited by Laura Crites. Lexington, MA: Lexington Books, 1978.

Halcon, Linda L., and Alan R. Lifson. "Prevalence and Predictors of Sexual Risks among Homeless Youth." *Journal of Youth and Adolescence* 33, no. 1(2004): 75–76.

Haq, Farquan. "U.S. Children: Street Kids Turn to Sex to Survive." *Inter-Press Service,* March 27, 1996.

Harlan, Sparky, Luanne L. Rodgers, and Brian Slattery. *Male and Female Adolescent Prostitution: Huckleberry House Sexual Minority Youth Services Project.* Washington, DC: U.S. Department of Health and Human Services, 1981.

Hazelhurst, Kayleen, and Cameron Hazelhurst, eds. *Gangs and Youth Subcultures: International Explorations.* New Brunswick, NJ: Transaction Publishers, 1989.

Heinzmann, David. "Some Men Say Using Prostitutes Is an Addiction." *Chicago Tribune*, May 6, 2008, 4.

Herbert, Bob. "Op-Ed Columnist; Fantasies, Well Meant." *New York Times,* September 11, 2007. http://query.nytimes.com/gst/fullpage.html?res=9E03E0DF1430F932A2575AC0A9619C8B63&sec=&spon=&&scp=8&sq= bob%20herbert+nevada%20brothel%20prostitution&st=cse.

Hersch, Patricia. "Coming of Age on City Streets." *Psychology Today* (July 20, 1986), 37.

High Road for Human Rights. "Sexual Slavery/Human Trafficking." (2008). http://www.highroadforhumanrights.org/education/slavery.html.

Hoag, Christina. "New Laws Treat Teen Prostitutes as Abuse Victims." *ABCNews*, April 19, 2009. http://www.abcnews.go.com/US/WireStory?id=7370496&page=2.

Hodgson, James F. *Games Pimps Play: Players and Wives-in-Law: A Qualitative Analysis of Street Prostitution.* Toronto: Canadian Scholars' Press, 1997.

Hollander, Xaviera. *The Happy Hooker.* New York: Dell, 1984.

Hollander, Xaviera, Robin Moore, and Yvonne Dunleavy. *Happy Hooker: My Own Story.* New York: HarperCollins, 2002.

Holzman, Harold, and Sharon Pines. "Buying Sex: The Phenomenology of Being a John." *Deviant Behavior* 4 (1982): 89–116.

Hooton, Earnest A. *The American Criminal.* Cambridge, MA: Harvard University Press, 1939.

Hooton, Earnest A. *Crime and the Man.* Cambridge, MA: Harvard University Press, 1939.

Hornblower, Margot. "The Skin Trade." *Time* 141 (June 21, 1993): 44.

Hubbell, John G. "Child Prostitution: How It Can Be Stopped." *Reader's Digest* (June 1984), 202, 205.

Hughes, Donna M., Janice G. Raymond, and Carol J. Gomez. *Sex Trafficking of Women in the United States: International and Domestic Trends.* North Amherst, MA: Coalition against Trafficking in Women, 2001.

HumanTrafficking.org. "U.S. Estimates Thousands of Victims, Efforts to Find Them Fall Short." http://www.humantrafficking.org/updates/711 (September 24, 2007).

Hunter, George, and Doug Guthrie. "Wayne Co. Profits from Police Property Seizures." *Detroit News,* November 13, 2009. http://detnews.com/article/2009 1113/METRO/911130372/Wayne-Co.-profits-from-police-property-seizures.

Hunter, Susan K. "Prostitution Is Cruelty and Abuse to Women and Children." *Michigan Journal of Gender and Law* 1, no. 91 (1993): 91–104.

Ignoto, Barbara. *Confessions of a Part-Time Call Girl.* New York: Dell, 1986.

Ingles, Jacquelyn A. "Caught in the Web of Internet Prostitution." *Medill Reports Chicago,* July 25, 2007. http://news.medill.northwestern.edu/chicago/news .aspx?id=41347.

The Internet Movie Database. *Love Ranch.* http://www.imdb.com/title/tt1125929/ (2010).

The Internet Movie Database. *American Gigolo.* http://www.imdb.com/title/ tt0080365/ (1980).

The Internet Movie Database. Box Office/Business for *Pretty Woman.* http://www .imdb.com/title/tt0100405/business (1990).

The Internet Movie Database. *Cathouse.* http://www.imdb.com/title/tt0359056/ (2002).

James, Jennifer. "Two Domains of Streetwalker Argot." *Anthropological Linguistics* 14: 174–75 (1972).

James, Jennifer. "Prostitute-Pimp Relationships." *Medical Aspects of Human Sexuality* 7 (1973): 147–63.

James, Jennifer. "Motivations for Entrance into Prostitution." In *The Female Offender*, edited by Laura Crites. Lexington, MA: Lexington Books, 1976.

James, Jennifer. "Prostitutes and Prostitution." In *Deviants: Voluntary Actors in a Hostile World*, edited by Edward Sagarin and Fred Montanino. Morrison, NJ: General Learning Press, 1977.

James, Jennifer. *Entrance into Juvenile Prostitution: Progress Report*. Washington, DC: National Institute of Mental Health, 1978.

James, Jennifer. *Entrance into Juvenile Prostitution*. Washington, DC: National Institute of Mental Health, 1980.

Johnson, Joan J. *Teen Prostitution*. Danbury, CT: Franklin Watts, 1992.

Johnson, Timothy P., Jennie R. Aschkenasy, Mary R. Herbers, and Stephen A. Gillenwater. "Self-Reported Risk Factors for AIDS among Homeless Youth." *AIDS Education and Prevention* 8 (1996): 308–22.

Jones, Deborah. "Pimped." *Chatelaine* 67 (November 1994): 111.

Jones, Kasey. "Los Angeles Porn Actor Now the First Legal Gigolo in the US." *LA Examiner*, January 22, 2010. http://www.examiner.com/x-28270-LA-Headlines-Examiner~y2010m1d22-Los-Angeles-porn-actor-now-the-first-legal-gigolo-in-the-US.

Joseph, Elizabeth. "Sex for Hire: Real Stories of Prostitution in America." *ABC News*, March 24, 2008. http://abcnews.go.com/2020/story?id=4495721&page=1.

Kandel, Minouche. "Whores in Court: Judicial Processing of Prostitutes in the Boston Municipal Court in 1990." *Yale Journal of Law & Feminism* 4 (1992): 329.

Kara, Siddharth. *Sex Trafficking: Inside the Business of Modern Slavery*. New York: Columbia University Press, 2008.

Karen, Robert. "The World of the Middle Class Prostitute." *Cosmopolitan* 202 (January 1987), 205.

Karlinsky, Neal, and Alyssa Litoff. "Economic Tough Times Hit Nevada Brothel." *ABC News*, November 22, 2008. http://abcnews.go.com/Business/Economy/story?id=6308834&page=1.

Kates, Brian. "Elaborate Hooker Ring Busted." *New York Daily News*, September 29, 2002. http://www.nydailynews.com/archives/news/2002/09/29/2002-09-29_elaborate_hooker_ring_busted.html.

Kaufman, Greg. "Human Trafficking: Not Someone Else's Problem." *CBS News*, June 15, 2010. http://www.cbsnews.com/stories/2010/06/15/opinion/main6586310.shtml?tag=mncol;lst;1 ().

Keppel, Robert. *The Riverman: Ted Bundy and I Hunt for the Green River Killer*. New York: Simon and Schuster, 2010.

Khan, Huma. "Child Sex Trafficking Growing in the U.S.: 'I Got My Child Taken from Me.'" *ABC News*. May 5, 2010. http://abcnews.go.com/US/domestic-sex-trafficking-increasing-united-states/story?id=10557194&page=1.

Kihara, David. "Giuliani's Suppressed Report on Homeless Youth." *The Village Voice* 44 (August 24, 1999): 33. http://village voice.com.

Kipke, Michele D., Susanne B. Montgomery, Thomas R. Simon, and Ellen F. Iverson. "Substance Abuse Disorders among Runaway and Homeless Youth." *Substance Use and Misuse* 32 (1997): 969–86.

Klass Kids Foundation. "The HT Report." http://www.klaaskids.org/pg-ht-report.htm (February 2009).

Kostash, Myrna. "Surviving the Streets." *Chatelaine* 67 (October 1994): 103–104.

Kristof, Nicholas. "The Pimp's Slaves," *New York Times,* March 16, 2008. http://www.nytimes.com/2008/03/16/opinion/16kristof.html?_r=2&oref=slogin&oref=slogin.

Kruks, Gabe. "Gay and Lesbian Homeless/Street Youth: Special Issues and Concerns." *Journal of Adolescent Health* 12 (1991): 515–18.

Kurtz, P. David, Gail L. Kurtz, and Sara Jarvis. "Problems of Maltreated Runaway Youth." *Adolescence* 26 (1991): 543–55.

Laczko, Frank, and Elzbieta M. Gozdziak. *Data and Research on Human Trafficking: A Global Survey.* Geneva, Switzerland: International Organization for Migration, 2005.

Lagorio, Christine. "Crackdown on Child Prostitution: Justice Department Charges More Than 30 across Several States." *CBS News,* December 16, 2005. http://www.cbsnews.com/stories/2005/12/16/national/main1133570.shtml.

Lange, W. Robert, Frederick R. Snyder, David Lozovsky, Vivek Kaistha, Mary A. Kaczaniuk, and Jerome H. Jaffe. "HIV Infection in Baltimore: Antibody Seroprevalence Rates among Parenteral Drug Abusers and Prostitutes." *Maryland Medical Journal* 36, no. 9 (1987): 757–61.

Launter, Kimberly, and Katie Escherich. "Ashley Dupré Exclusive: 'My Side of the Story.'" *ABC News/20/20,* November 19, 2008. http://abcnews.go.com/2020/story?id=6280407&page=1.

"Lawsuit Accuses Craigslist of Promoting Prostitution." *CNN,* May 5, 2009. http://www.cnn.com/2009/CRIME/03/05/craigs.list.prostitution/index.html.

LeBlanc, Adrian N. "I'm a Shadow." *Seventeen* 52 (March 1993): 214–16.

Lee, Linda. "The World (and Underworld) of the Professional Call Girl." *New Woman* (January 1988), 62.

Leidholdt, Dorchen A. "Prostitution and Trafficking in Women: An Intimate Relationship." *Journal of Trauma Practice* 2, no. 3/4 (2003): 167–83.

Lemert, Edwin M. *Social Pathology.* New York: McGraw-Hill, 1951.

Leuchtag, Alice. "Merchants of Flesh: International Prostitution and the War on Women's Rights." *The Humanist* 55 (1995), 2: 14.

Leung, Rebecca. "Porn in the U.S.A." *CBS News,* November 21, 2003. http://www.cbsnews.com/stories/2004/08/31/60minutes/main639674.shtml?tag=mncol;lst;10.

Leung, Rebecca. "Rescued from Sex Slavery: *48 Hours* Goes Undercover into the International Sex Slave Trade." *CBS News,* February 23, 2005. http://www

.cbsnews.com/stories/2005/02/23/48hours/main675913.shtml?tag=curren tVideoInfo;segmentTitle.

Lever, Janet, and Deanne Dolnick. "Clients and Call Girls: Seeking Sex and Intimacy." In *Sex for Sale: Prostitution, Pornography and the Sex Industry,* edited by Ronald Weitzer. New York: Taylor and Francis, 1999.

Li, Qing, Xiaoming Li, and Bonita Stanton. "Alcohol Use among Female Sex Workers and Male Clients: An Integrative Review of Global Literature." *Alcohol and Alcoholism* 45, no. 2 (2010): 188–99.

Lloyd, Robin. *For Money or Love: Boy Prostitution in America.* New York: Ballantine, 1976.

Lombroso, Cesare, and William Ferrero. *The Female Offender.* New York: Appleton, 1900.

Lowman, John. "Taking Young Prostitutes Seriously." *Canadian Review of Sociology and Anthropology* 21, no. 1 (1987): 99–116.

Lukman, Z. M. "The Prevalence of Running Away from Home among Prostituted Children in Malaysia." *Journal of Social Sciences* 5, no. 3 (2009): 158.

Malarek, Victor. *The Johns: Sex for Sale and the Men Who Buy It.* New York: Arcade Publishing, 2009.

Mallett, Shelley, Doreen Rosenthal, and Deborah Keys. "Young People, Drug Use and Family Conflict: Pathways into Homelessness." *Journal of Adolescence* 28, no. 2 (2005): 185–99.

Marcus, Ashtar A. "Lucy Liu, USAID Highlight Human Trafficking." *Frontlines,* November 2009. http://www.usaid.gov/press/frontlines/fl_nov09/p01_liu091103.html.

Marinucci, Carla. "S.F. Vice Squad Focuses on Pimps." *San Francisco Chronicle,* July 16, 1995. http://www.sfgate.com/cgi-bin/article.cgi?f=/e/a/1995/07/26/NEWS13830.dtl.

Markos, A. R., A. A. Wade, and M. Walzman. "The Adolescent Male Prostitute and Sexually Transmitted Diseases, HIV and AIDS." *Journal of Adolescence* 17 (1994): 123–30.

Marriot, Trevor. *Jack the Ripper: The 21st Century Investigation.* London: John Blake, 2005.

McClanahan, Susan F., Gary M. McClelland, Karen M. Abram, and Linda A. Teplin. "Pathways into Prostitution among Female Jail Detainees and Their Implications for Mental Health Services." *Psychiatric Services* 50 (1999): 1606–13.

McLaughlin, Eliott C. "Child Traffickers Target Runaways." *CNN,* November 18, 2009. http://www.cnn.com/2009/CRIME/11/18/domestic.child.trafficking/index.html?iref=allsearch.

McLennan, Natalie. *The Price: My Rise and Fall as Natalia, New York's #1 Escort.* Beverly Hills, CA: Phoenix Books, 2008.

Merriam-Webster Online. "Call Girl." http://www.merriam-webster.com/dictionary/call+girl.

Merriam-Webster Online. "Madam." http://www.merriam-webster.com/dictionary/madam.

Merriam-Webster Online. "Prostitution." http://www.merriam-webster.com/dictionary/prostitution.

Michels, Scott. "Craigslist Threatened with Criminal Investigation." *ABC News,* May 5, 2009. http://abcnews.go.com/TheLaw/story?id=7507090&page=1.

Miller, Eleanor M. *Street Woman.* Philadelphia: Temple University Press, 1987.

Miller, Jody, and Martin D. Schwartz. "Rape Myths and Violence against Street Prostitutes." *Deviant Behavior* 16, no. 1 (1995): 1–23.

Miller, Laura. "Prostitution." *Harper's Bazaar* 3400 (March 1995): 210.

Miller, Pamela, Peter Donahue, Dave Este, and Marvin Hofer. "Experiences of Being Homeless or at Risk of Being Homeless among Canadian Youths." *Adolescence* 39, no. 156 (2004): 741.

Milner, Christina, and Richard Milner. *Black Players: The Secret World of Black Pimps.* New York: Little, Brown, 1973.

Minnesota Attorney General's Office. *The Hofstede Committee Report: Juvenile Prostitution in Minnesota,* August 23, 2000, 6. http://www.ag.state.mn.us/home/files/news/hofstede.htm.

Mitchell, John L. "Prostitute with HIV Faces Felony." *Los Angeles Times,* July 22, 2002. http://articles.latimes.com/2002/jul/22/local/me-hooker22.

Molino, Alma C. "Characteristics of Help-Seeking Street Youth and Non-Street Youth." 2007 National Symposium on Homelessness Research, March 1–2, 2007. http://aspe.hhs.gov/hsp/homelessness/symposium07/molino/index.htm.

Monto, Martin A., and Steve Garcia. "Recidivism among the Customers of Female Street Prostitutes: Do Intervention Programs Help?" *Western Criminology Review* 3, no. 2 (2002): 1–10.

Moossy, Robert. "Sex Trafficking: Identifying Cases and Victims." *National Institute of Justice Journal* 262 (March 2009). http://www.ojp.usdoj.gov/nij/journals/262/sex-trafficking.htm.

Moran, Susan. "New World Haven of Oldest Profession." *Insight on the News* 9 (1993): 12–16.

Moreland, Jo. "Area Study Says Female Teen Prostitution 'Common.'" *North County Times,* November 2, 2005. http://nctimes.com/news/local/sdcounty/article_f7d2d30c-f678-5a86-855e-89843f668fd2.html.

Morse, Edward V., Patricia M. Simon, and Paul M. Balson. "Sexual Behavior Patterns of Customers of Male Street Prostitutes." *Archives of Sexual Behavior* 21, no. 4 (1992): 347–57.

Mosedale, Brenda, Christos Kouimtsidis, and Martina Reynolds. "Sex Work, Substance Misuse and Service Provision: The Experiences of Female Sex Workers in South London." *Drugs: Education, Prevention and Policy* 16, no. 4 (2009): 355–63.

Nadon, Susan M., Catherine Koverola, and Eduard H. Schudermann. "Antecedents to Prostitution: Childhood Victimization." *Journal of Interpersonal Violence* 13 (1998): 206–21.

National Center for Missing and Exploited Children. "What Is Child Pornography?" http://www.missingkids.com/missingkids/servlet/PageServlet? Language Country=en_US&PageId=1504.

National Center for Missing and Exploited Children. *Prostitution of Children and Child–Sex Tourism.* Alexandria, VA: National Center for Missing and Exploited Children, 1999.

National Center for Missing and Exploited Children. *Female Juvenile Prostitution: Problem and Response*, 2nd ed. Alexandria, VA: National Center for Missing and Exploited Children, 2002.

National Crime Victims' Rights Week. (April 10–16, 2005) "Human Trafficking." http://www.ojp.usdoj.gov/ovc/ncvrw/2005/pg5l.html.

National Network for Youth. "NN4Y Issue Brief: Unaccompanied Youth Overview," 5. http://www.nn4youth.org/system/files/IssueBrief_Unaccompanyed_youth .pdf.

National Runaway Switchboard. "NRS Call Statistics." http://www.nrscrisisline. org/news_events/call_stats.html.

National Runaway Switchboard. "Keeping America's Runaway and At-Risk Youth Safe and Off the Streets." http://www.1800runaway.org/.

National Survey on Drug Use and Health. *The NSDUH Report.* "Substance Abuse among Youths Who Had Run Away from Home," July 2, 2004. http://www .oas.samhsa.gov/2k4/runAways/runAways.htm.

Netter, Sarah. "Prostitution Not Just for Women: Nevada Brothel Cleared to Hire Men." *ABC News*, January 7, 2010. http://abcnews.go.com/Business/ shady-lady-ranch-cleared-legal-male-prostitutes/story?id=9493257& page=1.

New World Encyclopedia. "Prostitution." http://www.newworldencyclopedia.org/ entry/Prostitution.

Nixon, Kendra, Leslie Tutty, Pamela Downe, Kelly Gorkoff, and Jane Ursel. "The Everyday Occurrence: Violence in the Lives of Girls Exploited through Prostitution." *Violence against Women* 8 (2002): 1016–43.

Noell, John, Paul Rohde, John Seeley, and Linda Ochs. "Childhood Sexual Abuse, Adolescent Sexual Coercion and Sexually Transmitted Infection Acquisition among Homeless Female Adolescents." *Child Abuse and Neglect* 25 (2001): 137–48.

O'Neill-Richard, Amy. (1999) *International Trafficking in Women in the United States: A Contemporary Manifestation of Slavery and Organized Crime.* Washington, DC: Center for the Study of Intelligence.

"Oakland Battles Wave of Teenage Prostitution." *KTVU*, May 7, 2009. http://www .ktvu.com/news/19388341/detail.html.

Oliver, Pam. "A Review of Literature on Child Prostitution." *Social Policy Journal of New Zealand* 19 (2002). http://www.thefreelibrary.com/_/print/Print-Article.aspx?id=99849275.

Oprah Winfrey Show. "Inside the Moonlite BunnyRanch," April 29, 2009. http://www.oprah.com/oprahshow/Moonlite-Bunny-Ranch.

Oprah Winfrey Show. "Child Sex Trafficking: The Facts." November 15, 2005. http://www.oprah.com/oprahshow/Child-Sex-Trafficking-The-Facts.

Pike, Deidre "On the Run." *Las Vegas City Life*, August 11, 2004. http://www.lasvegascitylife.com/articles/2004/08/11/cover_story/cover.txt.

Pisarcik, Kristin. "Inside a Brooklyn 'John School.'" *ABC News/20/20*, March 20, 2007. http://abcnews.go.com/2020/story?id=4488623&page=1.

Plant, Martin A. Sex Work, Alcohol, Drugs, and AIDS." In *AIDS, Drugs, and Prostitution*, edited by Martin A. Plant. London: Routledge, 1990.

Pleak, Richard R., and Heino Meyer-Bahlburg. "Sexual Behavior and AIDS Knowledge of Young Male Prostitutes in Manhattan." *Journal of Sex Research* 27 (1990): 557–88.

Pollak, Otto. *The Criminality of Women.* Philadelphia: University of Philadelphia Press, 1950.

Pollock, Joy. "Early Theories of Female Criminality." In *Women, Crime, and the Criminal Justice System*, edited by Lee H. Bowker. Lexington, MA: Lexington Books, 1978.

"Police Use Craigslist in Prostitution Sting." *KCTV 5 News*, February 22, 2008. http://www.kctv5.com/news/15378677/detail.html.

Possession of Child Pornography. 18 U.S.C. §2252 (2008).

"President Signs H.R. 972, Trafficking Victims Protection Reauthorization Act." (January 10, 2006). http://www.whitehouse.gov/news/releases/2006/01/20060110-3.html.

Prestage, Garrett. "Male and Transsexual Prostitution." In *Sex Work and Sex Workers in Australia*, edited by Roberta Perkins, Garrett Prestage, Rachel Sharp, and Frances Lovejoy. Sydney: University of New South Wales Press, 1994.

"Prostitution in America: Diane Sawyer Special Examines World's Oldest Profession." *ABC News*, March 19, 2008. http://abcnews.go.com/2020/story?id=4480892&page=1.

"Prostitution Not Just for Women: Nevada Brothel Cleared to Hire Men." *ABC News*, January 7, 2010. http://abcnews.go.com/Business/shady-lady-ranch-cleared-legal-male-prostitutes/story?id=9493257&page=3.

PROTECT Act. P.L. 108–21, 117 Stat. 650, S. 151 (2003).

Quan, Tracy. "The Work Ethic." *CNBC*, October 26, 2008. http://www.cnbc.com/id/15840232?video=907167785&play=1.

Quan, Tracy. "Male Prostitution Comes to Nevada." *Guardian*, January 20, 2010. http://www.guardian.co.uk/commentisfree/cifamerica/2010/jan/20/male-prostitution-nevada-brothel.

Rader, Dotson. "I Want to Die So I Won't Hurt No More." *Parade Magazine* (August 18, 1985), 5–6.

RapeIs.org. http://www.rapeis.org/activism/prostitution/prostitutionfacts.html.

Rashbaum, William. "Spitzer Antagonist Advises Ex-Madam's Campaign." *New York Times,* April 16, 2010. http://www.nytimes.com/2010/04/17/nyregion /17stone .html.

Rasmusson, Anne. "Commercial Sexual Exploitation of Children: A Literature Review." Alliance for Speaking the Truths on Prostitution and Center for Urban and Regional Affairs. http://members.shaw.ca/pdg/exploitation_of_ children.html#_Toc452540114 (June 1, 1999).

Ray, Nicholas. *Lesbian, Gay, Bisexual, and Transgender Youth: An Epidemic of Homelessness.* New York: National Gay and Lesbian Task Force Policy Institute and National Coalition for the Homeless, 2006.

Raymond, Janice G. "Health Effects of Prostitution." In *Making the Harm Visible: Global Sexual Exploitation of Women and Girls,* edited by Donna M. Hughes and Claire M. Roche. New York: Coalition against Trafficking in Women, 1999.

"The Realities of Human Trafficking." *CBS News,* September 12, 2007. http:// www.cbsnews.com/stories/2007/09/11/earlyshow/main3250963.shtml? tag=mncol;lst;1.

Reynolds, Michael. *Dead Ends: The Pursuit, Conviction and Execution of Female Serial Killer Aileen Wuornos, the Damsel of Death.* New York: St. Martin's Press, 2003.

Ridley, Jane. "Secrets of the High-End Hookers." *New York Daily News,* August 10, 2006. http://www.nydailynews.com/archives/entertainment/ 2006/ 08/10/ 2006-08-10_secrets_ofthe_high-end_hooke.html.

Roane, Kit R. "Gangs Turn to New Trade: Young Prostitutes." *New York Times,* July 11, 1999, 23.

Robertson, Marjorie J., and Paul A. Toro. "Homeless Youth: Research, Intervention, and Policy." In *Practical Lessons, the 1998 National Symposium on Homelessness Research,* edited by Linda B. Fosburg and Deborah L. Dennis. Washington, DC: U.S. Department of Housing and Urban Development, 1999. http:// aspe.hhs.gov/ProgSys/homeless/symposium/3-Youth.htm.

Rosenblum, Karen E. "Female Deviance and the Female Sex Role: A Preliminary Investigation." *British Journal of Sociology* 26 (1975): 173–78.

Rosencrance, Linda. *Ripper.* New York: Pinnacle, 2008.

Rosenthal, Doreen, and Susan Moore. "Homeless Youths: Sexual and Drug-Related Behavior, Sexual Beliefs and HIV/AIDS Risk." *AIDS Care* 6, no. 1 (1994): 83–94.

Rotheram-Borus, Mary J., Heino Meyer-Bahlburg, Cheryl Koopman, Margaret Rosario, Theresa M. Exner, Ronald Henderson, Marjory Matthieu, and Rhoda Gruen. "Lifetime Sexual Behavior among Runaway Males and Females." *Journal of Sex Research* 29, no. 1 (1992): 15–29.

Roxburgh, Amanda, Louisa Degenhardt, Jan Copeland, and Briony Larance. "Drug Dependence and Associated Risks among Female Street-Based Sex Workers in the Greater Sydney Area, Australia." *Substance Use and Misuse* 43, no. 8/9 (2008): 1202–17.

Rule, Ann. *Green River, Running Red: The Real Story of the Green River Killer—America's Deadliest Serial Murderer.* New York: Free Press, 2004.

Russell, Michael. (July 13, 2009) "Springfield-Area School Superintendent Cited in Prostitution Sting." *OregonLive.com.* http://www.oregonlive.com/news/index.ssf/2009/07/springfield_school_super_cited.html.

Safe Schools Coalition. "Homeless LGBT Youth and LGBT Youth in Foster Care." http://www.safeschoolscoalition.org/RG-homeless.html (July 6, 2009).

Salett, Elizabeth P. "Human Trafficking and Modern-Day Slavery." *National Multicultural Institute* (2010). http://www.nmci.org/news/news_items/trafficking.html.

Salfati, C. Gabrielle, Alison R. James, and Lynn Ferguson. "Prostitute Homicides: A Descriptive Study." *Journal of Interpersonal Violence* 23, no. 4 (2008): 505–43.

Sanchez, Rebecca P., Martha W. Waller, and Jody M. Greene. "Who Runs? A Demographic Profile of Runaway Youth in the United States." *Journal of Adolescent Health* 39, no. 5 (2006): 778–81.

Sanders, Teela. *Paying for Pleasure: Men Who Buy Sex.* London: Wilan Publishing, 2008.

Saphira, Miriam. *The Commercial Exploitation of Children.* Auckland, New Zealand: ECPAT, 2001.

Schaffner, Laurie. "Searching for Connection: A New Look at Teenaged Runaways." *Adolescence* 33, no. 31 (1998): 619–28.

Schalet, Amy, Geoffrey Hunt, and Karen Joe-Laidler. "Respectability and Autonomy: The Articulation and Meaning of Sexuality among the Girls in the Gang." *Journal of Contemporary Ethnography* 32 (2003): 108–43.

Scott, Michael S., and Kelly Dedel. *Street Prostitution,* 2nd ed. Washington, DC: Office of Community Oriented Policing Services, 2006. http://www.cops.usdoj.gov/files/RIC/Publications/e10062633.txt.

Sealey, Geraldine. "Exposing America's Ugly Child Sex Secret." *ABC News,* December 13, 2009. http://abcnews.go.com/US/story?id=90557&page=1.

"Sex Trafficking Charges against Reputed Mobsters." *CBS News,* April 20, 2010. http://www.cbsnews.com/stories/2010/04/20/national/main6415114.shtml?tag=mncol;lst;3.

"Sex Trafficking Problem Growing Quicklyn." *Austin News,* December 1, 2009. http://www.kxan.com/dpp/news/national/sex-trafficking-problem-growing-quickly.

"Sex Work Emerges from Shadows." *CBS News,* March 12, 2008. http://www.cbsnews.com/video/watch/?id=3928272n.

Sherman, William. "Inside the World of High-Priced Hookers." *New York Daily News*, March 16, 2008. http://www.nydailynews.com/news/2008/03/16/2008-03-16_inside_the_world_of_highpriced_hookers.html.

Silbert, Mimi H. *Sexual Assault of Prostitutes: Phase One*. Washington, DC: National Institute of Health, 1980.

Silbert, Mimi H. "Delancey Street Study: Prostitution and Sexual Assault, Summary of Results." Delancey Street Foundation, San Francisco, 1982.

Silbert, Mimi H., and Ayala M. Pines. "Occupational Hazards of Street Prostitutes." *Criminal Justice and Behavior* 8 (1981): 397.

Silbert, Mimi H., and Ayala M. Pines. "Entrance into Prostitution." *Youth and Society* 13 (1982): 471–500.

Silbert, Mimi H., and Ayala M. Pines. "Victimization of Street Prostitutes," *Victimology* 7 (1982): 122–33.

Simons, Marlise. "Amsterdam Tries Upscale Fix for Red-Light District Crime." *New York Times*, February 24, 2008. http://www.nytimes.com/2008/02/24/world/europe/24amsterdam.html?_r=1&scp=1&sq=amersterdam%20tries%20upscale%20fix%20for%20red%20light%20district%20crime&st=cse.

Simons, Ronald L., and Les B. Whitbeck. "Sexual Abuse as a Precursor to Prostitution and Victimization among Adolescent and Adult Homeless Women." *Journal of Family Issues* 12, no. 3(1991): 361–79.

Skrobanek, Siriporn, Nattaya Boonpakdi, and Chutima Janthakeero. *The Traffic in Women: Human Realities of the International Sex Trade*. New York: Zed Books Ltd, 1997.

Slim, Iceberg. *Pimp: The Story of My Life*. Los Angeles, CA: Holloway House, 1969.

Smolenski, Carol. "Sex Tourism and the Sexual Exploitation of Children." *Christian Century* 112 (1995): 1080.

Snyder, Howard N., and Melissa Sickmund. *Juvenile Offenders and Victims: 1999 National Report*. Washington, DC: Office of Juvenile Justice and Delinquency Prevention, 1999.

Spangenberg, Mia. "Prostituted Youth in New York City: An Overview." *ECPAT-US*. http://www.libertadlatina.org/US_ECPAT_Child_Prostitution_NYC.htm (2001).

Sponsler, Connie. "Juvenile Prostitution Prevention Project." *WHISPER* 13, no. 2 (1993): 3–4.

Stein, Martha L. *Lovers, Friends, Slaves: The Nine Male Sexual Types, Their Psycho-Sexual Transactions with Call Girls*. New York: Berkley, 1974.

Sterk, Claire E. *Tricking and Tripping: Prostitution in the Era of AIDS*. Putnam Valley, NY: Social Change Press, 2000.

Sticof, R. L., L. F. Novick, and J. T. Kennedy. "HIV Seroprevalence in Facilities for Runaway and Homeless Adolescents in Four States: Florida, Texas, Louisiana, and New York." Paper presented at the Sixth International Conference on AIDS, San Francisco, June 20–24, 1990.

Stieber, Tamar. "The Boys Who Sell Sex to Men in San Francisco." *Sacramento Bee*, March 4, 1984, A22.

Stossel, John, Catherine Brosseau, and Andrew Kirell. "New Dating Web Sites Bring Sugar Daddies, Babies Together at Last." *ABC News*, August 20, 2009. http://abcnews.go.com/2020/Stossel/story?id=8364856.

Stransky, Michelle, and David Finkelhor. *How Many Juveniles Are Involved in Prostitution in the United States?* Durham, NC: Crimes against Children Research Center, 2008.

"Study: Ohio at Center of Child Sex Trade." *CBS News*, February 11, 2010. http://www.cbsnews.com/stories/2010/02/11/national/main6196454.shtml?tag=mncol;lst;4.

Strauss, Eric M. "Domestic Sex Trafficking in the U.S." *ABC News/Primetime*, July 14, 2008. http://abcnews.go.com/Primetime/story?id=5326721&page=1.

"Suspect Arrested in Call Girl Ring," *Houston News*, March 18, 2009. http://www.click2houston.com/news/18961545/detail.html

Tattersall, Clare. *Drugs, Runaways, and Teen Prostitution*. New York: Rosen, 1999.

Territo, Leonard, and George Kirkham. *International Sex Trafficking of Women & Children*. Flushing, NY: Looseleaf Law Publications, 2009.

Thomas, Ruth. "AIDS Risks: Alcohol, Drugs, and the Sex Industry." In *AIDS, Drugs, and Prostitution*, edited by Martin A. Plant. London: Routledge, 1990.

Thomas, William I. *Sex and Society: Studies in the Social Psychology of Sex*. Boston: Little, Brown, 1907.

Thomas, William I. *The Unadjusted Girl: With Cases and Standpoint for Behavioral Analysis*. New York: Harper and Row, 1923.

Trafficking Victims Protection Act. P.L. 106–386 (2000).

Traina, Meredith. "LI Motivational Speaker Murdered by Prostitute for Debit Card PIN." *WPIX*, July 18, 2009. http://www.wpix.com/news/local/wpix-motivational-speaker-prostitute,0,3703962.story.

Trujillo, Laura. "Escort Services Thriving Industry in Portland Area." *Oregonian*, June 7, 1996, B1.

"27 Charged in Child Porn Sting." *CNN*, March 16, 2006. http://www.cnn.com/2006/LAW/03/15/childporn.arrests/index.html.

Tyler, Kimberly A., Les B. Whitbeck, Danny R. Hoyt, and Ana Mari Cauce. "Risk Factors for Sexual Victimization among Male and Female Homeless and Runaway Youth." *Journal of Interpersonal Violence* 19 (2004): 503–20.

U.S. Department of Health and Human Services. Family Youth and Services Bureau. *Youth with Runaway, Throwaway, and Homeless Experiences:*

Prevalence, Drug Use, and Other At-Risk Behaviors. Silver Spring, MD: National Clearinghouse on Families and Youth, 1995.

U.S. Department of Health and Human Services. The Campaign to Rescue and Restore Victims of Human Trafficking. "Fact Sheet: Sex Trafficking," May 27, 2010. http://www.acf.hhs.gov/trafficking/about/fact_sex.html ().

U.S. Department of Justice. Child Exploitation and Obscenity Section (CEOS). "Child Prostitution." http://www.justice.gov/criminal/ceos/prostitution.html.

U.S. Department of Justice. Child Exploitation and Obscenity Section (CEOS). "Trafficking and Sex Tourism." http://www.justice.gov/criminal/ceos/trafficking.html.

U.S. Department of Justice. Child Exploitation and Obscenity Section (CEOS). "Child Pornography." http://www.justice.gov/criminal/ceos/childporn.html (November 6, 2007).

U.S. Department of Justice. Federal Bureau of Investigation. *Crime in the United States 2008.* http://www.fbi.gov/ucr/cius2008/data (September 2009).

U.S. Department of Justice. Office of Juvenile Justice and Delinquency Prevention. *Prostitution of Children and Child–Sex Tourism.* Alexandria, VA: National Center for Missing and Exploited Children, 1999.

U.S. Department of State. *Trafficking in Persons Report, Office to Monitor and Combat Trafficking in Persons.* http://www.state.gov/g/tip/ris/tiprpt/2005/46606.htm (June 3, 2005).

U.S. Department of State. "Trafficking in Persons Report 2010." http://www.state.gov/g/tip/rls/tiprpt/2010/index.htm (June 14, 2010).

U.S. Department of State. "Trafficking in Persons: Ten Years of Partnering to Combat Modern Slavery." Bureau of Public Affairs Fact Sheet (June 14, 2010). http://www.state.gov/r/pa/scp/fs/2010/143115.htm.

U.S. Immigration and Customs Enforcement. News Release. "Human Trafficking: 21st Century Slavery." http://www.ice.gov/pi/nr/1001/100107washingtondc.htm (January 7, 2010).

U.S. Legal Definitions. "Prostitution Law and Legal Definition." http://definitions.uslegal.com/p/prostitution.

Ugarte, Marisa B., Laura Zarate, and Melissa Farley. "Prostitution and Trafficking of Women and Children from Mexico to the United States." *Journal of Trauma Practice* 2, no. ¾ (2003): 147–65.

UN Protocol to Prevent, Suppress and Punish Trafficking in Persons, Article 3 (February 14, 2006). http://www.unodc.org/unodc/en/trafficking_human_beings.html.

Unger, Jennifer B., Michele D. Kipke, Thomas R. Simon, Susanne B. Montgomery, and Christine J. Johnson. "Homeless Youths and Young Adults in Los Angeles: Prevalence of Mental Health Problems and the Relationship between Mental Health and Substance Abuse Disorders." *American Journal of Community Psychology* 25, no. 3 (1997): 371–94.

United Nations in Frontline. "Sex Slaves." http://www.pbs.org/wgbh/pages/frontline/slaves/etc/stats.html (February 7, 2006).

Venema, Petrien, and Jan Visser. "Safer Prostitution: New Approach in Holland." In *AIDS, Drugs, and Prostitution,* edited by Martin A. Plant. London: Routledge, 1990.

Venetis, Penny. "International Sexual Slavery." *Women's Rights Law Reporter* 18, no. 3 (1997): 263–70.

Victims of Trafficking and Violence Protection Act. P.L. 100–386, Sec. 103 (8) (2000).

Volkonsky, Anastasia. "Legalizing the 'Profession' Would Sanction the Abuse." *Insight on the News* 11 (1995): 20–21.

Waldorf, Dan, and Sheigla Murphy. "Intravenous Drug Use and Syringe-Sharing Practices of Call Men and Hustlers." In *AIDS, Drugs, and Prostitution,* edited by Martin A. Plant. London: Routledge, 1990.

Walker, Nancy E. "Executive Summary: How Many Teens Are Prostituted?" fce. msu.edu/Family_Impact_Seminars/pdf/2002-2.pdf (2002).

Ward, Vicky. "The Business Side of Prostitution," *CNBC,* November 9, 2008. http://www.cnbc.com/id/15840232?video=924626302&play=1.

Wayne County. Asset Forfeiture Unit. http://www.waynecounty.com/wcpo_divisions_forfeiture.htm.

Weisberg, D. Kelly. *Children of the Night: A Study of Adolescent Prostitution.* Lexington, MA: Lexington Books, 1985.

Weitzer, Ronald, ed. *Sex for Sale: Prostitution, Pornography and the Sex Industry.* New York: Taylor and Francis, 1999.

Western Michigan University. "The Pimping Game." http://www.wmich.edu/destinys-end/pimping%20game.htm.

Whitbeck, Les B., Danny R. Hoyt, Kevin A. Yoder, Ana Mari Cauce, and Matt Paradise. "Deviant Behavior and Victimization among Homeless and Runaway Adolescents." *Journal of Interpersonal Violence* 16 (2001): 1175–1204.

"Why Serial Killers Target Prostitutes." *CBC News,* December 19, 2006. http://www.cbc.ca/news/background/crime/targeting-prostitutes.html.

Wikia Education. The Psychology Wiki. "Prostitution." http://psychology.wikia.com/wiki/Prostitution.

Wikia Education. The Psychology Wiki. "Prostitution of Children." http://psychology.wikia.com/wiki/Child_prostitution.

Wikipedia. "Aileen Wuornos." http://en.wikipedia.org/wiki/Aileen_Wuornos.

Wikipedia. "American Pimp." http://en.wikipedia.org/wiki/American_Pimp.

Wikipedia. "Brothel." http://en.wikipedia.org/wiki/Brothel.

Wikipedia. "Child Pornography." http://en.wikipedia.org/wiki/Child_porn.

Wikipedia. "De Wallen." http://en.wikipedia.org/wiki/De_Wallen.

Wikipedia. "Deborah Jeane Palfrey." en.wikipedia.org/wiki/Deborah_Jeane_Palfrey.

Wikipedia. "Eliot Spitzer Prostitution Scandal." http://en.wikipedia.org/wiki/Eliot_Spitzer_prostitution_scandal.

Wikipedia. "Emperors Club VIP." http://en.wikipedia.org/wiki/Emperors_ Club_ VIP.

Wikipedia. "Escort Agency." http://en.wikipedia.org/wiki/Escort_agency.

Wikipedia. "Estella Marie Thompson." http://en.wikipedia.org/wiki/Estella_ Marie_Thompson.

Wikipedia. "Forced prostitution." http://en.wikipedia.org/wiki/Forced_ prostitution.

Wikipedia. "Girlfriend Experience." http://en.wikipedia.org/wiki/Girlfriend_ experience.

Wikipedia. "Human Trafficking." http://en.wikipedia.org/wiki/Human_trafficking.

Wikipedia. "Human Trafficking in the United States." http://en.wikipedia.org/wiki/Human_trafficking_in_the_United_States.

Wikipedia. "John School." http://en.wikipedia.org/wiki/John_school.

Wikipedia. "Love Ranch." http://en.wikipedia.org/wiki/Love_Ranch

Wikipedia. "Male Prostitution." http://en.wikipedia.org/wiki/Rent_boy.

Wikipedia. "Mammary Intercourse." http://en.wikipedia.org/wiki/Mammary_ intercourse.

Wikipedia. "Moonlite BunnyRanch." http://en.wikipedia.org/wiki/Moonlite_ BunnyRanch.

Wikipedia. "Mustang Ranch." http://en.wikipedia.org/wiki/Mustang_Ranch.

Wikipedia. "Oral Sex." http://en.wikipedia.org/wiki/Oral_sex.

Wikipedia. "Pimp." http://en.wikipedia.org/wiki/Pimp.

Wikipedia. "Pornography in the United States." http://en.wikipedia.org/wiki/Pornography_in_the_United_States.

Wikipedia. "Prostitution." http://en.wikipedia.org/wiki/Prostitution.

Wikipedia. "Prostitution and the Law." http://en.wikipedia.org/wiki/Prostitution_ and_the_Law.

Wikipedia. "Prostitution in Australia." http://en.wikipedia.org/wiki/Prostitution_ in_Australia.

Wikipedia. "Prostitution in Canada." http://en.wikipedia.org/wiki/Prostitution_ in_Canada.

Wikipedia. "Prostitution in the Netherlands." http://en.wikipedia.org/wiki/Prostitution_in_the_Netherlands.

Wikipedia. "Prostitution in Nevada." http://en.wikipedia.org/wiki/Prostitution_ in_Nevada.

Wikipedia. "Prostitution in Rhode Island." http://en.wikipedia.org/wiki/Prostitution_ in_Rhode_Island.

Wikipedia. "Prostitution in the United Kingdom." http://en.wikipedia.org/wiki/Prostitution_in_the_United_Kingdom.

Wikipedia. "Prostitution in the United States." http://en.wikipedia.org/wiki/Prostitution_ in_the_United_States.

Wikipedia. "PROTECT Act of 2003." http://en.wikipedia.org/wiki/PROTECT_Act_of_2003.

Wikipedia. "Sex Tourism." http://en.wikipedia.org/wiki/Sex_tourism.

Wikipedia. "Sexual Slavery." http://en.wikipedia.org/wiki/Sexual_slavery.

Wikipedia. "Shady Lady Ranch." http://en.wikipedia.org/wiki/Shady_Lady_Ranch.

Wikipedia. "Street Prostitution." http://en.wikipedia.org/wiki/Street_prostitution.

Wilcox, Joseph D. (October 11, 2002) "Madam Offers Few Regrets about Demise of Brothel." *TribLive.com.* http://www.pittsburghlive.com/x/dailycourier/sports/s_96266.html.

Wilkins, Jeff, and Alison Gendar. "Vice Cops Raid Grimy Midtown Teen Sex Brothel." *New York Daily News,* August 14, 2009. http://www.nydailynews.com/news/ny_crime/2009/08/15/index.html.

Williamson, Celia, and Lynda M. Baker. "Women in Street-Based Prostitution." *Qualitative Social Work* 8, no. 1 (2009): 27–44.

Williamson, Celia, and Terry Cluse-Tolar. "Pimp-Controlled Prostitution: Still an Integral Part of Street Life." *Violence against Women* 8 (2002): 1074–92.

Wilson, Glynn. "New Orleans Abuzz with Canal Street Brothel." *The Southerner,* June 16, 2002. http://www.southerner.net/v3n1_2002/brothel.html.

Winick, Charles, and Paul M. Kinsie. *The Lively Commerce: Prostitution in the United States.* Chicago: Triangle Books, 1971.

Winslow, Ben. "Ogden Police Make Prostitution Bust." *Deseret News,* February 29, 2008. http://www.deseretnews.com/article/1,5143,695257579,00.html.

Wolak, Janis, David Finkelhor, and Kimberly Mitchell. *Child-Pornography Possessors Arrested in Internet-Related Crimes: Findings from the National Juvenile Online Victimization Study.* Alexandria, VA: National Center for Missing and Exploited Children, 2005.

"Wolseley Home Used as Brothel, ex-Prostitute Confirms." *CBC News,* September 10, 2009. http://www.cbc.ca/canada/manitoba/story/2009/09/10/ mb-brothel-leblanc-winnipeg.html.

Woolston, Howard B. *Prostitution in the United States.* New York: Century, 1921.

World Famous Mustang Ranch. http://www.worldfamousbrothel.com/wfhome.php.

Worth, Heather. "Up on K Road on a Saturday Night: Sex, Gender and Sex Work in Auckland." *Venereology* 13, no. 1(2000): 15–24.

Wortley, Richard, and Stephen Smallbone. "Child Pornography on the Internet." *Problem Oriented Guides for the Police.* http://www.cops.usdoj.gov/files/RIC/Publications/e04062000.txt (May 2006).

Wyman, June. "Drug Abuse among Runaway and Homeless Youths Calls for Focused Outreach Solutions." *NIDA Notes* 12 (1997), 3. http://www.nida.nih.gov/NIDA_Notes/NNVol12N3/Runaway.html.

Yi, Matthew. "Police Say Sex-Slave Ring Is Broken Up." *Associated Press,* November 14, 1998.

Yoder, Kevin A., Les B. Whitbeck, and Danny R. Hoyt. "Gang Involvement and Membership among Homeless and Runaway Youth." *Youth and Society* 34, no. 4 (2003): 441–67.

York, Frank, and Robert H. Knight. "Reality Check on Homeless Gay Teens." *Family Policy* (1998). http://www.frc.org/fampol/fp98fcv.htm.

YourDictionary.com. "Panderer Legal Definition." http://www.yourdictionary .com/law/panderer.

YourDictionary.com. "Streetwalker Definition." http://www.yourdictionary.com/ streetwalker.

Zelizer, Viviana A. *The Purchase of Intimacy*. Princeton, NJ: Princeton University Press, 2007.

Index

About the Author

R. BARRI FLOWERS is a literary criminologist with more than 40 published books and numerous articles to his credit. His book titles include *Street Kids, The Prostitution of Women and Girls, Runaway Kids and Teenage Prostitution, Sex Crimes,* and *The Victimization and Exploitation of Women and Children.*

Flowers has a BA and an MS in Criminal Justice and is the recipient of the Wall of Fame Award from Michigan State University's renowned School of Criminal Justice. He has been interviewed on the Biography Channel's *Crime Stories* and Investigation Discovery's *Wicked Attraction* series, as well as by ABC News.

The author lives with his wife in the Pacific Northwest.